NEITHER IN DARK SPEECHES NOR IN SIMILITUDES

NEITHER IN DARK SPEECHES NOR IN SIMILITUDES

Reflections *and* Refractions Between Canadian *and* American Jews

Barry L. Stiefel *and*
Hernan Tesler-Mabé, editors

WILFRID LAURIER
UNIVERSITY PRESS

Wilfrid Laurier University Press acknowledges the support of the Canada Council for the Arts for our publishing program. We acknowledge the financial support of the Government of Canada through the Canada Book Fund for our publishing activities. This work was supported by the Research Support Fund.

Library and Archives Canada Cataloguing in Publication

Neither in dark speeches nor in similitudes : reflections and refractions between Canadian and American jews / Barry L. Stiefel and Hernan Tesler-Mabé, editors.

Includes bibliographical references and index.
Issued in print and electronic formats.
ISBN 978-1-77112-231-3 (paperback).—ISBN 978-1-77112-232-0 (pdf).—
ISBN 978-1-77112-233-7 (epub)

1. Jews—Canada—History. 2. Jews—United States—History. 3. Canada—Ethnic relations. 4. United States—Ethnic relations. I. Stiefel, Barry, editor II. Tesler-Mabé, Hernan, editor

FC106.J5N47 2016   971.004'924   C2016-903690-1
                                                          C2016-903691-X

Cover design by Martyn Schmoll. Text design by Mike Bechthold.

This book is printed on FSC® certified recycled paper and is certified Ecologo. It is made from 100% post-consumer fibre, is processed chlorine free, and is manufactured using biogas energy.

Printed in Canada

RECYCLED
Paper made from
recycled material
FSC® C103567

In memory of my grandmother Doris Goodman Lapin, O.B.M.
(5 May 1918, Toronto, Ontario – 8 August 1994, Southfield, Michigan)
B.L.S.

To my family, who in their travels from the Old World to the New
and then throughout the Americas taught me that Jewishness
does not always respect national boundaries
H.T-M.

With him will I speak mouth to mouth, even apparently, and *neither in dark speeches nor in similitudes*, of the Lord shall he behold: Wherefore then were ye not afraid to speak against my servant Moses?
Numbers 12:8

Contents

Acknowledgements

Over the course of this binational project the editors encountered extraordinary assistance and guidance from several people, organizations, and institutions. To begin, we would like to acknowledge the Morris and Beverly Baker Memorial Foundation, the Institute for Canadian Jewish Studies at Concordia University, and the College of Charleston's School of Humanities and Social Sciences as well as the Historic Preservation and Community Planning Program for their financial support of this book. Also, Jonathan D. Sarna of Brandeis University and Ira Robinson of Concordia University provided sage advice and encouragement throughout the course of the project, from initial inception to completion, which we greatly appreciate. We are also incredibly grateful and indebted to David Koffman at York University and Stephanie Schwartz at Concordia University for their review of an earlier draft of this book, which was essential to its completion. As this project began, David Rittenberg provided exceptional assistance in articulating key ideas. Finally, the book could not have reached publication without the generous support of family members Carlos Tesler-Mabé, Karin Kemeny, Steven Silver, and Gabriela Tesler.

Introduction

How different are Canadian Jews from the Jews of the United States? This book explores the experiences of Jews in Canada and the United States so that we can better appreciate the similarities and differences that are so often overlooked. More often than not, scholars study Jews within the frameworks of specific nations, such as the United States or Canada, or in terms of province, states, or cities. When transboundary scholarship investigates Jewish heritage from a continental perspective, the region of study is often Europe or Latin America, not North America.[1]

An example from the United States of a national-oriented study of Jews is *Jews and Gentiles in Early America, 1654–1800*, by the late historian William Pencak, which looked closely at the Jewish communities of New York, Newport, Philadelphia, Charleston, and Savannah.[2] Pencak's study is impeccable, and his scholarship is extraordinary regarding the communities he examines. But he chose not to treat the Jewish community of Montreal, although it had developed connections with Jews along the entire North American Atlantic seaboard. This omission seems peculiar, given that the French and Indian War (1763) led to Quebec and all of French Canada being ceded to the British Empire.

The key point here is that the fates of many – including Jews – in Quebec, New England, and the American Middle Atlantic colonies were intertwined. That is why, between June 1775 and October 1776, the American Continental Army moved quickly to occupy Montreal, in the hope of adding Quebec to the thirteen colonies already in rebellion. The attempt failed. As American Loyalists travelled north to Quebec, Canadian supporters of the revolution, including Jews, went south. When the fighting came to an end in 1783, relations between Montreal's Jews and those in the new United States were vigorously restored. Additionally, between 1783 and 1825, when the Erie Canal was completed, the small population of Jews on the American side of the Great Lakes–St. Lawrence watershed was at least as dependent on Montreal's Jewish community as it was on New York's. In other words, the small groups of Jews living in Detroit (where there had been Jewish settlers since 1762), Mackinaw (1760s), Sandwich (now Windsor, 1794), and Green Bay (1794) were also satellites of Montreal's Jewish community, just like the Jews in Trois-Rivières and Quebec City. So Pencak's study might well have benefited from regarding Quebec, if not as a "fourteenth American colony," then certainly as a core element in a familial North American saga. In essence, Pencak's work would have borne an enhanced contribution to the academy had he – like many scholars on either side of the border – taken a binational perspective.

Notwithstanding the nationalist tendencies of journalists and historians along both sides of the world's longest undefended border, there has been a long tradition of binational studies. As the Canadian historian Bruce Hutchinson observed in his seminal work *The Struggle for the Border* (1955), "the historic, constitutional, and economic relationship of the two nations dividing between them most of North America has long been noted and much discussed by historians."[3] This volume focuses specifically on the Jewish experience, which has not received its due scholarly attention for some time. Hutchinson also postulated that "the American standpoint on the affairs of America has been amply set forth and that a Canadian viewpoint, often quite different, may be of interest [and vice versa] – not because it is more valid but because it may set things in better proportion; for assuredly more proportion is needed in a subject so important to every North American and too often distorted in our schools, by misguided patriotism, on both sides of the border."[4] This is part of the agenda we intend on exploring, with the focus on how transnational perspectives can more clearly elucidate Jewish history and heritage in Canada and the United States.

In recent years, border studies have become popular. Past scholarship in Jewish studies has focused on the boundaries between nations, peoples, cultures, and languages in continental Europe. Examples include Antony Polonsky's *Focusing on Jews in the Polish Borderlands* (2001); *Out of the Shtetl: Making Jews Modern in the Polish Borderlands* by Nancy Sinkoff (2004); and Amelia Glaser's *Jews and Ukrainians in Russia's Literary Borderlands* (2012). A borderlands study exclusive to Jews in Canada and the United States has yet to be conducted, however, despite the ripe opportunities for this. A localized example is the Detroit–Windsor area. These two

Figure 1: The central portion of North America, with English and Yiddish place names. Source: *John Foster Carr's Guide to the United States for the Jewish Immigrant* (1912). William A. Rosenthall Judaica Collection, Special Collections, College of Charleston Library.

cities, which are on opposite sides of the international border, have been the topic of scholarly analyses about their Jewish communities, such as *The Jews of Detroit: From the Beginning, 1762–1914*, by Robert A. Rockaway, and *The Jews of Windsor, 1790–1990*, by Jonathan V. Plaut.[5] However, the histories by Rockaway and Plaut are nation-oriented, and neither pays much attention to the community of Jews on the opposite side of the Detroit River. Can a local history ignore a constituency that is so geographically close? Indeed, shouldn't a research question have focused on the relations between Detroit's and Windsor's Jews? Mapping the Jewish community centres for the metropolitan area reveals that Windsor's Jews live geographically closer to downtown Detroit than Jewish Detroiters, who are concentrated in the northwestern suburbs. Judging from the likes of David Croll (1900–91), a former mayor of Windsor and Canada's first Jewish senator, to Carl Levin (1934–), a former US Senator from Michigan, the histories of the two communities appear even more closely intertwined. Indeed, Carl Levin is David Croll's nephew![6]

In *The Origins of Canadian and American Political Differences* (2009), Jason Kaufman makes a compelling argument for a borderlands approach: "In considering the effects of jurisdiction on political culture, what we are really asking is how certain aspects of a given society's legal institutions shape its larger and political climate. Unlike explanatory accounts of national political culture based on 'national values,' 'political structure,' or 'cultural repertoires,' a jurisdictional perspective lends itself particularly well to analyses of continuity and changes."[7]

While we embrace Kaufman's perspective, we hesitate to use the term "borderlands" due to the geographical constraints this can impose. For instance, in the essay "Re-evaluating Jew or Juif? Jewish Community and Life in Franco Heritage North America before ca. 1920," by Barry L. Stiefel, the Louisiana half of this case study is around 2,600 kilometers (1,605 miles) from Quebec.[8] But the similarities and differences between the Jewish experience in Louisiana and that in Quebec with respect to politics, economics, and culture would make for an intriguing and worthwhile study as well. In other words, a borderlands approach to American and Canadian Jews is a valid one, but scholarship need not be constrained to the international boundary region per se; geographically distant comparative approaches can also be utilized.

The Evolution of Contemporary Scholarship

Given the dearth of recent scholarship that treats North American history, politics, and economics holistically, it may surprise readers that as far back as the 1850s – more than a decade before the British North America Act of 1867 established the Dominion of Canada – some scholars envisioned their studies on a continental scale. On further reflection, these early studies point to one of the principal findings of this present book – namely, that in the 1850s, North America's political boundaries had yet to be firmly established and that greater fluidity existed across these now-hardened social frontiers. Examples include *A History of the War Between Great Britain and the United States of America, during the years 1812, 1813, & 1814*, by Gilbert Auchinleck (1853), and Charles Lanman's *Adventures in the Wilds of the United States and British American Provinces* (1856).[9] Auchinleck's work was published in Toronto and Lanman's in Philadelphia. Few, however, would argue that these monographs are influential among today's scholars.

A contender for the earliest seminal work on Canadian and American studies conducted together is *The Mingling of the Canadian and American Peoples* by Marcus L. Hansen and John B. Brebner, dating from 1940. In that book, Hansen and Brebner note how "there migrated from the United States groups of Austrians, Russians, Dutch, Belgians, and Jews" into Canada.[10] This book was followed by Hutchinson's monograph, which has enjoyed many reprints, the most recent in 2011 by Oxford University Press.[11] Hutchinson was a prolific Canadian historian and journalist who published many books between 1942 and 1988. But while Jews were mentioned in passing in this body of scholarship, the Jewish experience in North America has yet to be treated holistically.

To the inaugural issue of *American Jewish Historical Quarterly*, a journal published by the American Jewish Historical Society (both established in 1892), Andrew C. Joseph contributed the article "The Settlement of Jews in Canada."[12] While this article on Canadian Jewish history in a Jewish American scholarly journal is informative, it is – as per a common theme – nationalistic in orientation, similar to *Jews and Gentiles in Early America, 1654–1800*. It does not treat Canadian and American Jews as a single unit. The study of Jews in North America in Joseph's time was still relatively new.

Jewish studies at institutions of higher education have existed without interruption in North America since the founding of Hebrew Union College in 1875, in Cincinnati. While many non-Jewish institutions had instructors who taught Hebrew, such as Judah Monis at Harvard College (1720s–1760s, although he had to convert to Christianity), Jewish history beyond the Bible was not a primary topic of instruction.[13] That changed in 1925, when Harvard, now a university, established the Nathan Littauer Professorship of Hebrew Literature and Philosophy, a position that included instruction in both Hebrew and Jewish studies.[14] In 1930, the Nathan J. Miller Professorship of Jewish History was established at Columbia University, along with a Chair in Rabbinic Literature and Semitic Languages endowed by New York's Temple Emanu-El in 1887. Incrementally, courses and faculty positions in Jewish studies at other non-Jewish colleges and universities were established over the subsequent decades. For instance, two years after the independence of the State of Israel, Columbia University created the Center for Israel and Jewish Studies.[15] Then, in the 1960s, McGill University and the University of Toronto founded what were among North America's first stand-alone Jewish studies programs.[16] In 1969, the Association for Jewish Studies (AJS) was also founded, creating "the largest learned society and professional organization representing Jewish Studies scholars worldwide."[17] Academic Jewish studies in North America was becoming increasingly professionalized. Other academic programs followed at Indiana University (1972–73), Cornell University (1973–76), the University of Michigan (1976), and Harvard University (1978). Coincidentally, these programs, in addition to Jewish institutions of higher education, are mostly located relatively close to one another in the Great Lakes region of North America, not far from the Canada–US border.[18] That is where North America's Jews were clustered during this period. In raw numbers, there are more Jewish studies programs in the United States than in Canada, but this is a reflection of population – it doesn't point to a lack of interest.[19] For instance, the Canadian Jewish Historical Society / Société d'histoire juive canadienne was established in 1976, the precursor to the Association for Canadian Jewish Studies / l'Association d'études juives canadiennes.

In 2014, according to the AJS, there were around 215 institutions of higher education providing undergraduate or graduate Jewish studies education in one form or another in North America, with more being founded.[20] A dozen of these institutions are in Canada. While there are far fewer such programs in Canada than in the United States, with respect to population, the two countries are on par.[21] With this flourishing of Jewish studies in North America, beginning in the late 1960s, scholars began to specialize their research interests and reflect on modes of inquiry.

In 1970, Jacob Rader Marcus published the seminal three-volume series *The Colonial American Jew, 1492–1776*.[22] This was by no means the first work on American Jewish history, but within it Marcus covered the entire geographic span of the American Jewish experience during the colonial period, ending with the War of Independence in 1776, and he did so from an American-centred perspective. British North America, the area that would become Canada, was part of his analysis, but so were the Dutch and British colonies of the Caribbean and South America. While sharing colonial roots, the Jewish communities of North America had travelled very different cultural trajectories than those in the Caribbean and South America in terms of lifestyle, language, and geography.

In 1976, the same year the Canadian Jewish Historical Society was founded, the American Jewish historian Jonathan D. Sarna published "Jewish Immigration to North America: The Canadian Experience (1870–1900)" in *Jewish Journal of Sociology*. Breaking from some of the generalist assumptions made by Marcus (who was a mentor of Sarna), this article begins: "Historians of Canadian Jewry too often assume that the Jewish experience in the United States can serve as a model for understanding Canadian Jewish history. In the late eighteenth and nineteenth centuries, North America could be treated as a single large country, and historians seem to believe that this was also true of the late nineteenth century."[23] It is here that we see the beginnings of critical thinking pertaining to Jewish historiography in North America, with respect to Canadian and American Jews.

Even more forward thinking was an article published six years later by Sarna, "The Value of Canadian Jewish History to the American Jewish Historian and Vice Versa." In it he articulated how going beyond national-oriented studies of Jews in North America could bring about a richer understanding of what was taking place: "Realizing that there are many questions which historians cannot ask, let alone answer, unless their frames of reference extend beyond the narrow confines of just one country ... Canadian historians and United States historians [have much] to learn from one another. [Furthermore, the] virtue of comparative history lies in the new and fruitful lines of inquiry, which by its very nature, it helps to generate."[24]

That article has been the inspiration for the book at hand. Indeed, the editors asked Sarna to update it for this project, more than thirty years after its original appearance. The editors would also like to reiterate Sarna's sentiments from his first article in conjunction with the second regarding how "frames of reference extend beyond the narrow confines of just one country." Jews in Canada and the United States have some experiences in common, but others in which the contrast is great. However, whether any given case study is one of similarities or differences, it is always necessary to analyze matters from the perspectives of both sides of the border.

Around two years after Sarna's insightful article was published, a conference was held at the University of Toronto that brought together scholars from Canada, the United States, and Israel "to explore the Canadian and American Jewish experience as a North American totality."[25] A conference proceedings titled *The Jews of North America* was subsequently published by Wayne State University Press, edited by Moses Rischin (1987). Within this volume appeared contributions by seven Canadian, six American, and two Israeli scholars, covering such topics as Modern Migration; Continuity and Tradition; The Fathers of Jewish Ethnic Culture; and Jews, Community, and World Jewry. *The Jews of North America* was an outstanding contribution to the fields of Canadian and American Jewish studies, one that brought together scholars of both backgrounds (as well as Israeli scholars) and ambitiously looked beyond the borderland region of the United States and Canada.

No body of scholarship with respect to historiography has followed *The Jews of North America*, until now.[26] Nearly three decades later, the editors of this volume, one Canadian and the other American, decided to pick up the mantle of historical analysis where it had been left off. Wilfrid Laurier University Press, a Canadian academic press, was purposely selected to counterbalance the previous publication, which had been produced in the United States. A new generation of scholars in Jewish studies from Canada and the United States have been recruited to provide fresh analysis and perspective, especially on the eve of an important anniversary for Canada – its sesquicentennial in 2017. Like *The Jews of North America*, we hope that *Neither in Dark Speeches nor in Similitudes: Reflections and Refractions Between Canadian and American Jews* will serve as a fresh start in a growing chain of understanding. We look forward to what lies ahead in the teaching of North American Jewish studies and hope that work of the sort presented here can help it improve.

New Contributions to North America's Jewish Experience

To bridge the research of the first scholars who brought together Canadian and American Jewish studies into a single North American saga, we invited Jonathan D. Sarna to revisit his earlier article. Many of Sarna's ideas are highly relevant today despite the passage of time, which is why this first chapter is titled "The Value of Canadian Jewish History to the American Jewish Historian, and Vice Versa: Another Look."

Susan Landau-Chark contextualizes for us the early history of Jewish settlement in North America in her chapter titled "Traversing the 49th Parallel: The Canadian Jewish Experience Prior to 1867." Landau-Chark's study begins with the defeat of France on the Plains of Abraham during the Seven Years' War. With the signing of the Treaty of Paris in 1763, Great Britain acquired sovereignty over mainland North America north of the Spanish Viceroyalty of New Spain, which was then off limits to Jews. After American independence (1775–83), many borderland Jews travelled back and forth across the geopolitical boundary separating British North America from the nascent United States. They were "invisible immigrants," like the British and Americans among whom they lived, worked, and traded. This chapter explores the backgrounds and ties of marriage, family, and trade in the Jewish population living in North America from 1763 to 1881.

In the third chapter, "Re-evaluating *Jew* or *Juif?* Jewish Community and Life in Franco Heritage North America before ca. 1920," Barry L. Stiefel assesses the experience of Jews in bilingual localities in Canada and the United States, where both French and English were spoken. In 1987, the same year *The Jews of North America* was published, Michael Brown published *Jew or Juif? Jews, French Canadians, and Anglo-Canadians, 1759–1914.*[27] That monograph explored Jews' intricate relationship with anglo and francophone Canada, especially in Montreal. The book was impeccably well executed with respect to Quebec, but Stiefel asks what the situation had been elsewhere in francophone North America. For instance, was there a lasting legacy among Jews in Louisiana, part of France's former North American empire, even though they did not participate in the development of these colonies in any great numbers (pre-1760)? While the two locales are not geographically contiguous, Stiefel compares the Jewish experience in francophone Quebec and Louisiana.

In Howard Gontovnick's "Planting the Seed of Identity: The Contributions of the Early Jewish Farmers of North America," we learn how some of the increasing numbers of Jewish immigrants arriving in North America from Europe attempted to put down roots as farmers instead of urban dwellers. These immigrants represented nationalities from across the

European continent and well as a variety of professions and economic and educational backgrounds. Some started out as independent farmers; others became affiliated with distinct settlements in various regions. As the number of Jewish farmers increased after 1900, membership in this occupation started off strong before dwindling towards 1950 in both countries. Gontovnick argues that while Jewish farmers had a somewhat shared experience, overall, Jewish farmers in the United States played a more prominent role in society than Jewish farmers in Canada.

Lillooet Nördlinger McDonnell moves the analysis to the western frontier in "Bacon, Beans, and a Fine Dish of 'Ditto': Commonalities in Early Jewish Life and Religiosity along the Pacific West Coast." Focusing on the Jewish community in the urban frontier centre of Victoria, Nördlinger McDonnell argues that British Columbia's early Jewish history is linked as much to the American west coast as it is to the rest of Canada. British Columbia's founding during a later stage of state formation, its geographic remoteness from the rest of Canada's population centres, and its socio-economic links to California give the region a distinct place in Jewish Canadian history. Nördlinger McDonnell focuses on how the constant influx of migrants by way of California and the maintenance of north–south trade links greatly influenced the social and cultural flavour of British Columbia. For instance, members of Victoria's newly founded Jewish community had an abundance of family and business ties to San Francisco. Victoria's first synagogue, Congregation Emanu-El (founded 1863), was named after the central synagogue in San Francisco. Indeed, the nascent congregation received prayer books and Torah scrolls from their co-religionists in California. And Victoria's Jews integrated into local society in much the same way as their American counterparts, exhibiting parallel attitudes towards both reforming and reasserting tradition.

Continuing with the theme of Jewish life and religiosity, we turn to Zev Eleff's "They Who Control the Time: The Orthodox Alliance of Abraham De Sola and Jacques Judah Lyons and the Nineteenth-Century Jewish Calendar." Eleff explores how one of the earliest published Hebrew calendars in North America was a collaborative effort between an American Jew and a Canadian Jew, Jacques Judah Lyons and Abraham De Sola, respectively. Eleff also found in his research that De Sola and Lyons sought to create a work that would reinforce Orthodox life and weaken the momentum towards religious reform. For example, some religious reformers during the nineteenth century endeavoured to shorten Sabbath prayers by converting to a triennial cycle of Torah reading. The new calendar included the various weekly portions of Torah based on the traditional annual cycle to prevent the spread of this reform, and included a lengthy introduction that defended many other traditional Jewish practices. This chapter places North American Jewish history in the current scholarly discussion of "Jewish time" and material culture.

In Chapter 7, "Finding a Rabbi for Quebec City: The Interplay Between an American Yeshiva and a Canadian Congregation," Ira Robinson looks at another issue affecting Jewish life in North America. According to Robinson, no matter what the religious orientation of Canadian Jewish congregations, spiritual leadership generally has come from elsewhere. Historically, the first Canadian rabbis came from Europe, especially England. By the twentieth century, however, most Canadian rabbis had been trained in the United States. Several attempts to create rabbinical training institutions in Canada did not succeed in satisfying the Canadian Jewish demand for spiritual leadership. Thus the process whereby American rabbis become spiritual leaders of Canadian synagogues is worth investigating in the context of the commonalities and distinctive features among Canadian and American Jewries. This study portrays both connections and disconnections experienced by Jews in countries with close and lasting ties.

Besides spiritual and religious well-being we look at the physical health of Jews and communal public health policy in "'Chasing the Cure' on Both Sides of the Border: Jewish Tuberculosis Sanatoriums in Denver and Montreal," by Jeanne Abrams. Tuberculosis, also commonly known as "consumption," the "White Plague," or simply "TB," held the dubious distinction of being the leading cause of death in late-nineteenth- and early-twentieth-century North America. After Dr. Edward Trudeau opened his pioneer sanatorium in 1886 at Saranac Lake, New York, in the Adirondack Mountains, it became a model for tuberculosis treatment across the continent. By 1925 there were more than five hundred tuberculosis sanatoriums in the United States alone. High altitude and fresh mountain air were considered part of an especially healthful environment for consumptives, and Denver, Colorado, near the Rocky Mountains, and Sainte-Agathe-des-Monts, in the Laurentian Mountains outside Montreal, fit this prescription perfectly. By 1896, Colorado was being flatteringly referred to as "the World's Sanatorium," and by the early twentieth century, the Laurentians were attracting many Canadian tuberculosis patients seeking an informal cure. In 1899 the small but largely affluent German Jewish Reform community brought the sanatorium movement to Denver, when it founded the National Jewish Hospital for Consumptives. This was followed in 1904 by a second Jewish sanatorium, the Jewish Consumptives' Relief Society, organized by Eastern European immigrants. Similarly, in 1909 the modest-sized Montreal Jewish community opened the Mount Sinai sanatorium. All three institutions were founded by Jews to provide aid and relief primarily to their co-religionists.

Hernan Tesler-Mabé's contribution, "Performing Jewish?: Heinz Unger, Gustav Mahler, and the Musical Strains of German-Jewish Identity in Canada and the United States," shifts the focus yet again, allowing us to examine how artistic expression – in particular, musical culture – can help us understand the plurality within what is usually seen as a fairly rigid and precisely defined cultural "identity." In the early to mid-twentieth century, Canadian Jewish musical culture – like many other Canadian Jewish cultural expressions – stemmed from Eastern Europe. Thus, Canadian Jewish musical values were formed in a manner distinct from the values prevalent among the often more assimilated Central and Western European Jewish musicians who settled in the United States. Tesler-Mabé argues that this created a situation in which German Jews such as the German-Jewish musician Heinz Unger (1895–1965) failed to embed themselves in the Canadian Jewish communal milieu and were only able to find common ground with limited segments of the Canadian Jewish community. Just as critically, many of Unger's main affiliations lay beyond Canada, in the United States or in other parts of the world.

In the final chapter, "East Meets West: Sephardic and Mizrahi Jews in Canada and the United States," Kelly Train investigates the immigration of "Eastern Sephardim" and "Mizrahim" from North Africa, the Middle East, and India to North America. This historical framework provides a basis for examining the relations among Sephardim, Mizrahim, and Ashkenazim in both countries. In particular, Train explores how "Eastern Sephardim" and Mizrahim were marginalized and excluded from the construction of an *authentic* Jewish identity that helped unify and essentialize the broader American and Canadian Jewish community identities as synonymous with an Ashkenazi identity.

We would like to end with a plea similar to Sarna's of more than three decades ago. In his work, Sarna identified a number of areas of interest that he felt might help us better understand Jewish identity and experience across North America, and perhaps even shed new light on issues beyond this geographic area. He also speculated that "comparative and transnational approaches to history offer what the great French Jewish historian Marc Bloch once called 'a powerful magic wand'" and a hope that "more scholars will employ its magic in the service of North American Jewish history."[28] In this modest volume, we have attempted to do just that. But much work remains to invigorate the paradigm that Canadian Jewish studies and American Jewish studies not only can but should be pursued together on a more frequent basis.

Notes

1 See Bernard Wasserstein, *On the Eve: The Jews of Europe before the Second World War* (New York: Simon and Schuster, 2012), for an example of a continental exploration of Jews in Europe.

2 William Pencak, *Jews and Gentiles in Early America, 1654–1800* (Ann Arbor: University of Michigan Press, 2005).

3 Bruce Hutchinson, *The Struggle for the Border* (Toronto and New York: Longmans, Green, 1955), i.

4 Hutchinson, *The Struggle for the Border*, i–ii.

5 See Robert A. Rockaway, *The Jews of Detroit: From the Beginning, 1762–1914* (Detroit: Wayne State University Press, 1986); and Jonathan V. Plaut, *The Jews of Windsor, 1790–1990: A Historical Chronicle* (Toronto: Dundurn, 2007).

6 Plaut, *The Jews of Windsor, 1790–1990*, 99.

7 Jason Andrew Kaufman, *The Origins of Canadian and American Political Differences* (Cambridge, MA: Harvard University Press, 2009), 22.

8 The distance of 2,600 kilometers (1,615 miles) is that between New Orleans and Montreal, each having the largest Jewish community within its respective state/province.

9 Gilbert Auchinleck, *A History of the War Between Great Britain and the United States of America, During the Years 1812, 1813, & 1814* (Toronto: Thomas Maclear, 1853); Charles Lanman, *Adventures in the Wilds of the United States and British American Provinces* (Philadelphia: J.W. Moore, 1856).

10 Marcus L. Hansen and John B. Brebner, *The Mingling of the Canadian and American Peoples* (New Haven: Yale University Press, 1940), 233.

11 See Hutchinson, *The Struggle for the Border*.

12 Andrew C. Joseph, "The Settlement of Jews in Canada," *American Jewish Historical Quarterly* 1 (1892): 117–20.

13 Marvin R. Wilson, *Our Father Abraham: Jewish Roots of the Christian Faith* (Grand Rapids: W.B. Eerdmans, 1989), 129.

14 Louis S. Maisel, Ira N. Forman, Donald Altschiller, and Charles W. Bassett, eds. *Jews in American Politics* (Lanham: Rowman and Littlefield, 2001), 380.

15 Gil Anidjar, "The University without Walls: Jewish Studies, Holocaust Studies, Israel Studies," in *Traces 5: The Mental Labour of Globalization*, ed. Brett De Bary (Hong Kong: Hong Kong University Press, 2009), 229-52.

16 McGill University's program was founded in 1968. A specific date for the University of Toronto could not be found, but considering that in May 1970 they were planning on twenty-three Judaic Studies classes, a robust program had likely been established several years before. See Stanley B. Frost, *Mcgill University: For the Advancement of Learning*, vol. 2 (Montreal and Kingston: McGill–Queen's University Press, 1980), 284; and "University of Toronto Announces 23 Courses in Judaic Studies for 1970–71 Academic Year" (20 May 1970), http://www.jta.org/1970/05/20/archive/university-of-toronto-announces-23-courses-in -judaic-studies-for-1970-71-academic-year.

17 Association for Jewish Studies, *History, Mission, Strategic Plan*, http://www.ajsnet.org/mission.htm.

18 These institutions include Hebrew Union College–Jewish Institute of Religion (merger in 1950, Cincinnati and New York campuses); Jewish Theological Seminary (1886, New York); Yeshiva University (1886, New York); and Brandeis University (1948, Waltham, Jewish studies established in 1980).

19 See University of Toronto, *Centre for Jewish Studies*, http://www.cjs.utoronto.ca.

20 From individually assigned faculty that teach on the subject to fully developed departments offering undergraduate and graduate degrees. This count of 215 excludes the one program in Mexico.

21 Today, around 5.5 million Jews reside in the United States, and 315,000 in Canada. This gives Canada's Jews one program per 26,250, whereas there are 27,100 American Jews per program in their country. See Statistics Canada, *Ethnic Origins, 2006 Counts, for Canada, Provinces and Territories – 20% sample data*, 6 October 2010, http://www12.statcan.ca/census-recensement/2006/dp-pd/hlt/97-562/pages/page.cfm?Lang=E&Geo=PR&Code=01&Data=Count&Table=2&StartRec=1&Sort=3&Display=All&CSDFilter=5000; and Association for Jewish Studies, *AJS Directory of Programs in Jewish Studies*, http://www.ajsnet.org/programs.php.

22 Jacob R. Marcus, *The Colonial American Jew, 1492–1776*, 3 vols. (Detroit: Wayne State University Press, 1970).

23 Jonathan D. Sarna, "Jewish Immigration to North America: The Canadian Experience (1870–1900)" *Jewish Journal of Sociology* 18 (June 1976): 31-42.

24 Jonathan D. Sarna, "The Value of Canadian Jewish History to the American Jewish Historian and Vice Versa," *Canadian Jewish Historical Society Journal* 5, no. 1 (Spring 1981): 17–22.

25 Moses Rischin, ed. *The Jews of North America* (Detroit: Wayne State University Press, 1987), 14.

26 In 2008, Alex Pomson and Randal F. Schnoor published *Back to School: Jewish Day School in the Lives of Adult Jews* (Detroit: Wayne State University Press, 2008). The first of its kind in its approach, this was a sociological case study on the impact of contemporary Jewish day schools on the lives of parents and children, not a historical study.

27 Michael Brown, *Jew or Juif? Jews, French Canadians, and Anglo-Canadians, 1759–1914* (Philadelphia: Jewish Publication Society, 1987).

28 Marc Bloch, "Toward a Comparative History of European Societies," in *Enterprise and Secular Change*, ed. Frederick C. Lane and Jelle C. Riemersma (Homewood: R.D. Irwin 1953), 492–521.

ONE

The Value of Canadian Jewish History to the American Jewish Historian, and Vice Versa
Another Look

Jonathan D. Sarna

Seymour Martin Lipset, in an important essay written for an American audience in 1968, argued that "no one should work in United States history without also dealing with Canada." Robin Winks, speaking to Canadians a decade later, insisted that the reverse was no less true: "one cannot study the history of Canada without knowing United States history."[1] Both scholars were calling for comparative and what we now call transnational history.[2] Realizing that there are many questions that historians cannot ask, let alone answer, unless their frames of reference extend beyond the narrow confines of just one country, they urged historians of Canada and the United States to learn from one another.

Canadian Jewish historians and American Jewish historians should likewise strive to learn from one another. We too should be interested in analyzing the unique and common features of the Jewish experience in our respective countries. We too should be determining what shaped the Jewish communities on either side of our common border, and why they differed. We too should be broadening our horizons, asking new questions, and answering old questions based on fresh comparative and transnational studies.

What follows is a list of ten subjects that seem to me to lend themselves to comparative and transnational study. This is a tentative agenda, a starting point from which further analyses might take off. A prime virtue of looking beyond the constraints of national boundaries, it turns out, lies in the fruitful lines of investigation that altered visions generate. Widening the historical lens refocuses the historian's perspective, illuminating issues outside the frame of more narrowly conceived inquiries.

1. **Exceptionalism.** American Jewish historians generally buttress claims of uniqueness ("America is different") by pointing to the revolutionary heritage and the Bill of Rights. The one divided the United States from Europe, the other elevated religious liberty into a fundamental principle of constitutional law. Neither factor applies to Canada. Its development has proceeded along an evolutionary path, and it knows no "wall of separation" between church and state, at least not in the Jeffersonian sense of that term.[3] This opens up a host of tantalizing questions. How have different national experiences influenced American and Canadian Jewish history? Has the language of the US Constitution's First Amendment ("Congress shall make no law respecting an establishment of religion or prohibiting the free exercise thereof") affected the American Jewish experience in ways that render it distinct from its Canadian counterpart? What has been the impact of a revolutionary tradition upon Jews as against an evolutionary one? What factors nevertheless account for differences between Jews (and Judaism) in North America and in Europe?

2. **Leadership.** The Canadian Jewish Congress for many years proved far more influential and important than any single American Jewish organization. Likewise, Canada's Jewish leaders, by and large, have wielded more power and commanded more respect than their American counterparts.[4] These phenomena cry out for explanation. Does Canadian politics display greater tolerance for "elite accommodation" (i.e., for compromises made behind the scenes at the highest level)?[5] Does Canadian Jewish society, like Canadian society itself, retain remnants of hierarchical traditions left over from the days of the British? Or do differences stem more from the different Jewish immigration and settlement patterns in the two countries? As discussed below (see point 7), Canadian Jewry was until recent times more homogeneous than its American counterpart. The consequences of this would seem to be momentous, extending far beyond the realm of leadership. Yet these consequences have scarcely been studied.

3. **Tolerance of minorities.** Once scholars believed that the "melting pot" ideology of the United States stifled Jewish culture, while Canada's "social mosaic" permitted it to thrive. Nowadays, neither of these metaphors seems particularly apt, and evidence suggests that the United States and Canada actually

pursued similar national policies concerning immigrant assimilation and that both now espouse multiculturalism (which is official government policy in Canada). Nevertheless, a comparison of the American and Canadian Jewish immigrant experiences should shed light on key differences between the two countries, illuminating Morton Weinfeld's bold claim that "Canadian Jews ... enjoy a deeper cultural and communal life" than their American counterparts. Did immigrants and natives interact differently in both countries? How many differences are due to "time lag" – the fact that Jewish immigrants came to Canada after America's doors were shut and that Holocaust-era immigrants form a higher percentage of Canada's Jewish population – and how many are due to differences in national culture and social policy? And how did American and Canadian Jews react to other national minority groups? Were French Canadian/Jewish relations different from Black/Jewish ones?[6]

4. **Demography, geographical distribution, and power.** Canada's Jews have always formed a smaller percentage of their country's population than American Jews have of theirs. In 2012, Jews were around 1.09 percent of Canada's population but at least 1.74 percent of the population of the United States. Years ago, the density of Jews in the United States was many times that of Canada.[7] Still to be determined is how this difference in density affected history. Have Jews in both countries used similar strategies to overcome their numerical weakness? Have American Jews been able to exert more power than their Canadian brethren? Has the size of the community had any impact on anti-Semitism? Also, the regional distribution of Canada's Jewish population differs substantially from what is found in the United States. Canada's Jews are heavily concentrated in two metropolitan areas (Montreal and Toronto). A subtle comparative study tracing the links between community size, distribution, density, and power in North America might answer these questions, yielding insights of far-reaching significance.

5. **Occupations.** Historically, American Jews entered manufacturing and the professions to a somewhat greater degree than Canadian Jews, who took more jobs, relatively speaking, in the transportation and trade sectors.[8] How do we account for this? What does it teach us about Jewish economic habits and values? A rigorous comparative study could teach us much about the factors that have influenced Jewish occupational choices, driving Jews towards some lines of work and away from others.

6. **Language loyalty.** Canadian Jews long remained more attached to Yiddish and Yiddish culture than their American Jewish counterparts – so much so that David Roskies has described Yiddish in Montreal as a "Utopian Experiment." Does this reflect the later immigration of most Canadian Jews, the complex language politics of Montreal, or broader cultural factors? It is curious that the "ivrit b'vrit" ideology – teaching Hebrew in Hebrew – took hold in the United

States more firmly than in Canada. How can this be explained? Has Hebrew played a different symbolic role in the Jewish culture of Canada that in that of the United States?[9]

7. **Subethnic composition.** Canadian Jewry never experienced a "great German period" in the sense in which this term is used in the United States. For this reason, the community is, as we have seen, both more homogeneous and more heavily East European than the American Jewish community.[10] What impact has this had? What are the benefits of homogeneity as against a more heterogeneous admixture? Did German Jewry affect American Jewish history in a way that Canadian Jewish history was not? What about more recent *mizrachi* immigration, especially the immigration of francophone Jews to Montreal? Has that further distinguished the two communities from each other?

8. **Religion and Zionism.** In Canada, Reform Judaism has been weaker, Orthodoxy stronger, Conservative Judaism more right-wing, and Zionism less controversial than in the United States. This may again simply reflect the absence of German-Jewish influence, but considering that Christianity in Canada, according to Mark Noll, has also been "less fragmented, more culturally conservative, more closely tied to Europe [and] more respectful of tradition" than its American counterpart, one suspects that other factors too have been at work.[11] Have Canadian Jews, like Canadians generally, been more strongly linked to the Old World than their American counterparts? Has the United States demanded of its citizens a greater degree of assimilation and outward patriotism than Canada? Have Canadian Protestantism and Catholicism, both somewhat different from their American counterparts, influenced Canadian Judaism in distinctive ways? Many more of these kinds of questions need to be asked. Enlarging the comparative framework to encompass other diaspora lands – particularly Australia and South Africa – would also prove valuable.

9. **Intermarriage.** Morton Weinfeld has shown that Jewish intermarriage rates are only about half as great in Canada as in the United States (although the Canadian rate of intermarriage is rising).[12] Possibly this proves that the Jewish community in Canada is internally stronger than that of the United States. But might it not also suggest that Canadian Jews are less acculturated, more distant from non-Jews? In this regard, it would be interesting to know whether Jewish and non-Jewish attitudes towards intermarriage differ on the two sides of the border. Is there any correlation between Jewish intermarriage rates in the two countries and the intermarriage rates of Catholics and Protestants?

10. **Education.** Most twentieth-century American Jews obtained their elementary and high school education in non-sectarian public schools, where even before the outlawing of school prayer, displays of any form of religion were kept to a minimum. By contrast, Canadian public schools have been far more religiously oriented, especially in Quebec. Partly for this reason, comparatively

large numbers of Canadian Jews have long sent their children to Jewish day schools, something that until recent decades was rarely done in the United States. By all measures, Jewish education is stronger in Canada than in the United States.[13] Have these differences in upbringing affected Jewish–Christian relations and Jewish self-identity in Canada and the United States? Does Jewish education help account for the above-mentioned differences in intermarriage rates? Do community priorities differ north and south of the border? Note that these queries are of more than just historical significance. With the growing concern about "day school affordability" in the United States, they should be of interest to policy-makers as well.

In education, as in the other nine categories enumerated, the questions are better than the answers. Years of research lie ahead; dozens of new hypotheses need to be formulated; numerous old ones await rigorous testing. The phenomena discussed here are only some of the many that merit comparative and transnational study.

We would especially benefit from a university-based centre focused on North American Jewish studies: a forum where comparisons and contrasts could continually be charted, analyzed, and discussed. Such a centre would alert people to the enormous potential benefits of comparative and transnational studies. If successful, it would demonstrate both to American Jewish historians and to Canadian ones that they have much to learn from one another.

As I have tried to show here in preliminary fashion,[14] comparative North American Jewish history can yield new lines of inquiry where none previously existed. It can subject old lines of inquiry to more rigorous examination based on new data. It can generate and test theories of development. It can help scholars rid themselves of parochialism and tunnel vision.

Comparative and transnational approaches to history offer what the great French Jewish historian Marc Bloch once called "a powerful magic wand."[15] That wand must be employed cautiously and with due regard for potential abuses. But handled properly – as in this volume – it can work wonders. Here's hoping that more scholars will employ its magic in the service of North American Jewish history.

Notes

This essay began, half a lifetime ago, as a brief paper delivered at the First Annual Conference of the Institute of Academic and Communal Jewish Studies. It was subsequently published, in 1981, in Volume 5 of *Canadian Jewish Historical Society Journal*. Since then, it has been repeatedly cited, though more by Canadian Jewish scholars than by American ones, and a great deal of important historical scholarship bearing on the topics discussed here has appeared. The passage of more than three decades suggests the need for an entirely new article on the interplay of Canadian and American Jewish history, but that is a task for somebody else. Here I have confined myself to modest revisions in the text and the notes, without tampering with the original theme.

1 Seymour M. Lipset, "History and Sociology: Some Methodological Considerations," in *Sociology and History Methods*, ed. R. Hofstadter and S.M. Lipset (New York: Basic Books, 1968). 35; Robin W. Winks, "Cliché and the Canadian-American Relationship," in *Perspectives on Revolution and Evolution*, ed. Richard A. Preston (Durham: Duke University Press, 1979), 18.

2 For a brief, incisive treatment of transnational history, see Akira Iriye, *Global and Transnational History: The Past, Present, and Future* (New York: Palgrave, 2012); on its implications for American history, see Ian Tyrrell, *Transnational Nation: United States History in Global Perspective since 1789* (New York: Palgrave, 2007). For work in comparative history, see Raymond Grew ("The Case for Comparing Histories"), Shearer Davis Bowman ("Antebellum Planters and Vormarz Junkers in Comparative Perspective"), Peter Kolchin ("In Defence of Servitude: American Proslavery and Russian Proserfdom Arguments, 1760–1860"), and Alette Olin Hill's ("Marc Bloch and Comparative History") articles in *American Historical Review* 85 (1980): 763–857; and C. Vann Woodward, ed., *The Comparative Approach to American History* (New York: Basic Books, 1968). Examples in Jewish history include Todd M. Endelman, *Comparing Jewish Societies* (Ann Arbor: University of Michigan Press, 1997); Moshe Davis, "Centres of Jewry in the Western Hemisphere: A Comparative Approach," *Jewish Journal of Sociology* 5 (June 1963): 4–26; and Morton Weinfeld, "A Note on Comparing Canadian and American Jewry," *Journal of Ethnic Studies* 5 (Spring 1977), 95–103.

3 Preston, *Perspectives on Revolution and Evolution*, esp. 26–87; S.M. Lipset, *Revolution and Counterrevolution* (New York: Basic Books, 1968).

4 Daniel J. Elazar and Harold M. Waller, *Maintaining Consensus: The Canadian Jewish Polity in the Postwar World* (Lanham: University Press of America, 1990); Harold M. Waller, *The Governance of the Jewish Community of Montreal* (Center for Jewish Community Studies no. 5, Jerusalem, 1974); Davis, "Centres of Jewry," 7–9.

5 Robert Presthus, *Elite Accommodation in Canadian Politics* (New York: Cambridge University Press, 1973), 3.

6 Morton Weinfeld, *Like Everyone Else ... But Different: The Paradoxical Success of Canadian Jews* (Toronto: McClelland and Stewart, 2001), 347; Ruth Klein and Frank Dimant, eds., *From Immigration to Integration: The Canadian Jewish Experience: A Millennium Edition* (Toronto: Institute for International Affairs – B'nai Brith Canada, 2001); John Porter, "Melting Pot or Mosaic: Revolution of Reversion," in *Perspectives on Revolution and Evolution*, ed. Richard A. Preston (Durham: Duke University Press, 1979), 152–79; H. Palmer, "Mosaic versus Melting Pot? Immigration and Ethnicity in Canada and the United States," *International Journal* 31 (1975–6), 488–528; Leo Driedger, ed., *The Canadian Ethnic Mosaic* (Toronto: McClelland and Stewart, 1978).

7 Sergio DellaPergola, "World Jewish Population, 2012," 59, http://www.jewishdatabank.org/Studies/downloadFile.cfm?FileID=2941; Joseph Yam, "The Size and Geographic Distribution of Canada's Jewish Population: Preliminary Observations," *Canadian Jewish Population Studies* 3 (January 1974).

8 Joseph Kage, *The Dynamics of Economic Adjustment of Canadian Jewry – A Historical Review* (Montreal: Jewish Immigrant Aid Services of Canada, 1970), 35; Sidney Goldstein, "American Jewry, 1970," *American Jewish Year Book* 71 (1971): 68–79.

9 David G. Roskies, "Yiddish in Montreal: The Utopian Experiment," in *An Everyday Miracle: Yiddish Culture in Montreal,* ed. Ira Robinson et al. (Montreal: Vehicule Press, 1990), 22–38; Rebecca Margolis, *Jewish Roots, Canadian Soil* (Montreal and Kingston: McGill–Queen's University Press, 2011). See also Joshua A. Fishman, "Language Maintenance and Language Shift: Yiddish and Other Immigrant Languages in the United States," *YIVO Annual of Jewish Social Science* 14 (1969): 12–26; Nathan H. Winter, *Jewish Education in a Pluralist Society* (New York, NYU Press , 1966); and Jonathan B. Krasner, *The Benderly Boys and American Jewish Education* (Waltham: Brandeis University Press, 2011).

10 Jonathan D. Sarna, "Jewish Immigration to North America: The Canadian Experience (1870–1900)," *Jewish Journal of Sociology* 18 (June 1976): 31–41; Lloyd P. Gartner, "North American Jewry," *Migration and Settlements: Proceedings of the Anglo-American Jewish Historical Conference* (London, 1971), 114–27.

11 Mark A. Noll, *A History of Christianity in the United States and Canada* (Grand Rapids: Eerdmans, 1992), 284; Weinfeld, *Like Everyone Else ...,* 293–300, 359–61; Richard Menkis, "Both Peripheral and Central: Towards A History of Reform Judaism in Canada," *CCAR Journal* 51 (2004): 24–36. See also Albert Rose (ed.), *A People and Its Faith* (Toronto: University of Toronto Press, 1959); Michael Brown, "The Beginnings of Reform Judaism in Canada," *Jewish Social Studies* 34 (1972): 322–42; Samuel B. Hurwich, "Zionism (Canada)," *Encyclopedia Judaica*, 16 (1971): 109–11; and Stuart Schoenfeld, "The Jewish Religion in North America: Canadian and American Comparisons," *Canadian Journal of Sociology* 3 (1978): 209–31.

12 Weinfeld, *Like Everyone Else ...,* 372–75; Schoenfeld, "Jewish Religion in North America," 224; Moshe Davis, "Mixed Marriage in Western Jewry: Historical Background to the Jewish Response," *Jewish Journal of Sociology* 10 (1968): 177–220.

13 Weinfeld, *Like Everyone Else ...,* 226-252; Schoenfeld, "The Jewish Religion in North America," 221–23.

14 For other incisive comparisons, see Gerald Tulchinsky, *Canada's Jews: A People's Journey* (Toronto: University of Toronto Press, 2008), esp. 73–75, 178, 191–92; and Randal F. Schnoor, "The Contours of Canadian Jewish Life," *Contemporary Jewry* 31 (2011): 179–97.

15 Marc Bloch, "Toward a Comparative History of European Societies," in *Enterprise and Secular Change,*ed. Frederick C. Lane and Jelle C. Riemersma (Homewood: Irwin , 1953), 492–521.

TWO

Traversing the 49th Parallel
The Canadian Jewish Experience Prior to 1867

Susan Landau-Chark

Anyone crossing the Canada–US border today from either side has access to websites, Twitter feeds, and radio reports to help gauge border wait times.[1] It is estimated that every year, Canadians make 21 million visits to the United States,[2] over 20 million Americans visit Canada,[3] and more than 5 million commercial trucks cross the border to deliver goods between the two countries.[4] The high volume of border activity – wait times, document checks – is considered a natural aspect of trading with or visiting the other country. Two centuries ago, however, the border was far less difficult to traverse. Little attention was paid to those who crossed back and forth as they visited family and friends and plied their trades. The small community of Jews who had settled throughout Quebec easily visited the thirteen British North American colonies to the south (later the United States of America) to satisfy their economic, religious, and social needs without regard for the border between the two countries.

For the Jewish population living mainly in Lower Canada, ties of marriage, family, and trade were unhindered by treaty demarcations. The first Jewish arrivals in Canada were not fleeing religious and/or political persecution; rather, they were seeking new business opportunities (and per-

9

haps also some adventure). These newcomers to Canada were "invisible immigrants," similar to the British and Americans among whom they lived, worked, and traded; that they were able to "melt" into their host communities facilitated their ability to traverse the borders. While the outline of their settlement in Canada is well known to those in the field of Canadian Jewish history, in the wider community their story has often been overshadowed by the later arrival of their co-religionists from Eastern Europe. This chapter will illustrate the ease with which the various members of this community were consistently able to cross this contested yet fluid border. Despite the clashes between the United States and Great Britain, the early Canadian Jewish community unabashedly developed strong bonds with the already established American Jewish community through ties of marriage, friendship, and business. The regions under discussion here are the present-day provinces of Quebec and Ontario and the states of New York and Michigan; the time span examined is from 1760 (the end of French sovereignty in North America) to 1867, when Canada entered into Confederation and the United States and the new Canadian government both deemed it time to "take control" of the border. Indeed, for the interval between 1763 and around 1776, Lower and Upper Canada were all part of the same British North American polity that extended as far south as Florida.

Early Settlement

Prior to 1760, the population of what was then New France was wholly Roman Catholic.[5] After the Treaty of Aix-la-Chapelle (1748), which ceded Louisbourg to the French until the defeat of France on the Plains of Abraham (1759), traders and merchants who were openly Jewish could only be found at the shifting boundaries of New France and British Colonial America. Samuel Jacobs is listed as the earliest known Jew to live and trade (but not yet settle permanently) in what would eventually become Canadian territory.[6] Jacobs was an active trader between the ports of Bristol (England), Barbados, New York, and Newfoundland; the speculation is that he was with the British garrison at Louisbourg when it was evacuated to Halifax. Despite being allocated land, and having the opportunity to engage in trade without restrictions, the Jewish settlement of about twenty Jews, as of 1758, was unable to maintain itself economically.[7] Samuel Jacobs moved to Quebec shortly after the Battle of the Plains of Abraham, eventually settling (1763) in St-Denis-aux-Richelieu, a village on the river route to New York.[8]

Farther to the west, before 1760, five Jewish men (Ezekiel Solomon, Gershon Levy, Chapman Abraham, Levy Solomons, and Benjamin Lyon) had formed a consortium, Gershon Levy and Company, which was prominent in the New York Indian trade.[9] Initially, the French had controlled Detroit, at the western end of Lake Erie on the Detroit River. Detroit controlled the link between the lower and upper Great Lakes, and its hinterland included Lake Michigan and the confluence of the Illinois and Mississippi rivers.[10] By 1760, the consortium's activities had expanded to include the upper Great Lakes, Oswego, and Fort Niagara, which helped break the French monopoly of the Great Lakes fur trade with the native populations. With the end of France's domination of the fur trade, Jewish merchants and fur traders gained significant business opportunities. With the capture of Montreal (1760), the consortium was free to establish a new base there, much to the consternation of the merchants in Albany and New York.[11] Besides diverting business from New York and Albany, the consortium tended to favour trading with merchants whom they knew over those they did not. For example, the papers of Samuel Jacobs contain correspondence referring to trade between himself, Aaron Hart, Eleazar Levy, and Hyam Myers, who was still living in New York in the early 1760s.[12] One letter, dated 27 September 1761, was from Hyam Meyers, asking Samuel Jacobs to take charge of some goods being shipped to Montreal for Aaron Hart until he (Hart) could claim them.[13]

The Treaty of Paris, signed in 1763, gave Britain sovereignty over mainland North America, "the British victory [breaking] down both barriers and borders."[14] Like their Jewish counterparts in the American colonies, "openly Jewish officers, sutlers, and merchants could now trade, invest, and settle the new country."[15] The defeat of France was viewed with such "relish" that the *hazzan* at New York's Spanish and Portuguese synagogue (Shearith Israel) held a special ceremony to celebrate "the reducing of Canada to his Majesty's Dominions."[16]

As the British army made its way to Montreal, Frederic Haldimand, one of General Amherst's lieutenants, became friendly with one of the army's suppliers, Aaron Hart. When Haldimand was posted to Trois-Rivières, Hart, as a result of their friendship, opted to also settle there. Hart was later joined by his brother Moses and his cousin Uriah Judah. Other Jewish merchants came to Quebec as suppliers for the British troops: John (Jacob) Franks and his son David Franks, Joseph Simon, Gershon Levy, and Levy Andrew Levy.[17] Members of Gershon Levy's consortium also made their way to Montreal, where they extended their business operations and developed commercial connections within the city. By 1765, Ezekiel Solomon and his partner, Gershon Levy, were operating the Solomon-Levy Trading House at Fort Michilimackinac, and by 1779 he and his partners were managing a general store there.[18]

The many waterways enabled the traders to move with ease between Montreal, New York, Albany, Detroit, and Fort Michilimackinac. These waterways were vital to their ability to trade, travel, and visit, forming the beginnings of the future boundary between British North America and England's former colonies.[19] New arrivals spread and settled along the waterways. It would be almost a hundred years before the waterways were no longer needed to carry goods and people between the villages and towns as well as to the larger urban markets.

In 1768, the small group of Jews living in Montreal came together to form Canada's first congregation, also called Shearith Israel (Remnant of Israel).[20] Although the new congregation developed more formal ties with Bevis Marks, London, England's Sephardic synagogue, Montreal's Jews also sought assistance from their co-religionists in New York and Philadelphia. At different times throughout this initial settlement period, various members of the Montreal Jewish community sought refuge and support from their "mother" congregation in New York. In the first decade, services were tenuous as members moved around with the military or moved back to New York or returned to England. Many of the community's members moved to the larger American cities seeking wives and remained there, or married French Canadian women and became lost to the nascent Jewish community. Aaron Hart returned to London briefly to marry his cousin Dorothea Judah (1768), sister to Uriah and Samuel Judah.[21] Lazarus David, also an early settler in Montreal, and a supporter of the newly formed Shearith Israel, travelled to Rhode Island in 1761 to marry Phoebe Samuel, born in Arnwick, England.[22] Moses Hart married Esther Solomon, sister of Ezekiel Solomon, who married a Christian, Elizabeth Okimabinesikoue Dubois (b. 1743).[23]

The Thirteen Colonies Revolt: Canada Invaded

Many American settlers were angered by the ceding of the Indian Territory south of the Great Lakes between the Mississippi and Ohio rivers on the west, and by the Quebec Act. This was on top of other grievances, such as taxation without representation in the British Parliament, so they prepared to rebel against Great Britain. The Continental Congress urged the colony of Quebec to participate in their bid to overthrow the monarchy.[24] The majority of Jewish settlers valued their relationship with the British government and defended the towns where they lived.[25] Quebec City, unlike Montreal, managed to drive back the American forces. The lists of those who defended the city include Isaac Judah, Elias Solomon, and John Franks. This must have been particularly difficult for Franks, as his son, David Salisbury (Solebury) Franks, was very supportive of the American cause.[26]

Similarly, Hyam Myers, now living in Canada, was loath to assist in the defence of Quebec while his son Moses was serving in the New York militia. David Franks's cousin, Levy Solomons, husband of Rebecca Franks, whose New York family were staunch Loyalists, found himself cast as a supporter of the American cause by dint of circumstances. It was difficult for the citizens of Lower Canada to not aid the Americans as they occupied Montreal and Trois-Rivières, from the fall of 1775 to early summer 1776. Refusing to assist the invading force was a perilous choice. When Solomons was asked to undertake responsibility for the American hospitals, he did so, and it financially ruined him. With the evacuation of the Americans from Montreal, Solomons was ostracized, which not only socially isolated him but also made it impossible for him to recuperate his financial losses.[27] Despite he and his family being evicted from their home by British General John Burgoyne, and being publicly humiliated by having their possessions tossed into the street, Levy Solomons decided to stay in Canada, eventually returning to live in Montreal from Lachine, where he and his family had found refuge.[28]

Aaron Hart, in Trois-Rivières, found that, like Levy Solomons, he was left with worthless pieces of paper as a result of expenses incurred by the Americans. Besides piling up debts approaching almost £500, the invading Americans had confiscated various items, such as clothing, blankets, shovels, stoves, firewood, thousands of pounds of bread, and sleighs to transport these supplies.[29] Hart must also have been burdened personally, as his wife's brother Samuel Judah was very supportive of the American Revolution, and of George Washington in particular. Although the US government, many years later, acknowledged its debt to Aaron Hart, neither he nor his sons were able to recoup their losses.[30]

The American forces approached Samuel Jacobs, who lived between Montreal and St-Denis-aux-Richelieu, for aid. While engaging in trade with the Americans, he kept a journal of their occupation, and their interactions with his neighbours, with the intention of sharing his observations with the British.[31] Unfortunately, the journal was encoded so uniquely with Hebrew, Yiddish, and English words in Hebrew letters that it was of little use to anyone but Samuel Jacobs himself. Jacobs suffered severe financial losses when Colonel Moses Hazen, the American commanding officer in charge of Montreal during the invasion, demanded that Jacobs supply his troops. Hazen's duplicity and his active support of the American cause must have dismayed and shocked his Jewish neighbour; Hazen had entered Quebec with the British army twelve years earlier and had settled down to run his farm and other business interests. The Revolutionary War must have appealed to Hazen in a profound way, so much so that it cost him all he had worked for: home, lands, and businesses literally went up in smoke (he torched them) once he decided to join the Americans.[32]

Eleazar Levy, another early settler who had relocated from New York to Quebec City after 1760, worked closely with Aaron Hart (with whom he became friends) in supplying and feeding the British troops. An abuse of power on the part of the British resulted in a loss of goods valued at more than £1,500 for Levy. Disillusioned by the failure of the British to honour their debt, at the outbreak of the American Revolution Levy uprooted himself from Quebec, moving first to Philadelphia and then, once peace was re-established, back to New York. The fact that Levy now resided in the United States did not diminish his social and business ties with Aaron Hart.[33]

Re-establishing Connections: Trade Resumes

Soon after the War for American Independence, commerce and social relations resumed between those now divided by the international border between the United States and Canada. Samuel Judah, Hart's brother-in-law, realizing that the Americans would not be taking over Canada any time soon, sent $11,000 in Continental currency to a business friend in Philadelphia, asking him to sell it for whatever he could. Unfortunately, offloading his currency did not help his business; close to the end of the hostilities, his goods were seized at sea, and in 1784 he was forced to declare bankruptcy. He returned to New York shortly after. A combination of financial difficulties and personal loss resulted in Hyam Myers, a founding member of Shearith Israel in Montreal, returning to live in New York. The revolution affected the ability of the Montreal Jews to attend services in New York: as New York had been under control of the British, the Shearith Israel decided to disband, close the building, and retreat with its Torah scrolls and other religious items to Philadelphia, where it remained until 1782.[34] Lack of access to the services and clergy of the New York community provided the impetus for the community to formalize its presence in Quebec. Building a synagogue would signify their rootedness in the community, and hiring a *hazzan* would attract new members, ensuring continuity. While still living in Montreal, Hyam Myers was appointed to go to London (1778) to inquire of the London Sephardic community for a spiritual leader for the congregation, and to purchase a Torah scroll. Myers returned to Shearith Israel with the Torah scrolls and a contract detailing the hiring of Reverend Jacob Raphael Cohen to be the synagogue's spiritual leader.[35] Membership in the

Montreal synagogue was not restricted to Montreal but was drawn from Quebec City to the Straits of Michilimackinac.[36]

Jonathan Sarna has noted that the border created by the American Revolution did not affect Canadian and American Jews, who "continued to visit one another, trade with one another, and marry one another."[37] Several Jews who had straddled New York and Montreal returned to New York once relations between the two countries "normalized."[38] In these early years of the Canadian Jewish community, the Jews living in and around Montreal identified with the Anglo-Saxon elites due to similarities in language (lack of French) and socio-economic standing.[39] As this next generation established itself, Aaron Hart brought various relatives from England to continue the development of his business network along the Quebec waterways. He encouraged the Manuels, his sister-in-law Miriam Judah and her husband Emanuel, to settle in Yamachiche, and his nephew, Henry Joseph, to settle in Berthier. Another of Hart's business colleagues, Isaac Phineas (Pines), settled in Louisville (Rivière-du-Loup).[40] Everyday life continued despite living along an international border; Marcus Hansen has noted that "Americans and Canadians crossed the boundary to have their grinding done at the nearest mills, and all of them prepared potash and timber for the buyers of Montreal."[41]

By virtue of familiarity and availability, a number of the sons and daughters of these settlers married each other, or cousins who resided in the United States: finding someone of marriageable age, and Jewish, in Quebec was not easily done. Three of Hart's daughters married Jewish men: Catherine married Bernard Judah; Sarah, Samuel David; and Charlotte, Moses David. Samuel and Moses were brothers.[42] Elizabeth, the second-youngest Hart daughter, married a French Canadian, Augustin Laveau.[43] Ezekiel, the second son, was in business with his father but also spent time in New York, hoping to find himself a wife. He stayed with Ephraim Hart (no relation) and there met his wife, Frances Lazarus (niece of this New York Hart family). The couple returned to live in Trois-Rivières. The two younger sons of Hart, Benjamin and Alexander, were sent at a young age – eleven and eight, respectively – to Philadelphia and New York to complete their education. The manner of their travels underscores the importance of the waterways at these times. Aaron asked Moses to return home with his brothers for Passover. Moses met Benjamin and Alexander in Kingsbury, New York, where Aaron's brother Henry (their uncle) lived and worked. The boys were accompanied by Uriah Judah (relative of Bernard Judah) from Philadelphia, to New York, through the Hudson Valley and to Lake Champlain; Kingsbury was about fifty-five miles north of Albany, at the portage point between the Hudson River and the Lake George–Champlain chain. From this point the trio journeyed by horse and boat to Saint John, New Brunswick, to La Prairie, Quebec, and then to Montreal; from there, they travelled by boat up the St. Lawrence River to Trois-Rivières.[44] There is no indication of how many days were required for this particular trip: elsewhere it is stated that Moses David, brother of David David, was often in Detroit and Sandwich (a settlement opposite the Detroit River on British territory after 1783) on business, and mention is made of him returning to Montreal from Detroit in seven days.[45]

Finding marriage partners continued to be a challenge, and many went south seeking partners to bring north to Canada, thus adding to the numbers of those who freely crossed the border for visiting and business. For example, Benjamin Solomons, brother of Rachel, married Elkalah Seixas, daughter of Gershom Mendes Seixas, minister of New York's Shearith Israel, also called the Spanish and Portuguese Congregation. A further connection was created with New York and Philadelphia when Jacob Henry Joseph, a son of Henry Joseph, married Sara Gratz Moses, a niece of the famous author and activist Rebecca Gratz.[46] Levy Solomons, Jr., son of Levy Solomons, unable to establish himself in Cornwall, moved to Albany, where his father had lived and worked prior to his move to Montreal.[47] He married Catherine Manuel, daughter of the Manuels in Yamachiche, while her sister Hannah became the second wife of Reverend Gershom Mendes Seixas of Shearith Israel.[48] Benjamin married Harriott Judith Hart, daughter of Ephraim Hart, with whom he had sixteen children despite their arguments and separations. Alexander moved to Montreal after his father's death and married a Protestant, Mary-Anne Douglas. Moses Hart, the eldest son, was a bit of a rogue and womanizer. The network of friends/family illustrates itself in the solutions Aaron Hart tried to create for his wayward elder son. Initially he planned to send him to his (Aaron's) brother Henry, who lived in Albany; then he thought to set up apprenticeships in either Plattsburgh or Burlington. None of these transpired as Moses took himself off to New York. He eventually married his cousin Sarah Judah (daughter of his uncle, Uriah Judah). This was more a marriage of convenience (so that he would be permitted to enter his father's business), and they eventually separated.

Lazarus David and Phoebe Samuel (mentioned previously) had five children. Three were sons: David, who remained single; Samuel, who married Sarah Hart; and Moses, who married Charlotte Hart. Their two daughters, Abigail and Frances, married men living in Montreal who both had American connections. Abigail married Andrew Hays, son of Solomon and Gitlah Hays of New York; as Andrew Hays is listed among the first group of Jewish settlers to live in Montreal in 1764,[49] this suggests he was quite a bit older than Abigail, whose parents had only just married in 1764. Myer

Michaels, husband of Frances, was the son of Levy Michaels and Rachel Hays, who had moved from New York to Montreal in 1764.[50]

Congress Declares War

The Treaty of Paris (1783) ended the war between Great Britain and the newly established United States but did not bring a lasting peace: the War of 1812 broke out three decades later.[51] Thousands loyal to the British Crown were forced to abandon their possessions and were driven from the United States. Montreal quickly turned into a Loyalist centre, and members of the local Jewish community became concerned about the maintenance of British authority.[52] The War of 1812 also disrupted trade and communications between the Jewish communities in Lower Canada and the various cities and towns to the south. Former president Thomas Jefferson imprudently committed to paper that "the acquisition of Canada this year, as far as the neighbourhood, will be a mere matter of marching."[53]

Within the Canadian Jewish community, there was no support for the American invasion; by this time almost every known Jewish family had a member in the British militias. David David, his brother Samuel, and Myer Michaels were part of the Montreal militia; Ezekiel Hart, second son of Aaron Hart, was an ensign and then lieutenant in the Trois-Rivières militia, along with Isaac Phineas. Eleazar Hays, son of Andrew and Abigail Hays, was a quartermaster in the 1st Battalion of the Vaudreuil Division of the Montreal militia, and Samuel Seixas, brother of Elkalah Seixas and son of the minister of New York's Spanish and Portuguese Congregation, was quartermaster and sergeant of the Montreal militia.[54]

Along the border communities of Lower Canada, New England, and New York, the day-to-day social and business interactions that had existed prior to the American "call to arms" continued.[55] During the War of 1812, the Hart brothers, especially Moses, were providing supplies to the British army. While the war impinged on the Harts' trade with England, they did well selling beer, flour, and meat to the British troops and Canadian militia. It appears that most of the agricultural products Hart sold to the British were purchased in Vermont and northern New York.[56] Not only did Vermonters and Canadians trade without regard for the hostilities on either side of the border, but in some cases the American customs collector stationed in Vermont did little to stem the trade. The war failed to interrupt commercial and social relations between American and Canadian merchants with their customers on the opposite side of the border. In fact, it stimulated additional trade during those years due to an increased demand for supplies during wartime.[57] Marion Smith, writing on the US–Canada border, noted that despite a "principal line [being drawn] (on paper) between the new United States and British colonies to the North, following the American Revolution and the War of 1812, it held little meaning for a population ... maintaining a perpetual motion around the Great Lakes."[58] With the end of the War of 1812 and before the many border skirmishes that led to the Rebellions of 1837–38, there was a brief respite between the two countries.

Resumption of Trade and Growth of Montreal

Jewish settlers were an integral part of the financial and commercial landscape of Montreal. For example, David David was one of the promoters of a company to build a canal connecting Montreal and Lachine, which improved trade and communications between Montreal and Upper Canada. Very active in the commercial development of Montreal, David David was a founding director of the Bank of Montreal and, with Henry Joseph and Moses Hays, formed the Committee of Trade to strengthen the business community in its dealings with the government and the military. This eventually became the Montreal Board of Trade.[59]

Not all the children of the early settlers were able to find suitable employment in Canada, as it was vastly underdeveloped from a professional perspective compared to the United States. For example, Frank Hart, a grandson of Aaron Hart and one of Benjamin Hart's sons, was the first Jew to obtain his medical degree in Canada, from McGill University in 1835.[60] He left after graduating to work in St. Louis, Missouri, where his brother Henry N. Hart and his family lived.[61] Two cousins, Esdaile Cohen David and Abraham Pinto Joseph, also left for the United States, the former to live on Long Island and the latter to live in Pittsburgh.

During this period (1790–1830), the Montreal Jewish community set about re-establishing its synagogue. The lack of a viable economy affected the maintenance of Shearith Israel. Between the active participation of some Jewish members in the British militias, and the volatile political and economic climate, a number of Jewish commercial enterprises were flagging. Lacking sufficient funds, Shearith Israel was unable to sustain services on a regular basis or provide its members with their ritual requirements. By the nineteenth century, members of the Montreal Jewish community were once again travelling to New York for the High Holidays. As the community at this time was unable to act as a legal entity, the synagogue could not maintain its own register of births, marriages, and deaths, possess a piece of land for cemetery needs, or even build a house of worship. Benjamin Hart, Aaron's third son, had moved to Montreal, where he became active in the Jewish community. Initially, he opened his home for services, hosting the 1824 High Holiday services. Through his efforts, the community drew together and in December 1828 petitioned the House of Assembly for the legal right to maintain its own registry and to build a synagogue. In January 1832, the Bill for the Relief of Persons professing the Jewish faith received Royal Assent. Despite the political tensions in Montreal, members of the Jewish community came together in August 1838 to inaugurate the new synagogue.[62]

Upheavals in Canada

In 1832, the Declaratory Act of Lower Canada confirmed that Jews were entitled to rights equal to those of others who lived there. Within five years, Benjamin Hart and Moses Judah Hays had been appointed Justices of the Peace (1837), in time for Benjamin Hart to be the magistrate dealing with those charged in Lower Canada with fomenting the rebellions of 1837–38.[63] The upheavals that took place in 1837 and 1838 were motivated by the needs of two disparate groups. In Lower Canada, especially among the French Canadian population, the *Patriotes* were seeking economic and political reforms.[64] In Upper Canada, supported to some extent by Patriots in the United States, a number of Americans, especially those living in the bordering states, were convinced that their assistance to free Canada from Great Britain would be wholly supported by Canadians.[65] An unforeseen consequence of these raids was greater surveillance at the various border crossings: the US Treasury Department issued a statement (19 December 1837) ordering the customs officials at these crossings to be more vigilant in their prosecution of "citizens and other inhabitants" seeking to undermine relations between Canada and the United States.[66] The youngest of Henry Joseph's sons, Gershom, was studying in Toronto at the time and witnessed some of the events during the rebellion of 1837–38 in Upper Canada.[67] As he wrote to his brother Jacob in December 1837: "Toronto is in a bad state – the first story of every shop is nailed up & barricaded as strongly as possible. 2d stories, banks, etc., filled with armed men ready to defend their homes if the rebels should get into the town. An armed force Militia 3100 strong was [*sic*] to march under Sir F. Head against the rebels tomorrow morning."[68]

Both groups were quickly disabused of their notions. Curiously, despite engaging in treasonous actions, most of the rebels of Upper Canada were not tried for treason and were eventually released.[69] The *Patriotes* of Lower Canada were not as fortunate: twelve men were hanged despite only four initially being sentenced to death with recommendations for clemency, six recommended for deportation, and two found not guilty. Denis Vaugeois points out that as a result of Benjamin Hart's being "the harshest of magistrates" and his alignment with those in power, a rift grew between himself, his son (Aaron Philip), and his nephews, Ezekiel's sons, Samuel Bécancour, Ira Craig, and Adolphus Mordechai. Hart's inability to be flexible in the face of obvious injustice may have caused him to fall out of favour with the British. No recognition was accorded his actions, and when the government passed the Rebellion Losses Bill (1849) to compensate those who had experienced financial loss as a result of the government's repressive actions, Hart must have felt deeply betrayed.[70]

As a result of a downward-spiralling economy, Hart's business investments were failing, and his export business (flour for the British market) collapsed completely after the British repealed their Corn Laws and placed the Canadian flour market in competition with the United States.[71] In retrospect, Hart's response to his personal crises is understandable. He was the author of and a signatory to the Annexationist Manifesto of 1849: a call for Canada to leave Britain and join the United States. The resultant uproar resulted in the loss of his militia rank of lieutenant-colonel, as well as the loss of his magistrate's position. Hart left Montreal and moved to New York, where his son Arthur Wellington had settled earlier.[72]

A series of reciprocity agreements between the British Canadian provinces and the United States provided for mutual free exchange of natural products. This made for very active exchanges along the waterways and borders. Marcus Hansen and John B. Brebner write that "merchants and farmers crossed and re-crossed the boundary buying and selling wherever the greatest advantage could be found."[73] Throughout the 1830s, for example, Moses Hart had amassed land in the Eastern Townships, northern Vermont, and northern New York State. He also owned many cattle, which he provisioned on his farms in northern New York State. While these cattle were mainly marketed at Albany, they were also sometimes driven north to Lower Canada for sale. Like his cousin, Henry Joseph, and other Hart and Joseph family members, Moses Hart was also heavily involved in shipping. A main source of revenue for the family was transporting freight and operating towboats along the St. Lawrence waterways. A large part of their shipping was centred on receiving wood for their sawmills and then delivering finished lumber to various buyers.[74] Vaugeois, in his history of the Hart family, describes the method for towing timber; he notes that rafts being floated between Hull and Quebec had to survive 175 miles of rapids.[75] The Richelieu River rapids also possibly contributed to product loss. Canals helped bypass the rapids in spring, summer, and autumn; delivery of the wood suffered in the winter months, when the water level was low.[76]

The railway would circumvent the obstacles inherent in water travel. In 1836, the first Canadian rail line was built: the Champlain and St. Lawrence

Railway.[77] This line, sixteen miles long, linked the cities of La Prairie and St-Jean-sur-Richelieu in Quebec, bypassing the Richelieu River rapids.[78] Benjamin Hart was an investor in this line, as were his cousins, Jesse Joseph and Jacob Henry Joseph.[79] By 1852, the line had been extended to the boundary of New York State.[80] The shortened travel times also affected immigration. Throughout the 1840s and 1850s, mostly Central European Jews crossed the ocean, escaping the lack of economic and professional opportunities. While the majority of Jewish immmigrants went to the United States, a few made their way to Montreal and Toronto. Enough came to Montreal, much to the delight of Moses Hart, who saw financial possibilities; and to the chagrin of Benjamin Hart, who saw that great changes were about to take place. One major change was the formation of a second synagogue in Montreal; in 1846 the Corporation of English, German, and Polish Jews became a legal entity, and their synagogue actively began its life as Sha'ar Hashomayim (Gates of Heaven) in 1858.[81]

Canada Moves Towards Nationhood

Shortly after the second inauguration of Shearith Israel (1840), David Piza, from Bevis Marks in London, was hired to be its *hazzan*.[82] When he left Montreal (and Shearith Israel) to take up the position of *Hazzan Sheni* at Bevis Marks, he encouraged then twenty-one-year-old Abraham de Sola (son of David Aaron de Sola, *hazzan* of Bevis Marks) to apply for his now vacant position.[83] In 1852, Abraham married Esther, the youngest daughter of the aforementioned Henry Joseph. Even as the community increased with the new influx of German Jewish immigrants, members continued to travel to and from the United States, visiting family and seeking new business opportunities.

Gershom Joseph, previously mentioned, was "bitten by the gold rush bug" and left for California in 1849 to seek his fortune. There, he married an American of French heritage (Celine Lyons); in 1863, he returned with her to Montreal.[84] Joseph's return to Canada was timely, for 1863 was the same year the borders tightened between the United States and Canada, as draft dodgers and army deserters made their way into Canada to escape service in the Union Army during the American Civil War (1861–65). It is curious that in seeking trade and developing their commercial prospects, most Montreal Jews continued to look south to the United States rather than west towards Toronto. Other than the abovementioned three young men from Quebec, most of the first Jewish arrivals to Toronto were from England, although several came via the United States. These newcomers came with funds to establish their businesses. The outbreak of the American Civil War temporarily disrupted all trade. Soon, however, the needs of the war took over: Canadians were recruited to join the Union States, and advertisements for Canadian labour included financial rewards. Able-bodied men were needed for fishing, lumbering, shipping, mining, and farming, and Canadians rushed to take advantage of these employment opportunities.[85] Even during the Civil War, Canadian Jews could still be found visiting and touring through parts of the United States.[86]

The constant border activity, the loss of Canadian workers to the South, the Fenian raids, and the fear of invasion propelled the provinces to Confederation. The British North America Act called for an all-Canadian rail link from Halifax to Montreal and for the railway to be built as far as possible from the American border.[87] However, the construction of the Grand Trunk Railway of Canada had been planned prior to Confederation, and despite that it linked Montreal to Portland, Maine, it was completed. This line guaranteed Montreal year-round access to an open port.[88] The end result was that Portland became Montreal's winter port and for several decades remained Canada's principal partner in its grain trade[89] – directly undermining the Canadian wheat brokers and traders, several of whom were Jewish.

Conclusion

A cursory reading of North American history before 1867, especially that related to the Jewish contribution, demonstrates the extensive overlap between the families of the early Jewish settlers in both countries. As noted at the outset of this article, the similarities between American and English Jews, not to forget American and English Christians with whom they traded and socialized, outweighed any implied differences. The research of Hansen and Brebner demonstrates that during this period economic opportunities were prized over national affiliations, which enabled a culture of permeability at the border.[90] This simple ability to traverse the borders unmolested was a primary factor in the development of the relationship between the Jewish communities in New York and Lower Canada. As has also been illustrated throughout, the conflicts between the United States and Great Britain had little impact on those individuals who regularly travelled and engaged in trade on the other side of the border. The apparent ease with which British and American Jews were able to attain social, financial, and professional success in Lower Canada (partly as a consequence of their American and British connections) is in sharp contrast to the history of Canadian Jewry after 1881. This "ease" has led a number of historians of Canadian Jewry to describe this period of early Jewish settlement as the "golden age" of Canadian Jewry.[91]

The difficulties experienced by the Canadian Jewish community after 1881 are viewed as "normative" Canadian Jewish history and as such the period prior, with its open trade and lack of overt anti-Semitism, does indeed appear idyllic. While there were successes, there were also, as mentioned previously, bankruptcies, trade failures, and family breakdowns. Further research in several key areas would allow a more realistic assessment of the nascent Jewish community. To what extent was the border a noticeable factor in the commercial success of the Jewish community in Lower Canada? To what extent did the tightening of border controls affect regional trading (specifically for the Jewish merchants in Canada)? And to what extent were the cross-border ties loosened as a consequence of generational change? These questions delve into a very localized history that is also international in scope.

By the early twentieth century, the border as it is known today was in place. For example, where once there had been one immigration inspector in Detroit, by 1907 there were thirteen.[92] Despite the increased presence of immigration officers, then as today, Canadian Jews and American Jews continued to cross the borders to buy and sell, to marry and socialize, and to travel and learn.

Notes

1 Americans crossing the border can access the FAQs published by the Canada Border Services Agency (CBSA), http://www.cbsa-asfc.gc.ca/menu-eng.html. For Canadians heading south, there is the US Customs and Border Protection website, http://apps.cbp.gov/bwt/index.asp. Updated border times are also available on Twitter; each Canadian border crossing has its own hashtag. US CPB also provides access to Twitter contacts by border location. Local radio stations close to the border often provide news about delays.

2 Randy Boswell, "Canadian tourism to U.S. hits record level," *Postmedia News*, 26 March 2012.

3 "The Canada–U.S. border: by the numbers," *CBC News*, http://www.cbc.ca.

4 US Department of Homeland Security and Public Safety Canada, Traffic Disruption Management, *Considerations for United States–Canada Border*, http://www.securitepublique.gc.ca/prg/ns/ci/_fl/btdm-eng.pdf.

5 Anne Joseph, *The Heritage of a Patriarch: Canada's First Jewish Settlers and the Continuing Story of their Families in Canada* (Sillery: Septentrion, 1995), 17.

6 Sheldon J. Godfrey and Judith C. Godfrey, *Search Out the Land: The Jews and the Growth of Equality in British Colonial America, 1740–1867* (Montreal and Kingston: McGill–Queen's University Press, 1995), 73–74.

7 Ibid., 79–81.

8 Denis Vaugeois, *The First Jews in North America: The Extraordinary Story of the Hart Family, 1760–1860* (Montreal: Baraka Books, 2012), 12, 44. Also in Godfrey and Godfrey, *Search Out the Land*, 96.

9 Ibid., 88.

10 Lisa Philips Valentine and Allan K. McDougall, "Imposing the Border: The Detroit River from 1786 to 1807," *Journal of Borderlands Studies* 19, no. 1 (Spring 2004): 13–22.

11 Godfrey and Godfrey, *Search Out the Land*, 88–89.

12 "Correspondence & Other Papers of Samuel Jacobs," Library and Archives Canada here-after LAC], MG 19 A2, series 3, vol. 8, file 2, 1760–61.

13 Ibid.

14 Vaugeois, *The First Jews in North America*, 38.

15 Susan Landau-Chark, "Canada," in *The Jewish Emigrant for Britain, 1700–2000: Essays in Memory of Lloyd P. Gartner*, ed. Gabriel A. Sivan (Jerusalem: Israeli Branch of Jewish Historical Society of England, April 2013), 43.

16 Rabbi Pinto composed a five-page blessing to be read out during morning and afternoon services. Part of it states: "And given to all his Generals, such Power, Strength and Wisdom, to conquer the country of Canada and reducing the same to the happy Dominions of his Sacred Majesty King George the Second." A full copy is available though Memorial University. Joseph Yesurun Pinto (b. 1729), *The form of prayer, which was performed at the Jews synagogue, in the city of New-York, on Thursday October 23, 1760: being the day appointed by proclamation for a general thanksgiving to Almighty God, for the reducing of Canada to His Majesty's dominions*. Printed and sold by W. Weyman, at his new printing-office, in Broad-Street, not far from the Exchange, Pub date: 1760. (Price 4d.), 7.

17 Vaugeois, *The First Jews in North America*, 32–44.

18 Description of the Solomon-Levy Trading Post in notes received from Arthur Kiron via email, 18 February 2014. Kaplan Collection (Canadiana – 021813), ed. Amy Kaplan.

19 Thomas F. McIlwraith, "Transport in the Borderlands, 1763–1920," in *Borderlands: Essays in Canadian–American Relations*, ed. Robert Lecker (Toronto: ECW Press, 1991), 54–79.

20 Gerald Tulchinsky, *Taking Root: The Origins of the Canadian Jewish Community* (Toronto: Lester Publishing, 1992), 8.

21 Gerald Tulchinsky, *Canada's Jews: A People's Journey* (Toronto: University of Toronto Press, 2008), 16–18.

22 Joseph, *The Heritage of a Patriarch*, 29.

23 Vaugeois, *The First Jews in North America*, 75.

24 Ibid., 105.

25 Tulchinsky, *Canada's Jews*, 29.

26 Jacob Rader Marcus, *Memoirs of American Jews, 1775–1865*, vol. 1 (Philadelphia: Jewish Publication Society of America, 1955), 45–50.

27 Godfrey and Godfrey, *Search Out the Land*, 109–11.

28 "Levy Solomons," *Jewish Encyclopaedia*, http://www.jewishencyclopedia.com/articles/13905-solomons-levy.

29 Frederic Gaffen, *The Sons of Aaron Hart*, M.A. thesis, University of Ottawa, 2011, 14–15.

30 Vaugeois, *The First Jews in North America*, xvii, 63–65.

31 Godfrey and Godfrey, *Search Out the Land*, 110.

32 Joe King, *From the Ghetto to the Main: The Story of the Jews of Montreal* (Montreal: Montreal Jewish Publication Society, 2001), 43–46.

33 Gaffen, *The Sons of Aaron Hart*, 24–32.

34 Godfrey and Godfrey, *Search Out the Land*, 116–23.

35 Tulchinsky, *Canada's Jews*, 21.

36 Godfrey and Godfrey, *Search Out the Land*, 114–15.

37 See Jonathan Sarna, "The Canadian Connection of an American Jew: The Case of Mordecai M. Noah," *Canadian Jewish Historical Society Journal* 3, no. 2 (Fall 1979): 117–29.

38 Godfrey and Godfrey, *Search Out the Land*, 122–25.

39 Tulchinsky, *Canada's Jews*, 23.

40 Vaugeois, *The First Jews in North America*, 60.

41 Marcus L. Hansen and John B. Brebner, *The Mingling of the Canadian and American Peoples* (New Haven: Yale University Press, 1940), 76.

42 Joseph, *The Heritage of a Patriarch*, 113, 142–44.

43 Vaugeois, *The First Jews in North America*, 90.

44 Gaffen, *The Sons of Aaron Hart*, 20–23.

45 Arthur D. Hart, *The Jew in Canada* (Montreal: Canadian Jewish Publications, 1926), 321.

46 Michael Brown, *Jew or Juif? Jews, French Canadians, and Anglo-Canadians, 1759–1914* (Philadelphia: Jewish Publication Society, 1987), 87.

47 Godfrey and Godfrey, *Search Out the Land*, 162. Solomons Jr.'s failure to succeed in Cornwall was more a result of the attitude of John Elmsley, Chief Justice of Upper Canada, towards Jews. The Constitutional Act of 1791 was an Act of the British Parliament designed to accommodate the thousands of United Empire Loyalists who had moved to Canada after the American Revolution. It divided Quebec into Upper and Lower Canada, and even though governed by the same laws, the interpretation of these laws was wholly the province of the ruling Chief Justice. The majority of Jews (100) lived in Lower Canada, where they could own land and had integrated with their British and French neighbours; whereas in Upper Canada, Jewish landownership was denied for several decades. Thus only a dozen Jews had settled in Toronto by 1846. See Stephen A. Speisman, *The Jews of Toronto: A History to 1937* (Toronto: McClelland and Stewart, 1979), 15.

48 Anne Joseph, "Montreal – In Days Gone By: The More Personal Life of Levy Solomons," *Montreal Forum: Quarterly Publication of Jewish Genealogical Society of Montreal*, 3, no. 2 (December 2007): 8.

49 Godfrey and Godfrey, *Search Out the Land*, 238n31.

50 Joseph, *The Heritage of a Patriarch*, 47, 283n30.

51 Solomon Frank, *Two Centuries in the Life of a Synagogue* (Montreal: Spanish and Portuguese Synagogue: 1968), 47–48.

52 Ira Robinson, Lecture, 24 January 2006, for *Reli-498L: The Canadian Jewish Experience: Jewish Identity and Religious Life in Canada*, Concordia University, Montreal, Winter 2006. See also Frank, *Two Centuries*, 48.

53 Thomas Jefferson, [Letter] *To Colonel Duane*, Monticello, Virginia, 4 August 1812. Thomas Jefferson and Henry A. Washington, *The Writings of Thomas Jefferson: Being His Autobiography, Correspondence, Reports, Messages, Addresses, and Other Writings, Official and Private*, vol.5 (Washington, DC: Taylor & Maury, 1854), 75.

54 Godfrey and Godfrey, *Search Out the Land*, 183–84.

55 Hansen and Brebner, *The Mingling*, 92–93.

56 Gaffen, *The Sons of Aaron Hart*, 39.

57 H. N. Muller, "A 'Traitorous and Diabolical Traffic': The Commerce of the Champlain–Richelieu Corridor during the War of 1812," *Vermont History* 44, no. 2 (Spring 1976): 78–96.

58 Marian L. Smith, "The Immigration and Naturalization Service (INS) at the U.S.–Canadian Border, 1893–1993: An Overview of Issues and Topics," *Michigan Historical Review* 26, no. 2 (Fall 2000): 127–47.

59 Joseph, *The Heritage of a Patriarch*, 153; Tulchinsky, *Taking Root*, 29–31.

60 Brown, *Jew or Juif?*, 79.

61 Frank Hart is a conundrum. While Michael Brown lists him as "a member of Canada's oldest Jewish family" (*Jew or Juif*, 79), there are no Franks listed in the third generation of Harts. Anne Joseph, in email correspondence, 16 August 2013, notes that Benjamin's son Frederick might have used the name Frank. It is known that Frank Hart/Frederick W. Hart graduated from the McGill University Faculty of Medicine in 1835 (*The Jew in Canada*, 536). According to Anne Joseph, the information available about Dr. Hart is somewhat fragmentary and disconnected. It has been noted that he moved to St. Louis and later to Colorado. One wonders about the choice of St. Louis and whether there were any family already living there. I have speculated that he had a brother there as the 1880 census for St. Louis, Missouri, lists Henry N. Hart, lawyer, son of Benjamin Hart. Unfortunately, we do not know which year either Hart actually moved there.

62 Godfrey and Godfrey, *Search Out the Land*, 148–53, 180–86, 256.

63 Ibid., 204.

64 Allan Greer, *The Patriots and the People: The Rebellion of 1837 in Rural Lower Canada* (Toronto: University of Toronto Press, 1993).

65 J.I. Little, *Loyalties in Conflict: A Canadian Borderland in War and Rebellion, 1812–1840* (Toronto: University of Toronto Press, 2008).

66 Orrin Edwin Tiffany, *Relations of the United States to the Canadian Rebellion of 1837–1838* (Buffalo: Buffalo Historical Society, 1907), 78.

67   Benjamin G. Sacks, *History of the Jews in Canada*, trans. Ralph Novek (Montreal: Harvest House, 1965), 116. According to Sacks, Gershom Hart enrolled at the University of Toronto in 1838 for the purpose of taking his BA, and then prepared for the bar. However, it appears that no instructional courses were offered at the University of Toronto until 1842.

68 Letter from G. Joseph to J. Henry Joseph, December 1837, privately held by Anne Joseph, Montreal. Anne Joseph also mentioned her intention to give the documents pertaining to her family history to the National Jewish Archives in Montreal, although she did not specify when.

69 Little, *Loyalties in Conflict*, 94.

70 Vaugeois, *The First Jews in North America*, 162.

71 Gaffen, *The Sons of Aaron Hart*, 74.

72 Vaugeois, *The First Jews in North America*, 163.

73 Hansen and Brebner, *The Mingling*, 139.

74 Gaffen, *The Sons of Aaron Hart*, 44–57.

75 Vaugeois, *The First Jews in North America*, 187.

76 Gaffen, *The Sons of Aaron Hart*, 54, 72.

77 "The Canadian National Railways Museum Train Collection," LAC, RG 30-8, vol. 591, B, "The Company of proprietors of the Champlain and Saint-Lawrence Railroads, 1836–1931," 21.

78 Gaffen, *The Sons of Aaron Hart*, 72.

79 Hart, *The Jew in Canada*, 323; Joseph, *The Heritage of a Patriarch*, 268. Anne Joseph notes that Jacob Henry Joseph was an active shareholder and director of the Champlain and St. Lawrence Railroad Co. and was one of a handful of merchants who helped design and construct the railway.

80 "The Canadian National Railways Museum Train collection," 21.

81 Wilfred Shuchat, *The Gate of Heaven: The Story of Congregation Shaar Hashomayim of Montreal, 1846–1996* (Montreal and Kingston: McGill–Queen's University Press, 2000), 17–18.

82 Tulchinsky, *Taking Root*, 17–18.

83 Joseph, *The Heritage of a Patriarch*, 198, 219. Anne Joseph notes that as a result of the strong personal ties between the founding members of Shearith Israel and Bevis Marks, a special healing prayer (*misheberach*) on behalf of the synagogue is offered every year at the evening service prior (Kol Nidre) to the Day of Atonement (58).

84 Joseph, *The Heritage of a Patriarch*, 79, 88.

85 Hansen and Brebner, *The Mingling*, 13–17, 143–57.

86 Brown, *Jew or Juif*, 92.

87 Donald G. Janelle, "The Maine Connection: Quebec to New Brunswick," in *Borderlands: Essays in Canadian–American Relations*, ed. Robert Lecker (Toronto: ECW Press, 1991), 113–26.

88 Ève Préfontaine, "Railways in Canada, 1830–1918," McCord Museum, 2013, http://www.mccord-museum.qc.ca/scripts/explore.php?elementid=4__true&tableid=11&contentlong.

89 Janelle, "The Maine Connection," 113–26.

90 See Hansen and Brebner, *The Mingling*.

91 Steven Lapidus, "The Golden Century?: Jews in Nineteenth-Century British North America," in *Canada's Jews: In Time, Space, and Spirit*, ed. Ira Robinson (Boston: Academic Studies Press, 2013), 29.

92 Bruno Ramirez, *Crossing the 49th Parallel: Migration from Canada to the United States, 1900–1930* (Ithaca: Cornell University Press, 2001), 44.

THREE

Re-evaluating *Jew or Juif?*
Jewish Community and Life in Franco
Heritage North America before ca. 1920

Barry L. Stiefel

In 1987, historian Michael Brown published *Jew or Juif? Jews, French Cana-dians, and Anglo-Canadians, 1759–1914*, which explored the intricate rela-tionship between Jews and anglophone and francophone Canada, particu-larly in Montreal.[1] The book was informative and well written. However, the former Viceroyalty of New France, which created a lasting North American francophone landscape, was by no means confined to the contemporary borders of Quebec, or Canada for that matter. Other areas once part of the old French empire, such as Louisiana, are in the United States. Further-more, Louisiana and New Orleans in particular have a contemporary Jew-ish presence that has had contact with this patrimony. The cultural environ-ments and societies of Quebec and Louisiana have many similarities rooted in the shared French colonial experience. So, while the geopolitical union of the United States and Canada was dissolved after the American War of Independence (1775–83), the destinies of these countries continue to be intertwined.

I will use Brown's mode of analysis regarding the relationship between Jews and French peoples, but with a perspective that spans the entirety of

North America. In other words, I will be asking whether there has been a shared experience among Jews in Quebec and Louisiana even though Jews did not participate in the development of these territories when they belonged to France. For example, beginning with the building of the first synagogue in Quebec in 1778, we find that Montreal's Shearith Israel composed its bylaws *only* in English, while the bylaws of New Orleans's first congregation, Shaarei Chessed, were written in English *and* French when it formed in 1827. What accounts for this difference?[2] Thus, as a case study, this investigation can be an important model for future scholarship on North American cultural heritage studies as they relate to Canada and the United States. This comparative study will reveal the exceptionalities and commonalities of the Jewish experience in Quebec vis-à-vis Louisiana, and bring a more holistic understanding of what "Jew or Juif" means north and south of the international border.

I have limited my study to before 1920 for several reasons. It was around that year that the United States began restricting its flow of immigrants (Immigration Restriction Act of 1921), which also significantly affected immigration to Canada as an alternative destination. Xenophobia was on the rise across the United States. In Louisiana, the state government banned the teaching of French in public schools, and this had a strong adverse impact on the French aspect of its cultural environment. In addition to this, racial discrimination – especially against African Americans – was on the rise across the South. Lastly, 1920 was two years after the end of the First World War. The Treaty of Versailles, signed on 28 June 1919 by the Allies and Germany had returned Alsace and Lorraine to France, which significantly affected the immigration of francophones from that region to North America – a subtopic that will also be discussed from the pre-1920 period.

Historic Context: Jews in French North America before 1763

French colonization in North America began in 1600 with the founding of Tadoussac, a settlement and trading post at the mouth of the St. Lawrence River. Quebec City, the province's capital, was founded in 1608. A year earlier, in 1607, the British had founded Jamestown, their first North American colony, in what is now Virginia. During the early seventeenth century, Jews were legally prohibited from both empires, having been expelled long before from England (in 1290) and France (in 1394), although there were some exceptions. After Judaism was made illegal in Spain and Portugal during the 1490s, Henry II (1519–59) admitted some Jews into Bordeaux, France, but they had to live as Catholics. Not until the early eighteenth century (1723) could Jews in France officially identify themselves as such, although by this time their Catholic appearance was scarcely more than lip service. However, due to the positive contributions Jews made to the Bordeaux economy, and the resulting tax revenue, the Crown was hardly offended.[3] The Jews of Avignon had been exempted because they were within a Papal State. This was in contrast to England, where around 1655, the Lord Protector, Oliver Cromwell (1599–1658), unilaterally ceased enforcing the 1290 expulsion edict. When Charles II (r. 1660–85) ascended to the throne, he continued to permit Jews within his realms. Jewish settlement in British North America began in the mid- and late seventeenth century, in Rhode Island and South Carolina, as well as in New York after it was acquired from the Dutch (1664).

In the mid-seventeenth century, descendants of the Iberian refugees became involved in France's Caribbean exploits. Sephardic Jews from the Netherlands joined them. Their success in the Caribbean – most notably in Martinique, Guadeloupe, and Cayenne – as producers of sugar and other luxury commodities did not go unnoticed. French colonial officials and entrepreneurs desired the presence of Jews in French colonial society, and especially valued their economic contributions. The Catholic Church, though, did not appreciate their presence, and the Jesuits found it especially repulsive (as indeed they did the presence of all non-Catholics).[4] Meanwhile, in France, a power struggle was playing out, beginning with the French Wars of Religion (1562–98), an extension of the Reformation and subsequent Counter-Reformation. The Edict of Nantes (1598) forged a temporary peace that returned civil unity to the war-torn nation. That unity applied primarily to France proper, less so to her colonies. Those who were against civil unity with France's Protestant minority began to chip away at the freedom of conscience and toleration extended to them by the Nantes edict. The Jesuits, among others, desired full unity, including that of faith. In 1627 and 1659, edicts were declared forbidding non-Catholics to settle in Quebec and Acadia respectively.[5] These prohibitions were directed towards Protestant Huguenots, although it did not trouble the Jesuits that Jews were adversely affected. Indeed, the Jesuits had been calling for Jews to be banned from the Caribbean as well. Thus, in 1685, the Code Noir and the Edict of Fontainebleau (which revoked Nantes) were promulgated. These statutes supporting Catholic hegemony applied across France and in her overseas empire. Huguenots were expelled from France and were no longer permitted anywhere under the fleur-de-lis.[6]

The Sephardic crypto-Jews in Bordeaux were permitted to remain, as were the Ashkenazim in Alsace after the conclusion of the Thirty Years' War (1618–48). The Crown held them to be non-threatening and economically beneficial. Confined to small towns and hamlets until emancipation in 1791, Alsatian Jews were the bulk of French Jewry after the territory was annexed in 1648. Over the subsequent centuries, Alsace and Lorraine would change hands between France and Germany, creating a Franco-Germanic cultural environment to which the peoples of the region had to adapt. This would provide a slight advantage for Alsatian Jewish immigrants who chose to settle in North America in the nineteenth century, where francophones and anglophones converged.

In 1685, the Jews were expelled from France's colonies, having been singled out by the first article of the Code Noir.[7] The Crown had acquiesced to the Jesuits and their agenda of converting heathen African slaves and Native Americans (the Jews being a distraction to these efforts). Thus, when the colony of Louisiana was founded in 1699, near the present-day site of Biloxi, Mississippi, French law already prohibited Jewish settlement. New Orleans, the colony's capital and largest metropolitan centre, was established in 1718. Unlike the Edict of Fontainebleau, the Code Noir was not strictly enforced, especially regarding the prohibition of Jews. This was for multiple reasons. Some colonial administrators could be enticed to look the other way, perhaps because they were bribed, or for the sake of the colony's economic security. In many colonies, administrators developed a laissez-faire attitude towards their positions and tasks. So, as long as the few Jews residing within their jurisdiction were discreet and paid their taxes (or bribes), little fuss was made. This perhaps is why the Code Noir was declared a second time in 1724.[8]

A select number of Jews received special permission to settle in Martinique and Saint-Domingue (now Haiti). Most significant was the Gradis family, headed by David and (later) Abraham Gradis (1700–80), based in Bordeaux, France. They conducted extensive mercantile activities with the Caribbean, New France, and (to a certain extent) Louisiana during the eighteenth century. During these years, the Gradis family syndicate established offices on Martinique and Saint-Domingue, although not on North American shores.[9] So well known were the Gradis in the francophone Atlantic world that Abraham's death, in 1780, was reported in the *Gazette Françoise*, a French-language newspaper published in Newport, Rhode Island.[10]

The first Jew to establish a presence in Louisiana, in 1757, was Isaac Monsanto, a Dutch Sephardic merchant. He soon brought members of his extended family to reside near him in New Orleans. During the 1760s, Monsanto became so successful that he often dealt with high-ranking officials such as Chevalier Louis Billouart de Kerlerec (1704–70), Louisiana's governor. Monsanto also purchased the Trianon plantation, a short distance from the colonial capital. Purchasing land was a very bold move that would draw the attention of later authorities. Elsewhere, Isaac Henriques, from Bordeaux, settled in Baton Rouge during the 1760s.[11] However, Jewish settle-

Figure 3.1: *Carte du Canada et de la Louisiane qui forment la Nouvelle France et des colonies angloises ou sont representez les pays contestez* / Map of Canada and Louisiana that make up New France and the English colonies in which the territories under dispute are shown, by Jean-Baptiste Nolin, Paris, 1756. Library of Congress Geography and Map Division.

ment in French Louisiana would be short-lived. With the conclusion of the French and Indian War (1754–63; in Europe, referred to as the Seven Years' War), Louisiana was given to Spain, France's ally, in compensation for the loss of Florida to the British. In 1769, Alejandro O'Reilly (1722–94) arrived in Louisiana as the Spanish governor and Captain General. Soon after his arrival he set about reorganizing the colonial administration, especially combating what the Spanish perceived as corruption and mismanagement. This also entailed imposing Spanish bureaucracy and policies. Among other things, this meant expelling the small number of Jews residing there, especially the very successful Monsantos. However, O'Reilly's removal of Louisiana's Jews was not an enforcement of the Code Noir so much as of the Alhambra Decree of 1492, which was still in effect across New Spain. Not until Louisiana's purchase by the United States in 1803, with a brief conveyance to France (lasting around one month), were Jews allowed by law to return to the territory.[12] Meanwhile, when Aaron Hart (1724–1800) entered Montreal in 1760 with the British Army as a commissary officer, following the city's capture in the French and Indian War, it launched continuous Jewish settlement in the Quebec portion of former New France.[13]

Jewish Immigrants in Franco-Heritage North America after 1763

In a strict sense, the only ethnically "French" Jewish congregation in North America – that is, according to custom and language – was New York's Shaarey Beracha, founded in 1859 by Ashkenazic immigrants from Alsace and Lorraine. Shaarey Beracha flourished until 1909, when it merged with Temple Israel, a Reform congregation.[14] However, the members of Shaarey Beracha should be seen as a (Ashkenazi) French-ethnic immigrant community that was separate from the franco-heritage environment established under North American French rule, akin to any other immigrant ethnic enclave. Other ethnic French enclaves like this (Catholic and Huguenot) were founded during the late eighteenth and nineteenth centuries in Boston, Charleston, New York, and San Francisco.[15] North American franco-heritage is not strictly Caucasian either. In Canada, many of the Métis people, descendants of European fathers and Indigenous mothers, are French-speaking. Along the Gulf Coast are the *gens de couleur libres* – free people of colour – who originated from the union of Europeans and emancipated African slaves. Thus, after 1783 and the formal creation of the border between the United States and British Canada, francophones could be found throughout the continent. North American francophones are Catholics and Protestants and are of European, Native American/First Nation, and African descent, and some are Jews.

Multilingualism is the feature I wish to home in on among North America's Jews who resided in or conducted business with francophone communities. It is highly probable that when Jews like Isaac Monsanto and Aaron Hart first arrived in New Orleans and Montreal in the 1750s and 1760s respectively, they knew some French. Indeed, after the French and Indian War, Aaron Hart settled in the French community of Trois-Rivières, Quebec, and stayed there the rest of his life. Multilingualism was also important for those who ventured into the lands in between before they became heavily anglicized. An example is Montreal-based Gershon Levy and Company, a fur trade syndicate involving Gershon Levy and Ezekiel Solomon (1735–1809) at Fort Michilimackinac (near Mackinaw, Michigan), Chapman Abraham (ca. 1723–83) in Detroit, Benjamin Lyons in Albany, and Levy Solomons (1730–92) at Fort Niagara.[16] Since the predominant occupation of Jews in North America from the 1760s to the 1840s was commerce (merchant, pedlar, shopkeeper, etc.), they certainly had to know the local language(s) in order to succeed in this highly competitive environment. Those languages included French, but immigrants not arriving from Great Britain also had to learn English, of course. During the eighteenth and nineteenth centuries, various pockets of northeastern North America spoke German and/or Dutch. To the south, along the US–Mexico border as well as in Florida and the short-lived Republic of Texas (1836–45), facility in Spanish was necessary. We also cannot forget the multitude of Indigenous languages that immigrants encountered as the continent's frontier was pushed west by Anglo-European expansion. North America was as much a Tower of Babel as the Old World. To succeed economically in such a landscape, one had to be multilingual.

Furthermore, even when there were positive relations between Jews and French-speaking Canadians, Jews had little if any interest in exposing French Canadians to Judaism, nor did francophone Canadians take much interest in being exposed. For example, Ezekiel Solomon – mentioned earlier as a member of Gershon Levy's fur trade syndicate – married a French Canadian Métis (in 1769), Elizabeth Okimabinesikoue Dubois (b. 1743), in a Montreal church, despite being an active member of Shearith Israel. They had several children, all baptized. Their son William (1777–1850) served as a translator for the British. William was probably familiar with, if not fluent in, English, French, and an Indigenous language, all a circumstance of his upbringing. However, Judaism does not seem to have been an interest for William or for the rest of the Solomon family.[17]

As English-speakers settled in what had been French North America, divergent trajectories of societal evolution emerged between the people of these language groups. This is reflected in the relations that Jewish immigrants developed with their neighbours. As noted earlier, Montreal's Shearith Israel composed its bylaws *only* in English in 1778. Contrastingly, Shaarei Chessed of New Orleans wrote its bylaws in English *and* French when it formed in 1827.[18] Both congregations were the first in their respective localities, and both followed the Sephardic *minhag* despite having Ashkenazic majorities (although Shaarei Chessed changed to Ashkenazic traditions in 1842), with nearly all of the congregants coming to Quebec or Louisiana from either Britain or the English-speaking Americas. Why would Shaarei Chessed offer its bylaws in both languages, when Shearith Israel did not?

In Louisiana, the Americans were merely the "purchasers" of the territory that had previously been passed from France to Spain and back to France again. For the French Cajuns and Creoles, the Americans were just another passing administration. The rivalry here was strictly socioeconomic and political, not one between a conquered people and a conqueror. On occasion, economic alliances formed across linguistic and ethnic boundaries, such as the one between Maurice Barnett, who speculated in real estate, and H.J. Domingue.[19] When Jews first appeared on the docks of New Orleans around 1803 they were among a diverse group of other Yankee and European immigrant settlers who had come to seek their fortunes on the American frontier. In fact, Jews may have been hardly noticeable as a distinct group during this formative period in Louisianan social history. In this heterogeneous, laissez-faire environment, all that was needed to succeed was an enterprising spirit.

In contrast, the British were the "victors" over the French and Indians in Quebec and thus formed the postwar government and administration over the "defeated" French-speaking Canadians. The first Jews to settle in Quebec, and the founders of Montreal's Jewish community, such as Aaron Hart, were first employed by or worked closely with the British Army. They were fully enmeshed with the occupying force, which evolved into Quebec's political anglophone elite, which was alien to the Québécois populace. Aaron Hart and Gershon Levy and their Jewish colleagues affiliated and identified with the English-speaking ruling class for a very simple reason – the Jews in Canada wanted to be part of that (new) upper echelon. Also, many had family economic connections with their co-religionists in Britain; in contrast, few if any had ties to France or the Québécois. Hence, since almost no Jews in Canada (if any at all) were *only* fluent in French (and not English) during the late eighteenth and nineteenth centuries, there was no need to provide a French translation of Shearith Israel's bylaws, nor was there any interest in doing so. And unlike today, when French is *de rigueur* in Montreal, during the late eighteenth and nineteenth centuries it was important to identify with the anglophone rulers. This was not the case in Louisiana. The Jews of New Orleans were proactively engaged in social and economic relationships with anglophones *and* francophones. Having a French copy of Shaarei Chessed's bylaws showed that the Jewish community was a welcoming member of Louisiana's pluralistic society. A second reason, probably, is that French-speaking Jews from Alsace and Lorraine came to Louisiana after the American purchase.

Many Louisiana francophones may have also held a different opinion of Jews than French Canadians. Louisianans have a reputation for being live-and-let-live in social and religious matters, in addition to economic ones. Indeed, a popular Cajun expression is *laissez les bons temps rouler* (let the good times roll), which expresses Louisianans' relaxed cultural inclinations.[20] Although few in number during the French colonial period, a small number of Jews frequented and settled in Louisiana, such as the Monsantos. In Quebec, in contrast, there was strict enforcement of the bans on Jews, and the Catholic Church was rigidly pious. The Québécois proverb *je me souviens* (I remember) – in reference to the French colonial period – suggests a very different cultural attitude and outlook.[21] The Québécois were completely cut off from the liberalizing effects of the French Revolution, and so harboured many sentiments held over from the *ancien régime*, including anti-Semitic dispositions encouraged by the Jesuits, even if the average Québécois had never met a Jew in his or her own life.[22] Anti-Semitic incidents were reported in Quebec newspapers as early as 1775, just fifteen years after Aaron Hart first came to Montreal.

An incident co-reported in the *Connecticut Journal* and *Connecticut Gazette* was the defacement of a bust of King George III at the Place d'Armes, Montreal's first important public square.[23] Since the American Declaration of Independence would not come about for another year, Quebec and Connecticut were both British. To summarize, on the bust of George III, in addition to the defacements, was a sign that read, "Behold the Pope of Canada and the English Fool." Jacob R. Marcus continues the story: "A French Canadian declared that the scoundrel who had done this ought to be hanged. [David S.] Franks hearing the remark answered: 'In England men are not hanged for such small offenses.' A fight ensued in which Franks rashly struck the remonstrant, which cost him a week's incarceration."[24] The incident also continued: "Another affair happened between Ezekiel Solomons, the Jew, and de Pallieur, the latter accused the Jews of having disfigured the bust, upon which some words ensued, and Solomons knocked him down; he has been apprehended and has given bail."[25]

The precise identity of "de Pallieur" cannot be determined; however, there was a "Le Pallieur" family of merchants in Montreal, who also participated in commerce with Fort Michilimackinac, in present-day Michigan, where the Solomons was sometimes located.[26] We can surmise that Solomons and "de Pallieur" were most likely acquaintances, if not downright competitors. Their commercial rivalry may have fuelled de Pallieur's anti-Semitism, leading to the baseless accusation that a Jew had committed this act against the Crown. Considering Quebec's social environment, the early members of Shearith Israel possibly saw no point in having the bylaws available in French.

The Ezekiel Hart Affair is another example of the relationship between Jewish and British colonists in nineteenth-century Canada in the eyes of the Québécois. To summarize, Ezekiel Hart (1767–1843), the son of Aaron Hart of Trois-Rivières, was elected in 1807 to the Quebec Legislative Assembly to represent his district. However, he refused to swear "upon the true faith of a Christian" as a precondition of taking office since he was Jewish; in any case, that clause was in violation of the Naturalization Act of 1740, passed by the imperial Parliament in London. The Québécois-dominated assembly would not allow him to take his seat in the legislature, even after he was elected a second time. Anti-Semitism was a factor, although this was complicated by political rivalries between British colonists and French Canadians. The *Parti Canadien* made a point of characterizing Hart's anglophone supporters as Jew lovers. This was taken by some in society as a slur, even though many of Hart's constituents in Trois-Rivières were Québécois.[27] In many ways, Hart was viewed by the Québécois as simply another British politician: his family had come to Canada by way of London, and by excluding him as non-Christian there would be one less English speaker in the Quebec Assembly. The affair animated the assembly, whose overwhelmingly French Catholic majority tried to pass a bill excluding not only Jews but also, more importantly, all Protestants (who were, coincidentally, mostly anglophones). In response, the colonies' chief executive, Governor General Sir James Craig (1748–1812), temporarily dissolved the assembly due to its infringement of the Naturalization Act. Twenty years later, the politics of the situation had changed. The *Parti* were seeking support from non-English minority groups to strengthen their political base. In the early 1830s, Samuel B. Hart (1759–1859) of Trois-Rivières – Ezekiel Hart's son – petitioned the assembly to remove the detestable oath that excluded non-Christians from the legislative body. When the Declaratory Act was passed in 1832, giving Jews equal rights with all other Canadians, there was neither amendment nor dissenting discussion.[28]

Jews in both Canada and the United States served loyally in their respective militaries. During the War of 1812, in the United States the achievements of Judah Touro (1775–1854), Uriah Phillips Levy (1792–1862), and others were celebrated. Canadian Jews who volunteered to defend their homes against American aggression included Quebec legislator Ezekiel Hart, who became a lieutenant in the 8th Trois-Rivières Battalion, and Samuel David (1766–1824) of the 2nd Montreal Battalion, who fought at the Battle of Chateauguay and rose to the rank of major.[29] However, there was significant divergence when it came to internal conflict within each respective country. During the American Civil War (1861–65), scores of Jews volunteered and fought valiantly on both sides, including many from Louisiana who supported the Confederate States of America, such as Alexander Hart of New Orleans, who rose to become a major in the 5th Louisiana Regiment. American Jews were both Yankees and Confederates. In contrast, in Canada, Jews were almost universally supportive of the anglophone government and Crown during the rebellions of 1837 and 1838. Few if any of Canada's Jews sympathized with the rebellions. Indeed, Eleazar David served in the Royal Montreal Cavalry at the battles of St-Charles-sur-Richelieu and St-Eustache to oppose it, rising to the rank of major.[30] Actions such as his may have reinforced the opinion that Canada's Jews did not see themselves as part of the other half of the coin, the subjugated Québécois.

In Louisiana, the economic situation was different. While they certainly competed against each other, the anglophone Americans also worked with the local francophones. Unlike in Quebec, Louisiana's wealthy French Creoles were only slowly pushed out of positions of political authority and influence by anglophone elites. Clearly, many intermarried, given that there were anglophone Cajuns and Creoles. *The New Orleans Tribune / La Tribune de la Nouvelle-Orléans*, a triweekly newspaper (1864–68), was bilingual in order to appeal to all Louisianans.[31] French speakers remained important in local politics and society, besides being important to the consumer economy. The larger issue of discrimination, brought by anglophone Americans, had more to do with skin colour. So when Judah P. Benjamin (1811–84), Louisiana's most renowned Jewish politician (although not very observant), entered politics in 1842, there was no "Christian oath," nor was there any protest. This is not to say there was no anti-Semitism. In a quick response to an anti-Semitic comment made by another politician when Benjamin was a Louisiana senator, he is reputed to have said, "It is true that I am a Jew ... and when my ancestors were receiving their Ten Commandments from the immediate hand of Diety, amidst the thunderings and lightnings of Mount Sinai, the ancestors of my opponent were herding swine in the forests of Great Britain."[32]

Like many of his fellow Southerners, Benjamin was a slave owner. But according to Eli Faber's seminal work, *Jews, Slaves, and the Slave Trade: Setting the Record Straight*, Jewish ownership of slaves was proportionately no different than in the rest of the population, until the end of the Civil War brought emancipation.[33] Prior to that, Benjamin owned around 140 slaves, most of whom worked in the sugarcane fields of the Bellechasse plantation.[34] It is less commonly known that chattel slavery of Africans also existed in British Canada until the Slavery Abolition Act of 1833. While Faber's study does not include Canada, focusing mainly on the United States and the British Caribbean, his findings appear to be consistent in Canada as well. Samuel Judah (1725–89), a Jewish merchant in Montreal in the late eighteenth century, was a slave owner.[35] The uncomfortable fact of Jewish slave ownership points to a major difference between the Jewish communities of Quebec and Louisiana: Jews in French Canada, like Samuel Judah, owned slaves when it was legal to do so; but it was of course legal far longer in Louisiana than in Quebec. Also, in both Canada and the United States after slavery ended, there persisted racism towards those of African descent, besides the anti-Semitism under discussion.[36]

With the outbreak of the Civil War, Judah P. Benjamin sided with the Confederate States of America, serving in the cabinet as Secretary of War and Attorney General (simultaneously) and later as Secretary of State. In

Figure 3.2: Judah P. Benjamin (1811–84), Louisiana's distinguished Jewish planter and politician. Library of Congress Prints and Photographs Division.

these positions, he had dealings with the British government, often via Canada, to lobby for financial, diplomatic, and military support. After the Civil War, Benjamin fled to England, where he embarked on a second career as a lawyer, eventually serving on the Queen's Counsel in 1872. Coincidentally, he also was involved in several appeals from Canadian courts to the Judicial Committee of the Privy Council.[37]

Benjamin's constituents and admirers were both anglophone and francophone. Notwithstanding his Sephardic upbringing, he was not a highly observant Jew, and when he married Natalie Bauché de St-Martin in 1833, it was in a Catholic ceremony. Natalie Bauché was the daughter of a prosperous French Creole family. They had one daughter, Ninette Benjamin, born in 1842. Five years later he and his wife separated (although they did not divorce), and his wife and daughter moved to Paris, where he visited on occasion. After his second career in England, Benjamin retired to Paris to be near his daughter and grandchildren.[38]

Judah P. Benjamin's relations with French-speaking Louisianans were nothing out of the ordinary. Because there were so few possibilities in Louisiana for Jews to marry within their faith, intermarriage was widespread.

The nineteenth-century Jewish infrastructure in New Orleans was similar to Montreal's, in that it was slow to develop. Wanting to be part of both sides of Louisiana's society – English as well as French – was reason enough to have New Orleans congregation Shaarei Chessed draft its bylaws in both languages. Nineteenth-century politicians cultivated votes from both sides of the language divide, just as businessmen tried to appeal to both English- and French-speaking customers. There are other reflections of bilingualism and biculturalism elsewhere in Louisianan society. Reported in *The New Orleans Tribune / La Tribune de la Nouvelle-Orléans* was the death of B.J. Wolf in November 1867, who was buried at "Hebrew Temma Dereche" cemetery.[39] A death notice is different from a commercial advertisement (the most frequent occurrence of Jewish names within the New Orleans press), and it was reported to both French- and English-speaking Louisianans.

A popular cultural event among French- and English-speaking Louisianans is the annual Mardi Gras, which is observed every spring during Carnival season. While the festivities are of French Catholic origin, by the 1850s the city's English speakers, many of whom were Protestant, had also embraced the tradition. The anglophone elite were also the first to establish Mardi Gras social clubs, called krewes, in 1856, beginning with the Mistick Krewe of Comus. The pageantry grew with the encouragement of the English-speaking elite, with the lower classes of both language groups participating in the revelry. In 1872 it was decided that a "King of Carnival" would be elected from among the elite. The first king was Lewis Salomon, a Jew. For the next twenty years, Jews served as kings and queens of Mardi Gras krewes, before anti-Semitism infiltrated the Catholic-originated festivities in the late nineteenth century. Later, in the twentieth century, anti-Semitism in Mardi Gras subsided and Jews returned to some krewes.

Finally, we must consider a minority demographic among the waves of Jewish immigrants who came to North America. Some Jewish immigrants were from Alsace and Lorraine; it is estimated that over the course of the nineteenth century, around 10,000 of them spread across the North American continent.[40] Coming from a cultural and geopolitical frontier between France and Germany, many were at least somewhat fluent in both French and German. Jewish Alsatians had a complex identity that adapted easily to life in North America. Besides joining the Shaarey Beracha community in New York, Alsatian Jews in North America were absorbed into the broader German-Jewish immigrant community as they Americanized or Canadianized.

Familiarity with the French language had its advantages.[41] For example, John Mayer, from Landau in Alsace, arrived in Natchez, Mississippi, across the river from Louisiana, where he worked as a cobbler during the

1830s and 1840s. Many more would come, and establish themselves as pedlars, shopkeepers, tradesmen, and businessmen. The most significant was Leon Godchaux (1824–99), who started out as a pedlar and gradually built up a commercial empire that included the Godchaux Sugar Company and its vertical monopoly (from sugarcane plantations to finished products). He also founded the Godchaux Department Store on New Orleans's Canal Street, which eventually had more than a dozen branches. Godchaux appears many times, in both languages, in *The New Orleans Tribune / La Tribune de la Nouvelle-Orléans*.

Alsatian Jews also made their way to Quebec. Jacques Bloch helped found Montreal's Young Men's Hebrew Benevolent Society in 1863. A few travelled around the province as pedlars; outside Montreal, though, the only Jewish community in Quebec (i.e., with a congregation) was in Quebec City. Economic opportunities were such that even when they spoke French, Alsatian Jewish immigrants to Canada were more drawn to anglophone localities. For instance, Edmund Scheuner made his fortune as an industrialist in Toronto during the early twentieth century.[42]

In rural Louisiana, and in much of the American South, Alsatian Jews were among the early-nineteenth-century pioneers. Many of them started as pedlars and later traded in their packs for their first small shop, often specializing in dry goods. These first Jewish settlers became the nuclei around whom later Jewish immigrants from Central and Eastern Europe chose to settle. Gerald L. Gold observed the details of these socio-economic dynamics in Opelousas, Louisiana, where the Jews "became brokers between the rural Cajun farmers and an emerging national market for cotton and rice ... They formed the nucleus of a group that had much in common culturally, even though they were too much apart from the planter milieu to be involved in the creation of separate Jewish institutions. Most were francophones, many from Alsace, giving them a linguistic bond with both the dominant French-speaking elites of Opelousas ... French also provided a linkage with the French-speaking white Cajuns and black Creoles who filled the unilingual agricultural communities of the surrounding prairie."[43]

A survey of Louisiana's nineteen small-town Jewish communities (including four in Mississippi, on the opposite bank of the river) found that a dozen were founded in this manner between the 1820s and the 1870s. Of the seven established by Jews not from Alsace or France, four were by Central and Eastern European Jews (Germany, the Czech lands, Poland), two by Americans from Charleston, South Carolina, and one by a Jew from England. Alsatian Jewish immigrants also played a significant role in other parts of the francophone Gulf Coast region: Mississippi, Alabama, the Florida panhandle, southern Arkansas, and eastern Texas.[44]

In contrast to Louisiana, Quebec did not have a culture of small-town Jewish life before 1920. Jewish-owned resorts in the Laurentians, Quebec's equivalent of the Catskills, did not come about until the 1930s and 1940s. In *Jew or Juif?*, Brown argues that endemic anti-Semitism in Quebec was responsible for this.[45] However, French Canadian xenophobia did not limit itself to Jews or Protestants. Hostility towards foreigners was also extended to other non-French-speaking Catholic groups as well, especially Irish Catholics, who spoke English. Thus, immigration to Quebec was primarily limited to Montreal, a heterogeneous urban enclave within a homogenous agrarian province.[46]

And Montreal was by no means a New Jerusalem on the St. Lawrence. Xenophobia and anti-Semitism were present there as well. In the city's French-language newspapers, Jews were discussed on occasion, most significantly during the Dreyfus Affair (1894–1906). Although that scandal took place in France, the issues it raised – patriotism, French nationalism, and anti-Semitism – interested many in North America. (Captain Alfred Dreyfus [1859–1935] was a French army officer accused of spying for the Germans.) Most French Canadian newspapers took an anti-Semitic position, viewing Dreyfus and indeed most Jews as untrustworthy and treacherous. For instance, in addition to articles and editorials, *La Libre Parole* published a poem by Jean de Reguiny, titled "L'Ame Juive" (The Jewish Soul), and without a rebuttal to accompany it. The last stanza concluded:

> Le Juif a vendu Dieu, le Juif vend sa patrie:
> Pour lui tout est objet de lucre et d'industrie;
> L'honneur, les sentiments, les devoirs, l'amitié,
> Il faut qu'il les transforme en argent monnayé.[47]

> [The Jew has sold God, the Jew sells his homeland:
> For him everything is an object of lucre and industry;
> Honor, feelings, duties, friendship,
> He must turn them into silver coin.]

Only rarely did French Canadian newspapers defend Jewish rights. An example is an article in *Le Courrier* by Henri Roullaud (1856–1910), who was not Québécois, but an immigrant and intellectual from Nord Pas-de-Calais, France.[48] Roullaud had settled in Montreal and was merely continuing the debate over the Dreyfus Affair in Canada in an objective way.[49] Meanwhile, reporting that presented both sides of the Dreyfus Affair appeared in Louisiana newspapers.

How did French Canadian anti-Semitism compare to elsewhere? To begin with, most Alsatian Jews came from small towns where there was pervasive anti-Semitism. This is evident in the waves of Alsatian Jewish immigration to North America around the times of the July Revolution of 1830, the French Revolution of 1848, and the Franco-Prussian War of 1870–71; during all of these events, there had been anti-Semitic riots in Europe. For instance, in 1832, two Jews were killed and twenty injured during a riot in Bergheim, Alsace.[50] The *shtetls* and *dorfs* of Central and Eastern Europe – the origin places of most Ashkenazim who came to North America in the nineteenth and early twentieth centuries – were also hot spots of anti-Semitism. At times, the southern *Goldene Medina* (United States) was no safe haven either. Jews in the American South had to contend with the Ku Klux Klan; they also witnessed the 1915 lynching of Leo M. Frank (1884–1915) by a mob in Marietta, Georgia. Canada around this time may have had a reputation for anti-Semitic rhetoric from fanatical clerics, and its immigration policies may have been punitive, but there were no lynch mobs.[51] Incidents such as the burning of the synagogue in Val David in the mid-1930s were shocking, but Canada's Jews were not being killed or maimed.[52] Rural Quebec was anti-Semitic in its own way, but it was "tame" compared to the American South, Alsace, and Lorraine.

The rural economies in Louisiana and Quebec during the nineteenth and early twentieth centuries were predominantly agricultural. In Louisiana, that included sustenance food production, but also cash crops like cotton, sugarcane, and rice. In the Mississippi watershed, which extended into the North American breadbasket, foodstuffs were a significant export. Rural Louisianans, both white and black, as well as English and French speaking, needed access to extra-regional markets to sell their produce and purchase supplies. Jewish immigrants, first as pedlars and then as owners of dry goods stores, filled this economic niche. The most successful ones, like Godchaux, opened department stores. Many Jewish merchants accepted cotton in place of cash (of which there was a shortage in the rural economy) and shipped the cotton to market in New Orleans or New York.[53] Those who knew both English and French, and especially the small number of Alsatian Jews who were native French speakers (including Godchaux), had a slight advantage. Also, the disposable income that rural Louisianans produced generated demand for imported luxury goods, which reinforced the need for Jewish mercantile connections.

In contrast, Quebec only had sustenance farming, which only required a local market economy. While profitable, Quebec's fur and lumber industries did not involve a large percentage of the rural population. There was no rural economic niche for large numbers of Jewish pedlars and merchants to fill in Quebec. The "Jew's store" that was so common in Louisiana was almost unheard of in the small towns of Quebec. Jews involved themselves in Canada's nineteenth and early twentieth century fur trade mainly as furriers in Montreal, where they settled in anglophone and Yiddish-speaking enclaves. Spurred by the rhetoric of the Catholic Church, the Québécois could "afford" to be anti-Semitic, boycotting Jewish merchants. The few Jews who engaged in rural trade in Quebec did not prosper as much as their counterparts in Louisiana, so small-town Jewish communities never took root. In Louisiana, economic prosperity allowed for a levelling of differences and a softening of social strains between Louisiana francophones and immigrants.

One would expect Louisiana to have more Jews than Quebec, with New Orleans as its metropolitan heart. And indeed, for much of the nineteenth century, Louisiana's Jewish population was larger; by 1910 it was spread across fifteen cities and towns in every corner of the state, with New Orleans having the highest concentration. Outside of metropolitan Montreal (including Westmount, Outremont, and Lachine), Quebec City was the only other municipality to have a Jewish community, and it was relatively small. But after 1880, immigration and urbanization, spurred by the socio-economic conditions in each locality, had a profound affect. In 1903, the Jewish population for all of Louisiana was around 12,000, in contrast to Quebec, where in Montreal alone there were 6,941 Jews in 1901 – a figure that had grown to 28,807 by 1911.[54]

Jewish Connections Between French Canada and the United States

This chapter has so far covered the flow of Jews from Europe to the opposite ends of France's former North American empire. What about exchanges between French Canada and the Gulf Coast? The Cajuns are descended from Acadians expelled by the British during the eighteenth century – none were Jews. This was the largest migration between the two polities. Many American Jews, including the author, have some ancestors who came to the United States after a temporary sojourn in Canada. But many of these immigrants – who passed through Montreal, Toronto, and Winnipeg – settled in the Northeast, Midwest, and Great Plains. Very few ventured to the American South, let alone Louisiana. There are Canadian Jews with ancestors who came through the United States by way of New York, Philadelphia, and San Francisco, but the flow north was very small. Among the more established Jews in Montreal and New Orleans there were some connections, although nothing that could be classified as a migration.

With respect to communal relations, in 1853, Montreal's Shearith Israel sent aid to Shaarai Chessed to help with the yellow fever epidemic in New Orleans that year.[55] There is also Nathan Gordon (b. 1882), who grew up in

Figure 3.3: Temple Emanu-El of Westmount, Montreal, built in 1911 while Nathan Gordon, a Louisianan by birth, served as rabbi. William A. Rosenthall Judaica Collection, Special Collections, College of Charleston Library.

New Orleans and went on to become rabbi of Montreal's Temple Emanu-El, whom Gerald Tulchinsky considered to be one of the three pre-eminent rabbis in that city, along with Meldola de Sola at Shearith Israel and Sha'ar Hashomayim's Herman Abramowitz.[56] Gordon presided over the congregation when it built its imposing Sherbrooke Street edifice in suburban Westmount, in 1911. He was also an active Zionist in Canada, which was unusual for Reform rabbis of that era, and may have conversed on the topic with Rabbi Max Heller (1860–1929), the leading Zionist Reform rabbi in the United States, who coincidentally was based in New Orleans.[57] In addition to his pulpit duties, Gordon taught Hebrew at McGill University and was heavily involved in the founding of the Mount Sinai Sanatorium, built for Canada's Jewish tuberculosis patients (see Jeanne Abrams in her chapter "Chasing the Cure"). While in Montreal he attended Université de Laval à Montréal as a part-time law student, qualifying for the Quebec bar in 1916. As can be inferred from the name of the institution he attended, his legal education was in French, the language he sometimes used in his legal practice after he changed careers and left Temple Emanu-El. Many of his clients were anglophone Montreal Jews.[58] Besides the similarities in language environments, Quebec law may have also been somewhat familiar to Gordon from his previous life in Louisiana. While not identical, Quebec and Louisiana are unique within their respective countries in having French-based civil legal codes; the rest of North America's provinces and states use common law of British origin.[59]

Since this analysis has focused so much on relations between Jews and non-Jews, we must also consider this relationship dynamic. Coming south in 1872 was the builder and architect Peter Rollo Middlemiss (1826–1887), a Presbyterian Montrealer by birth. In 1847, Middlemiss came to Louisiana. He would spend much of his career in New Orleans, where he designed and built many of that city's synagogues during the middle and late nineteenth century. In 1852, he formed a partnership with Robert Little, until Little's retirement in 1860. Their firm built Nefuzoth Yehuda in 1857, a Greek Revival Sephardic synagogue designed by W.A. Ferret, Jr. Their most renowned non-residential buildings were St. Anna's Asylum and the St. Charles Hotel, both built around 1853. In 1872, Middlemiss built Temple Sinai, a Reform congregation, at a cost of US$104,000.[60] According to his obituary in 1887, he built "nearly all the synagogues and a number of churches" in New Orleans.[61] No names are mentioned in relation to Shaarai Chessed, the first synagogue erected in the city in 1851. However, its

Figure 3.4: Temple Sinai of New Orleans, designed and built by architect Peter Rollo Middlemiss (1826–87), was originally from Montreal. William A. Rosenthall Judaica Collection, Special Collections, College of Charleston Library.

builder may have also been Little and Middlemiss, given their reputation among New Orleans's Jews, especially Judah Touro, a financial supporter of the project as well as a frequent client of the builders.[62] Middlemiss had a successful career in New Orleans, adjusting well to his new home after moving from Montreal. Might Middlemiss's early success have been due to his connections with Judah Touro? Unfortunately, Touro's papers were destroyed at his own request after he died in 1854.[63] Little is also known about Middlemiss's life before he came to the United States. However, considering that Montreal's Jews socialized with their anglophone neighbours, the anglophone Middlemiss may have known some Jews in Canada prior.

Conclusion

Jews in Quebec, Louisiana, and adjacent areas shared the unique circumstance of living in francophone cultural environments. That said, by the nineteenth century the French-speaking Cajuns and Creoles had diverged in many ways from the Québécois, despite their commonalities in motherland, language, and religion. Even the migration of Acadians to Louisiana did not create a bond between these two regions. The common experiences for Jews in Quebec and Louisiana today are merely a heritage remnant – something that has been passed down by the ancestors of the local francophone inhabitants.

Political and economic changes strongly shaped these two regions. Louisiana profited from its expanding sugarcane and cotton economy, while Quebec remained relatively stagnant. In Louisiana, financial prosperity allowed for cordial relations between the previous francophone inhabitants and immigrant groups, including the Jews. Immigrants felt that opportunity could be found in rural areas as well as in New Orleans, even though there was anti-Semitism to be confronted. In contrast, Jews and other non–French-speaking foreigners in Quebec were only able to establish themselves in urban Montreal, where the anglophone elite had entrenched itself. That is why the French language and cultural contexts of these two places matter, besides improving our understanding of North American Jewry for these specific regions.

Jews did not migrate to any great degree across the international border between the francophone environments of Quebec and Louisiana. There were only a handful of exceptions to this, such as Nathan Gordon, who was born and raised in New Orleans and went on to become a prominent Montrealer. Even non-Jews, like Peter Rollo Middlemiss of Montreal, who was very influential in the development of synagogues in New Orleans, were unusual.

Lastly, there is a very particular francophone minority that immigrated to anglophone North America, as well as to anglophone-governed Quebec and Louisiana. These immigrants were mainly Catholic and Huguenot, although there were some Jews, especially from Alsace and Lorraine. Although francophone North America was governed by British Canadian and American anglophones, French-speaking Alsatian Jews had some advantages that their immigrant co-religionists from Central and Eastern Europe did not. In Quebec and Louisiana, these people were the seeds from which Jewish communities (with immigrants from elsewhere) would grow.

Notes

I am very grateful to Lee Shai Weissbach and Emily Ford for their assistance on earlier drafts of this chapter.

1 See Michael Brown, *Jew or Juif?: Jews, French Canadians, and Anglo-Canadians, 1759–1914* (Philadelphia: Jewish Publication Society, 1987).
2 The New Orleans congregation "Gates of Mercy" went by several different spellings of the transliteration of "שערי חסד," including "Shaarei Chessed," "Shangarai Chasset," and "Shenarai-Chasset." In this chapter I give preference to "Shaarei Chessed." See Bertram Wallace Korn, *The Early Jews of New Orleans* (Waltham: American Jewish Historical Society, 1969), 192–208; and *Congregation Shearith Israel Minutes, 1778–1779*, Document SC-8355, Small Collections, American Jewish Archives, Cincinnati.
3 See Esther Benbassa, *The Jews of France: A History from Antiquity to the Present* (Princeton: Princeton University Press, 1999), a thorough study of French Jewry.
4 Mordechai Arbell, *The Jewish Nation of the Caribbean: The Spanish-Portuguese Jewish Settlements in the Caribbean and the Guianas* (Jerusalem: Gefen Publishing, 2002), 36–57.
5 Susan Broomhall, "The Convent as Missionary in Seventeenth-Century France," in *Gender, Race, and Religion in the Colonization of the Americas*, ed. Nora E. Jaffary (Aldershot: Ashgate, 2007), 57–66.
6 Gerard Lafleur and Lucien Abenon, "The Protestants and the Colonization of the French West Indies," in *Memory and Identity: The Huguenots in France and the Atlantic Diaspora*, ed. Bertrand Van Ruymbeke and Randy J. Sparks (Columbia: University of South Carolina Press, 2003), 267–84.
7 Most of the Code Noir deals with the treatment of African slaves.
8 Emily Ford and Barry Stiefel, *The Jews of New Orleans and the Mississippi Delta: A History of Life and Community along the Bayou* (Charleston: History Press, 2012), 15–23.
9 Jacques Langlais and David Rome, *Jews and French Quebecers: Two Hundred Years of Shared History* (Waterloo: Wilfrid Laurier University Press, 1991), 17; Arbell, *The Jewish Nation of the Caribbean*, 36–57.
10 "De Paris, Le 17 Août," *Gazette Françoise*, 8 December 1780, 2.
11 Ford and Stiefel, *The Jews of New Orleans*, 15–23.
12 Ibid., 15–23.
13 Irving M. Abella and Harold Martin Troper, *None Is Too Many: Canada and the Jews of Europe, 1933–1948* (Toronto: University of Toronto Press, 2012), 10.
14 Hyman Bogomolny Grinstein, *The Rise of the Jewish Community of New York, 1654–1860* (Philadelphia: Porcupine Press, 1976), 477n25, 496n24.

15 Francophone newspapers in the United States, outside of Louisiana, included Newport's *Gazette Françoise,* the *Courier de Boston,* and the *Gazette Française* of New York. In San Francisco the French community was established shortly after the 1849 Gold Rush, centred on the Notre Dame des Victoires Church. In Charleston there is the French Huguenot Church, a congregation established during the 1680s.

16 Sheldon J. Godfrey and Judy Godfrey, *Search Out the Land: The Jews and the Growth of Equality in British Colonial America, 1740-1867* (Montreal and Kingston: McGill–Queen's University Press, 1995), 88–89.

17 Godfrey and Godfrey, *Search Out the Land,* 115; "First Jewish Settler in Michigan Informational Historical Marker," *Detroit: The History and Future of the Motor City,* 1 July 2012, http://www.detroit1701.org/First%20Jewish%20Settler.html.

18 Korn, *The Early Jews of New Orleans,* 192–208; *Congregation Shearith Israel Minutes, 1778–1779,* Document SC-8355, Small Collections, American Jewish Archives, Cincinnati.

19 "Auction Sales: Sale of Metairieville," *The Picayune* [New Orleans], 23 March 1837, 3.

20 See the essays in John Lowe, *Louisiana Culture from the Colonial Era to Katrina* (Baton Rouge: Louisiana State University Press, 2008), for further insights on Louisiana culture.

21 Richard Handler, *Nationalism and the Politics of Culture in Quebec* (Madison: University of Wisconsin Press, 1988), 17. *Je me souviens* was also coined by Eugène-Étienne Taché in 1883 as the Quebec motto, officially adopted in 1939.

22 Brown, *Jew or Juif?,* 133.

23 An incident studied in Godfrey and Godfrey, *Search Out the Land,* 103; and in Jacob R. Marcus, *United States Jewry, 1776–1985,* vol. 1 (Detroit: Wayne State University Press, 1989), 57.

24 Ibid.

25 "Intercepted Letter, dated 'Montreal, 6th May, 1775,'" *Connecticut Journal,* 31 May 1775, 3.

26 Frank Mackey, *Done with Slavery: The Black Fact in Montreal, 1760–1840* (Montreal and Kingston: McGill–Queen's University Press, 2010), 404–5.

27 Michael Brown, "The Beginning of Jewish Emancipation in Canada: The Hart Affair," *Michael: On the History of the Jews in the Diaspora* 10 (1986): 31–38.

28 Godfrey and Godfrey, *Search Out the Land,* 186–89, 232.

29 Jacques Langlais and David Rome, *Jews and French Quebecers: Two Hundred Years of Shared History* (Waterloo: Wilfrid Laurier University Press, 1991), 18.

30 Tulchinsky, *Canada's Jews: A People's Journey* (Toronto: University of Toronto Press, 2008), 31.

31 Thomas J. Davis, *Plessy v. Ferguson* (Santa Barbara: Greenwood, 2012), 93.

32 See Eli N. Evans, *Judah P. Benjamin: The Jewish Confederate* (New York: Free Press, 1988), 97, who quotes Max J. Kohler, *Judah P. Benjamin Statesman and Jurist* (Baltimore: Lord Baltimore Press, 1905), 83–84, who cites *Senate Debates.*

33 See Eli Faber, *Jews, Slaves, and the Slave Trade: Setting the Record Straight* (New York: NYU Press, 1998).

34 Evans, *Judah P. Benjamin,* 32.

35 Mackey, *Done with Slavery,* 126–33.

36 Kristin McLaren, "'We had no desire to be set apart': Forced Segregation of Black Students in Canada West Public Schools and the Myth of British Egalitarianism," in *The History of Immigration and Racism in Canada: Essential Readings,* ed. Barrington Walker (Toronto: Canadian Scholars' Press, 2008), 69–81.

37 Robert Douthat Meade, *Judah P. Benjamin: Confederate Statesman* (New York: Oxford University Press, 1943), 372.

38 See ibid.; and Evans, *Judah P. Benjamin.*

39 "Chronique Locale," *La Tribune de la Nouvelle-Orléans / New Orleans Tribune*, 30 November 1867, 2.

40 Lee Shai Weissbach, "Contextualizing the Franco-Jewish Experience in the South," *Southern Jewish History* 14 (2011): 1–35.

41 Anny Bloch, "Mercy on Rude Streams: Jewish Emigrants from Alsace-Lorraine to the Lower Mississippi Region and the Concept of Fidelity," *Southern Jewish History* 2 (1999): 81–110.

42 Ruth A. Frager, *Sweatshop Strife: Class, Ethnicity, and Gender in the Jewish Labour Movement of Toronto, 1900–1939* (Toronto: University of Toronto Press), 64.

43 Gerald L. Gold, "A Tale of Two Communities: The Growth and Decline of Small-Town Jewish Communities in Northern Ontario and Southwestern Louisiana," in *The Jews of North America*, ed. Moses Rischen (Detroit: Wayne State University Press, 1987), 227.

44 See Goldring/Woldenberg Institute of Southern Jewish Life, "Louisiana," *Encyclopedia of Southern Jewish Communities* (2006), http://www.isjl.org/history/archive/main_la.htm.

Place	Date	Place of Origin of Founders
Alexandria	1830	Charleston, South Carolina
Bastrop	1840s	not clear, though Alsatians present
Baton Rouge	1850s	Alsace and Bavaria
Donaldsonville	1840s	Alsace and France
Houma	1872	Czech
Lafayette	1850s	Alsace
Lake Charles	1879	Alsace
Monroe	1861	Germany and Poland
Morgan City	1850s	not clear, though Alsatians present
Natchitoches	1830s	England
Jeanerette/New Iberia	1871	Alsace
Opelousas	1852	France
Plaquemine	1850s	Alsace
St. Francisville	1850s	Germany
Shreveport	1840s	Alsace and Germany
Osyka, MS	1850s	Alsace
Woodville, MS	1820s–30s	Charleston, South Carolina
Natchez, MS	1840s	Alsace-Lorraine and Bavaria
Port Gibson, MS	1839	Germany

45 Brown, *Jew or Juif?*, 133–52.

46 See the excellent essays in Terrence Murphy and Gerald J. Stortz, eds. *Creed and Culture: The Place of English-Speaking Catholics in Canadian Society, 1750-1930* (Montreal and Kingston: McGill–Queen's University Press, 1993).

47 Jean de Reguiny, "L'Ame Juive," *La Libre Parole* (22 August 1896), 4.

48 Henri Roullaud, "Verdict," *Le Courrier,* 10 September 1899, 1.

49 Académie canadienne-française, "Henri Roullaud (1856–1910)," *Galerie des chroniqueurs* (2011), http://catfran.flsh.usherbrooke.ca/chroque/chroniqueurs_roullaud.php.

50 Stephen Wilson, "Antisemitism in France at the Time of the Dreyfus Affair," in *Hostages of Modernization: Studies on Modern Antisemitism, 1870–1933/39,* ed. Herbert A. Strauss (Berlin: W. de Gruyter, 1993), 541–92.

51 Michael Posluns, "Canada" in *Antisemitism,* vol. 1, "A–K," ed. Richard S. Levy (Santa Barbara: ABC-CLIO, 2005), 94–95.

52 Irving Abella, "Anti-Semitism in Canada in the Interwar Years,"in *The Jews of North America,* ed. Moses Rischen (Detroit: Wayne State University Press, 1987), 235–46.

53 Elliott Ashkenazi, *The Business of Jews in Louisiana, 1840–1875* (Tuscaloosa: University of Alabama Press, 1988), 23–24.

54 John Alexander Dickinson and Brian J. Young, *A Short History of Quebec* (Montreal and Kingston: McGill–Queen's University Press, 2000), 206; Louis Rosenberg, *Canada's Jews: A Social and Economic Study of Jews in Canada in the 1930s* (Montreal and Kingston: McGill–Queen's University Press, 1993), 308; Cyrus Adler and Henrietta Szold, eds. *American Jewish Year Book,* vol. 7 (Philadelphia: American Jewish Committee, Jewish Publication Society of America, 1905), 151.

55 Brown, *Jew or Juif?,* 104.

56 Gerald J.J. Tulchinsky, *Canada's Jews: A People's Journey* (Toronto: University of Toronto Press, 2008), 161.

57 William H. Atherton, *Montreal, 1535–1914* (Montreal: S.J. Clarke, 1914), 389.

58 Gerald J.J. Tulchinsky, "'Justice and Only Justice Thou Shalt Pursue': Considerations on the Social Voice of Canada's Reform Rabbis," in *Religion and Public Life in Canada: Historical and Comparative Perspectives,* ed. Marguerie Van Die (Toronto: University of Toronto Press, 2001), 313–28.

59 See Joseph Dainow and Pierre Azard, *Two American Civil Law Systems: Quebec Civil Law and Louisiana Civil Law* (Ottawa: Canadian and Foreign Law Research Centre, 1964).

60 Max Heller, *Jubilee Souvenir of Temple Sinai, 1872–1922* (New Orleans: American Print Co., 1922), 55.

61 "Death of Peter R. Middlemiss," *Daily Picayune,* 13 September 1887, 4.

62 S. Frederick Starr, Robert S. Brantley, and Jan White Brantley, *Southern Comfort: The Garden District of New Orleans* (New York: Princeton Architectural Press, 1998), 110–12.

63 Leon Hühner, *The Life of Judah Touro (1775–1854)* (Philadelphia: Jewish Publication Society of America, 1946), xii.

FOUR

Planting the Seed of Identity
The Contributions of the Early Jewish Farmers of North America

Howard Gontovnick

In the 1880s, life for Jews in Eastern Europe was hard. The challenges included demoralizing social and economic restrictions, ongoing accusations of political terrorism, and pogroms that were increasing in frequency. After the assassination of Tsar Alexander II (1855–81), Jews began to leave Eastern Europe in significant numbers. Some became part of the first wave of settlers in Palestine, and others made their way to Latin America, but the majority chose to make the difficult journey to the United States – the "Goldene Medina." And then there were those who chose Canada.

The question of how to settle the thousands of poor, uneducated Jews arriving from Eastern Europe was a critical one, both for the newcomers and for the Jewish communities receiving them. One creative response to these penniless refugees was to establish farming settlements in Canada and the United States. It is unlikely that those who founded these settlements gave any thought to the role they would play in the emergence of a Jewish identity in North America. Aside from providing Jewish refugees with productive vocations, these settlements would serve as "social test tubes" – as places where Jews learned to be what they were and how to contribute to the North American Jewish identity.

These settlements influenced the lives of the newcomers with regard to work, residence, income, and security. I would suggest that a strong sense of community also emerged in the same environment. According to Sheva Medjuck, "the greater the extent to which an ethnic group has its own structures to serve the needs of the group, the more likely the group is to be able to maintain a higher sense of group identification and to counter integration into the larger host society."[1] As I will show in this chapter, the farming settlements fostered an environment that contributed to the emergence of a distinctive community lifestyle, besides adding and reinforcing characteristics of the North American Jewish identity.

For many newcomers, life in the farming colonies was not unlike what they had left behind in the small towns and villages of Eastern Europe. In both Europe and North America, such communities were built around small groups of people who shared cultural similarities and who provided one another with commodities and some services. This way of life led to the formation of a number of behaviours and perceptions that would become associated with a distinctive Jewish identity. Clearly, these settlements were not just sites for disseminating farming knowledge; they also contributed greatly to the Jewish identity in North America.

Jewish Refugees Overflowing

As Jewish refugees continued arriving at Canadian and American seaports, various Jewish philanthropic organizations met to discuss the sheer numbers arriving and what could be done to integrate them into North American society. In writing about this period, historian Samuel Joseph acknowledged, "social attitudes of the native population must be taken into consideration. The danger of direct stimulation of anti-Jewish sentiments cannot be disregarded."[2] Joseph was simply echoing the fears held by many local Jews that American nativist parties would bring a halt to immigration and stir up antipathy against Jews. The rise of anti-Semitism in Europe, and in North America as well, made the American and Canadian Jewish communities hyper-vigilant in terms of avoiding situations that could trigger any kind of anti-Jewish backlash. These concerns certainly influenced the actions of some Jewish organizations as they developed programs to assist newcomers to North America.

Reflecting on the concerns of this period, Theodore Norman acknowledged that in the early years of the Jewish Colonization Association, many were aware that the "intellectual apostles of productivising Jews, of which the Baron de Hirsch was one, believed that, if enough of their brethren became productive workers, making and growing things by manual labour, anti-Semitism would be alleviated."[3] A key supporter of the farm settlement movement as well as one of its financial contributors, the Jewish industrialist Baron Maurice de Hirsch was an early supporter of what would ultimately become the Jewish Colonization Association. As the political and social situation continued to deteriorate in Eastern Europe in the 1880s, Hirsh came to believe that the way to strengthen a community was to help "human beings who are capable of work ... that would otherwise become paupers."[4] Helping a fellow Jew was not a new idea, but creating projects of this size *was* new. For most Jews in Eastern Europe, the social reality was poverty, with little opportunity to improve one's life. In Russia, the pogroms and the "May Laws" (imposed solely on the Jews) provided strong incentives to immigrate. Initially, Hirsch tried to offer funds to the Russian government, but eventually decided it would be better to fund the farming settlements directly. One has to wonder what would have happened to the Jews trying to leave Eastern Europe at that time if not for Hirsch's efforts. Hirsch was confident that by encouraging the development of agricultural settlements, he would be helping Jewish refugees become important to agriculture. He also believed in giving these new farmers direction and a sense of hope.

The Productivization of the Jewish Farmer

On one level, "productivization," or "occupational restructuring," was an ideological term, one that pointed to an important theme of the Jewish emancipation.[5] Generally, it referred to Jews distancing themselves from involvement in commerce and taking up more physically challenging livelihoods. In other words, they were to become associated with businesses or occupations that involved them in society as equals to gentiles. Put another way, productivization referred to a process whereby Jews would take up work that showed them to be hard working and industrious. As a consequence, Jewish immigrants would be seen as contributing to their communities through engagement, effort, and commitment. For many, there was no better example of productivization than the farming colony, where Jewish immigrants would find a livelihood and alter the anti-Semitic perceptions of North American society.

So instead of settling in the overcrowded cities and competing with the locals for work, some newcomers chose to join the new farming communities. In some cases, as part of a government relocation program, these newcomers were sent to virgin territories where there was strong agricultural potential. Most Jewish aid organizations were certain that agricultural labour would provide work and at the same time convey to non-Jews that Jews were not just newcomers – they were pioneers taking up the challenge of spreading agriculture throughout North America.

The Expanding Farming Option

In the late 1880s the Canadian government passed a law, the Dominion Lands Act, to encourage Europeans to settle on the Canadian frontier. This program offered land for sale at very low prices, the only drawback being the location, which was often the unsettled wilderness of western Canada. Clearly, there were benefits to this program, as well as questionable motives. The program favoured immigrants from English-speaking countries. The placement of these immigrants in predetermined unsettled areas seemed deliberate. Many believed that the Canadian government's main priority was to secure the sparsely settled Canadian frontier against American incursions.

Successive Canadian governments would support and promote this policy until the 1920s. Largely, it was an agricultural development policy. Although English-speaking immigrants were preferred, it attracted all kinds of European pioneers, especially Jews from Eastern Europe.[6] Radical as it may have seemed, the idea of Jewish settlement on farms in North America had actually been attempted earlier by agriculturalists from Russia. Prior to the modern era of farming programs, the Jewish socialist movements *Hibbat Zion* and *Am Olam* had during the late 1870s believed that the best way to address the persecution of Jews in Eastern Europe would be to set up farming colonies far away. In the United States, from Florida to Utah, these scattered experimental farming communities were "intrinsically valuable as models of courage, determination and discipline against all odds. Their histories speak not merely of achievements by Jews but of Jewish achievements."[7] Although most of these early settlements were short-lived, they were well intended and seemed to augur well. So despite the combination of poor agricultural technology and challenging environmental conditions that contributed to these failures, years later, when American organizations returned to the idea of farming settlements, past efforts contributed to new, more successful results. As for the earlier groups of Russian farmers, they did not stay long: most of them returned to Eastern Europe before advances in agriculture could be helpful and settlement in Palestine had begun.

During the early years of this program of placing Jewish refugees in farming colonies, immigrant aid organizations and some supportive individuals such as the philanthropist Baron Maurice de Hirsch grew confident that farming could contribute to the normalization of the Jewish immigrant population. If these colonies succeeded, immigrants would be provided with professions and many would be able to integrate into the expanding urban middle class.[8] In light of this, it seems that the significance of the Jewish farming movement is that it provided what could be called an "entry level occupation." Given the limited availability of job training, farming was an obvious means for Jewish immigrants to work, support a family, and interact with the host population. Since farming was a developing industry and one perceived as productive, immigrant Jews who took it up would gradually integrate into the larger society. It was widely hoped that as the number of Jews visibly increased, positive perceptions of them as farmers would improve their image in North America society.

Realizing the integrative role that agriculture could play, some philanthropic organizations cautiously supported the expansion of such programs. Extensive documentation reveals that throughout Canada, the Jewish Colonization Association was actively involved in this project.[9] In the United States, the Jewish Agricultural Society played a similar role for many years in analogous programs. Evidence of the successes (and failures) of American Jewish farmers can also be found in the extensive communications among various regional organizations such as the Federation of Hotelmen and Farmers of Ulster and Sullivan Counties, in addition to their national organization.[10] And although this historical era can be considered short, the number and types of files that have been archived in both Canada and the United States testifies to the presence of Jewish farmers during this era, and to their significance. Even if there were only small pockets of successful farming settlements throughout North America, these communities were large enough to make a difference as significant starting points for many new arrivals. According to Ellen Eisenberg, who documented the farming colonies in New Jersey, "the dissolution of the Jewish colonies does not indicate a failing of the Jews as farmers ... [Rather,] it might indicate a failure of colonization ideology and movements."[11]

Perhaps in this context, one must ask what success means and how we understand history. Not surprisingly, the accomplishments of Jewish farmers in North America have always been downplayed, and it has been easier to blame their failures on the participants rather than on a system that had minimal organizational experience in such matters. Gabriel Davidson, a managing director of the Jewish Agricultural Society, wrote that what was significant was that "Jews on America's farmland signify a major social phenomenon not to be measured by numbers alone. They represent a positive gain in normalization ... within a comparatively short span of years."[12] In essence, even though there has been some scholarly research into farming settlements, most of it has described these efforts as failures that had little impact on the broader community. Perhaps this conclusion is premature.

As Jewish farming settlements gradually took hold in North America, some hoped this would disprove the ancient myth that Jews were not farmers – that it would show them to be a productive people. A Russian writer, Vladimir Grossman, published an early commentary on these settlements in the 1930s while visiting Canada. According to him, Jews involved in agriculture were making gains and becoming acknowledged as significant players in that industry. Grossman described Jewish farmers as having acquired considerable knowledge that had elevated their status in their communities: they were becoming "an important factor in Jewish life." For Grossman, this signified a natural movement towards "social reconstruction."[13] With a long history of living on the periphery of society, Jews have long found social integration a challenge. For Grossman, Jewish farmers were contributing to a modern economic relationship. This was a notable transformation: Jews were making an effort to fit into society instead of remaining outsiders or strangers in a new land.

Settlements: More Than Farming

According to German Zionist Arthur Ruppin, colonization could be more than an exercise in promoting agriculture. If handled correctly, building farm colonies could create "genuine communities ... of people living together with a minimum of friction."[14] For Ruppin, farming was much more than just a group of people working together. Farmers, along with others, were part of a foundation that would gradually become a "community" and a source of long-term growth. A farm was a place where people could share powerful life experiences that bound them together. These experiences would in turn forge a community's identity.

Farming settlements provided a sense of security and sustenance that could strengthen the incentive for some East European Jews to settle in strange and unknown lands. For the Jews who had been arriving from Eastern Europe, the land was very different and so were the people of North America. They found themselves in a new social environment in which they no longer faced mistreatment or political restrictions. A land that offered social peace and economic opportunity was highly attractive to them. According to the Jewish pioneer Rachel Calof, "two weeks after setting foot on the 'goldene medina' of America, I was on my way to become a pioneer woman and to help build my new country."[15] In her memoir, Calof expresses a sense of being freed from her former life in Russia and of belonging to a new community in the United States.

Canadian pioneer Jacob Baltzan's personal history conveys a comparable message. According to him, he "was no professional and certainly no carpenter, but in Canada I had become a builder."[16] For him, the idea of new opportunities was deeply empowering. His writings convey his excitement about and appreciation for his new home. As a newcomer, Baltzan dreamed of a better future, free of persecution and with endless opportunities. He emphasized with pride the value of "people living on a Jewish colony and look[ing] ahead to a brighter future."[17] Baltzan's brother Moishe noted that even though people had to work hard, they would surely benefit from enduring hardships, no matter what came next: "We will show them [the non-Jews] that we can open avenues, which they will imitate. And the colony will show that everything can be overcome with time. We only need patience and the manpower."[18]

Both Baltzan brothers were optimistic and articulated how freedom was the essence of life. They believed this new life for Jews in Canada would eventually fall into place no matter how difficult homesteading was at the time. "You are your own boss," wrote Jacob Baltzan, "not another's tenant to be wary of supervisors such as we had back home in Russia."[19] Baltzan put it most clearly when he wrote "the farm represented social and economic freedom."[20] For the Baltzans and many of their contemporaries, to be independent and to live free from persecution was a great incentive that would not only strengthen their resolve to become part of the community but also influence what they would eventually become as Canadians.

Agrarianism became popular within the Jewish immigrant refugee community, for it was viewed as a means to achieve economic and social freedom while retaining one's ethnic Jewish identity. The growth of the Jewish farming settlements encouraged a shift in attitudes towards Jewish immigrants and their contributions to society. Joseph Brandes wrote "agrarianism formed a bridge on which the disparate Jewish communities from the East and West met and mingled, even if the partnership was uneasy."[21] Here I think Brandes is suggesting that even though farming did at times divide people based on type of farming, skills, and economic status, overall it buttressed the idea of farmers as "pioneers" or "pilgrims." In a certain sense, farming served as a unifying factor rather than a divisive one for communities.

Jewish farmers recognized that life in North America was very different and learned that it was important to "band together for mutual aid and a strengthened cooperative movement."[22] Jewish farmers, wrote Joseph Brandes, were made to feel that they were working not just for themselves, "but rather for the cause of proving that Jews could be farmers."[23] For the Jewish philanthropists who supported and directed the settlement movement, farming "would speed the process of transition from visitor/outsider, to citizen/insider," wrote J. Sanford Rikoon.[24] As such, the placement of these immigrants on farms was beneficial in many ways and influenced the greater Jewish community. For whatever reason one accepted, the placement of these Jewish newcomers on farms "would not only turn immigrants into useful citizens, it would also aid in their Americanization."[25] For the new immigrants, to fit in – to become like others and avoid remaining on the periphery of society – became of paramount importance.

Years later, Simon Belkin acknowledged that the farming option contributed to the growth of the Jewish community in Canada and served as a positive factor for continued growth.[26] In the United States, according to Gabriel Davidson, a manager of the Jewish Agricultural Society of America, the future held great promise. Davidson was hopeful that the successful development of agriculture in America would lead to "the gradual creation of a real class of farmers ... and a lasting movement to be developed."[27] If Jews engaged in a practical and developing vocation like farming, their place in American society would become secure and recognized.

Verification of Productivization

As farming settlements expanded and the number of independent Jewish farmers increased, did the perception of Jews change among the non-Jewish population? And if the perception of Jews was changing, did productivization play a role in this, and how could this be shown?

From 1905 to 1920, around twenty articles appeared in the *New York Times* describing the activities and achievements of Jewish immigrant farmers. Although each told a slightly different story, most were bound by the common theme under discussion here – namely, all of these articles related back to the productivity of Jewish agricultural labour. In other words, Jewish immigrants were strongly involved in a sort of labour that proved they were contributing to the common American good.

For example, on 5 June 1905 the *New York Times* published a major feature on Jewish farmers. In it, the writer begins by emphasizing the success of Jewish immigrants who have ventured into farming and highlighting their accomplishments. Acknowledging the benefits to be derived from agriculture, the writer indicates that one can attain great wealth by following this career path. Quoting Nathan Bijur, the writer describes how "the farming industry in this country ... is so enormous and the revenue derived there so great that it is not surprising that so enterprising and industrious a citizen as the Jew has always shown himself ... to make his way in that field of labour."[28] Referring to Jewish people who have chosen farming, the writer suggests that these newcomers have shown themselves to be dedicated and hard working. The article presents the reader with a gloss on the successful undertakings of Jewish farmers and how their agricultural labours are a sign of their industriousness and hence their ability to contribute to the United States not *despite* being Jewish immigrants but *precisely* because they are.

In early March 1910, the *New York Times* published an article titled "Jewish Farmers Succeed Here." In this piece – part of a regular review of the annual meeting of the Jewish Agricultural and Industrial Aid Society held yearly in New York City – the writer describes the successes of Jewish farmers in the United States. According to this article, those successes serve as an open invitation for other Jews to follow them into farming. The writer considers it important to note that Jews are not opposed "to the hard manual labour involved in agricultural pursuits" and have clearly flourished in this line of work.[29]

In the *New York Times* of 28 November 1911, there is an article discussing how "the success of Jewish farmers in America was hailed as an introduction that Jews were coming into their own after forced and unnatural pursuits in commerce and finance."[30] Besides a recounting of the successes of Jews in agriculture, we find a reference to how Jews had in the past been associated with finance. This is part of a more general slant in the article emphasizing how Jewish immigrants are integrating into the workforce, leaving poverty behind, and striving to avoid becoming a burden on society. And while the article concludes by opining that it is the moral responsibility of Americans "to prevent the doors of our country being closed against those who flee from unspeakable persecution in foreign lands," its core emphasis is on how the Jewish farming population and its achievements represent "the best argument to combat the prejudice against immigration."[31] In other words, Americans' attitude towards Jewish immigrants is changing.

In Canada, as in the United States, concerns about immigrant placement programs pointed to an anxiety not to increase the ranks of the underprivileged. In an article published on 16 November 1892, the *Winnipeg Free Press* discussed the activities of the Jewish farmers in Oxbow in what was then the Northwest Territories. Detailing the newcomers' efforts to build a secure life, the article addresses the challenges facing these new settlers. It includes considerable discussion concerning the visit of "a commissioner" from Montreal, sponsored by the Baron de Hirsch Fund (soon to become the Jewish Colonization Association), who arrives to survey and where possible provide assistance to this large group of settlers. The settlement's future will be determined by how this group is doing. According to the article, the inspector finds that everyone is doing well; most people are happy and seem surprisingly good at their work.[32] The reporter concludes that the community's future looks bright, and notes that more settlers will soon be arriving from the east to join their families and friends. On the basis of its success so far, the author anticipates that the colony will soon expand.

In the summer of 1892, an article titled "Hirsch Is a Success" appears in the same newspaper. Referring to a settlement named after the Baron de Hirsch, it discusses the progress made so far by this colony of immigrant Jewish farmers near Souris, Manitoba (outside Brandon). Hirsch has more than two hundred settlers, who are committed to building a strong and vibrant community. According to the writer, "efforts to assist their poor Russian brethren were not thrown away, and promised to bring forth good fruits."[33] The settlers are content with their efforts, the reporter notes, and are committed to producing good crops and bountiful harvests, including oats, potatoes, and plenty of hay. In terms of relations with their non-Jewish neighbours, "the character of the little Jewish colony" is acknowledged "in the highest terms."[34] People work and live together with little if any friction.

A 1902 article in the same newspaper titled "Happy Jewish Farmers" details the life and times of another thriving community, this one near Wapella, Manitoba. The unnamed writer discusses the settlement's growing population and its farming successes. One part of the main colony seems to be doing better than a smaller nearby group. This dedicated and productive group of about thirty farmers has fields in the "highest state of cultivation."[35] The writer mentions visiting on the Sabbath and finding the village peaceful, without any activity. On this day, the community "remember[s] the Mosaic law" and all its members attend the "Jewish church."[36] According to the article, the Jewish farmers are working hard to build a community and a better life for all, all the while remaining respectful of their religious traditions. In considerable detail, this article reveals how the people live as well as the important qualities associated with farming.

In the above article and in other newspaper stories about Jewish farmers, the writers suggest that Jewish farming communities are good examples of how some immigrants integrate, and describe how they have worked hard to build their communities. Clearly, most Jews were dedicated to building a new life from the ground up, wherever they found themselves and whatever the circumstances.

A 1912 feature in the *Winnipeg Free Press* describes how Jewish farmers are proliferating and responding creatively to the difficulties they encounter. Whether it is the weather or something else, the problems they must confront are sometimes extremely challenging. A later article titled "Jewish Farmers Are Numerous in Canada" details the efforts of the Jewish Colonization Association in Canada to help new immigrants adjust to farming life. According to the article, the JCA [Jewish Colonization Association] is involved with 850 Jewish farming families comprising 3,720 individuals. The story adds "the type of farming ... varied according to the locality ... raising wheat in Saskatchewan, engaged in mixed farming in Alberta, truck gardeners in Manitoba and dairymen in the eastern provinces."[37] It is clear that this "back to the land movement" is continuing to attract more immigrants seeking security and opportunity.

Considering the diversity of work associated with agriculture – living in a farming settlement is only one type of agricultural labour, which can include work in related commercial areas – all of these news items are sending the clear message that newcomers from Eastern Europe are settling down on farms and becoming productive citizens. The problems they face are not at all the same as those facing Jewish refugees in large cities. The articles referred to above reflect an effort to dispel the idea that "Jews prefer[] settling in congested cities rather than following agricultural pursuits."[38] Although this resembles a public relations exercise, there is no evidence that it is a deliberate one. The many newspaper stories are merely stating the facts about the positive achievements of Jewish farmers.

Further Considerations on How Jewish Farmers Contributed to North American Jewish Identity

Jewish farmers contributed to how non-Jewish communities viewed Jewish immigrants. Whether it was a man selling produce at a market in Montreal or the pedlar going door to door selling fresh farm produce on the Upper East Side of New York, Jewish farmers were well known for their produce and services at a time when there were few supermarkets. In addition to this, the economic situation for Jewish farmers played a role often acknowledged but only rarely recognized as affecting the community's formation. More specifically, some farmers began taking in boarders, and in some regions this led to their opening summer hotels.

As Jewish agricultural settlements began to expand, some farmers looked for ways to bring in extra income. It was a time when people needed to be creative about supplementing their income, and summer hotels were one such way. "From the very beginning, friends and relatives from New York City visited in the summertime and on holidays ... For Jewish immigrants living in New York City, the farm offered an inexpensive vacation, wholesome food, and sorely missed contact with nature ... a pattern later followed by other farmers."[39] In Canada, the Laurentian Mountains north of Montreal served much the same purpose. A farmer would begin renting rooms to boarders from Montreal, then expand by building a separate rooming house that could accommodate a considerable number of people."[40] Most "city Jews" knew about these summer getaways, which were especially widespread in the Catskills in New York State. The Catskills had "the largest rural and small town Jewish population in the United States, [resulting in] a combination of Jewish farming and resort keeping."[41]

More and more farmers began renting out rooms in their homes and farmhouses, then raising new buildings to accommodate the increasing business. These places offered something experientially unique. According to Gertrude Dubrowsky, "the farmers' city friends and relatives helped to advertise the accommodations, spreading the news to coworkers and neighbours by word of mouth."[42] In the Catskills and places like it, "the farmers' summer enterprise was so successful that it turned into a major vacation resort industry."[43] Abraham D. Lavender and Clarence B. Steinberg wrote that "like many other Jewish farmers, they took in summer boarders in order to help meet their expenses ... Some of these farmers were to become famous success stories."[44] In hindsight, these destinations in Canada and the United States became sanctuaries for Jews as they adjusted to life in the New World, especially given the social restrictions they faced as to where they could vacation.

These experiences provided an atmosphere expressed in Yiddish as *haimisha*, in that they reflected a lifestyle similar to living in an Eastern European *shtetl*. Since many of these boarders were newcomers, farmers and guests would speak Yiddish and discuss matters related to Jewish life and religious duties. I suggest that this atmosphere contributed strongly to the development of a vibrant identity. In the Catskills, "a kind of spontaneous colonizing developed ... aided but not initiated by the society. The rural colonies were like a series of shells around small operating towns whose economies included Jewish artisans, craftsmen, merchants, food vendors, farm suppliers, farm produce buyers, barbers, tailors, glazers, mechanics, and physicians. Jews lived with their rural Christian counterparts as in the Russo-Polish shtetls."[45] It would seem, then, that Jewish farming settlements were compact little communities that contained everything, their contours becoming similar to those of a "typical Jewish rural settlement in the Old Country, but so unlike the native American village."[46] From this, one might conclude that these colonies also served as places where immigrants could smooth the transition from their home country to the New World. They were places where people lived in a way that provided familiarity in a strange new world.

These experiences must have provided an influential social climate for people to live and behave as if they were living in their home country – that is, to live without the social distress they encountered in the New World. In practice, when we change our circumstances or social environment, we must modify our way of living, and this affects our identity. Here, let us consider the premise offered by in Robert P. Amyot and Lee Sigelman that "lower levels of religiosity and social contact are associated with a weaker sense of Jewish identity."[47] It follows that living in a Jewish environment, speaking Yiddish, following Jewish religious life and practices, keeping kosher, and so on, no doubt builds and strengthens one's Jewish identity.

I would argue that Jewish farming settlements had a profound impact as crucibles for the growth, maintenance, and enhancement of "Jewish identity" prior to and up to the 1970s. Nathan Glazer wrote that "the combination of religious Judaism and ethnic Jewishness has always been a key to Jewish identity ... [and] Jewish kinship groups and organizations provide daily confirmation of their Jewishness."[48] Living in a Jewish environment "plays some part in the formation of Jewish identity, forming a base that does not atrophy with neglect."[49] Evidence suggests that the religious dimension of Judaism is significant to the formation of the Jewish identity, but so is "close interpersonal relations with other Jews."[50]

Conclusion

Although the activities of Jewish farmers and their settlements have been recognized and documented, there is still no comprehensive account of this period. There is ample evidence that Jewish farming settlements played a significant role in the development of the Jewish community in both Canada and the United States. These colonies provided work and settlement opportunities for Eastern European Jewish immigrants escaping persecution between 1880s and 1940s. These newcomers did not have an easy time building new communities where none had previously existed, in sparsely settled regions of North America. Farming unsettled lands was a means for Jews to display to other North Americans their commitment to their new home and their capacity for hard work.

Over time, these farmers began taking in boarders to generate extra income. Later, they began opening small hotels, mostly famously in the Catskills of New York State, which became associated with the development of the Jewish community in America. Indeed, the Catskills also served as a model for resort development and the entertainment industry more broadly.

It is difficult today to measure the contributions of Jewish farmers and the settlements they built; that said, it would be a mistake to underestimate their contribution to North America's Jewish community as a whole.

As shown in this chapter, the Jewish farming movement strengthened the foundations of the broader North American Jewish community. In turn this strengthened the ever-evolving Jewish identity – something Michael Myers refers to as "a complex sociological phenomenon central to the modern Jewish experience."[51] Unfortunately, scholars cannot agree on one universal model that explains how the "modern Jewish experience" came to be. Even so, most accept that "a healthy identity, like a healthy body, depends on what one consumes or absorbs during the period of maximum growth in childhood and adolescence. A healthy diet of Jewish experiences and education at this time helps to produce a strong Jewish identity."[52] In an era when Jewish immigrants were establishing who and what they were as a community, the lifestyle and contributions of Jewish farmers clearly played a role. Perhaps if one considers the presence and contributions of Jewish farmers, what on the surface might seem minor may have indeed been significant as a whole.

Notes

1 Shva Medjuck, "Maintaining an Identity: A Focus on the Smaller Communities," in *From Immigration to Integration – The Canadian Jewish Experience: A Millennium Edition*, ed. Ruth Klein and Frank Dimant (Toronto: Printed for B'nai Brith Canada Institute for International Affairs, 2001), 228.

2 Samuel Joseph, *History of the Baron de Hirsch Fund: The Americanization of the Jewish Immigrant* (Philadelphia: Printed for Baron de Hirsch fund by the Jewish Publication Society, 1935), 18.

3 Theodore Norman, *An Outstretched Arm: A History of the Jewish Colonization Association* (London: Routledge and Kegan Paul, 1985), 2.

4 Norman, *An Outstretched Arm*, 1.

5 David J. Sorkin, *The Transformation of German Jewry, 1780–1840* (Detroit: Wayne State University Press, 1999), 27.

6 Ibid., 76.

7 Robert A. Goldberg, *Back to the Soil: The Jewish Farmers of Clarion, Utah, and Their World* (Salt Lake City: University of Utah Press, 1986), 149.

8 Ibid., 149.

9 The vast majority of this correspondence can be found in the Archives of the Canadian Jewish Congress in Montreal.

10 Abraham D. Lavender and Clarence B. Steinberg, *Jewish Farmers of the Catskills: A Century of Survival* (Gainesville: University Press of Florida, 1995).

11 Ellen Eisenberg, *Jewish Agricultural Colonies in New Jersey, 1882–1920* (Syracuse: Syracuse University Press, 1995), 173.

12 Gabriel Davidson, *Our Jewish Farmers: And the Story of the Jewish Agricultural Society* (New York: L.B. Fischer, 1943), 192.

13 Vladimir Grossman, *The Soil's Calling* (Montreal: Eagle Publishing, 1938), 126.

14 Uri D. Herscher, *Jewish Agricultural Utopias in America, 1880–1910* (Detroit: Wayne State University Press, 1981), 28.

15 Rachel Calof and J.S. Rikoon, *Rachel Calof's Story: Jewish Homesteader on the Northern Plains* (Bloomington: Indiana University Press, 1995), 22.

16 Jacob A. Baltzan, *Memories of a Pioneer Farmer in Western Canada at the Dawn of the 20th Century* (Toronto: Published privately, 1991), 248.

17 Ibid., 72.

18 Ibid., 52.

19 Ibid., 49.

20 Ibid., 49.

21 Joseph Brandes and Martin Douglas, *Immigrants to Freedom: Jewish Communities in Rural New Jersey since 1882* (Philadelphia: University of Pennsylvania Press, 1971), 336.

22 Ibid., 336.

23 Ibid., 86.

24 Calof and Rikoon, *Rachel Calof's Story*, 110.

25 Ibid., 110.

26 Simon Belkin, *Through Narrow Gates: A Review of Jewish Immigration, Colonization, and Immigrant Aid Work in Canada (1840–1940)* (Montreal: Canadian Jewish Congress and Jewish Colonization Association, 1966), 76.

27 Davidson, *Our Jewish Farmers*, 13.

28 "Farming Needs Brains No Less the Business," *New York Times*, 5 June 1905.

29 "Jewish Farmers Succeed Here," *New York Times*, 6 March 1910.

30 "Schiff Calls Jews Farmers by Origin," *New York Times*, 28 November 1911.

31 Ibid.

32 "Jewish Farmers," *Winnipeg Free Press*, 16 November 1892.

33 "Hirsch Is a Success," *Winnipeg Free Press*, 10 August 1892.

34 Ibid.

35 "Happy Jewish Farmers," *Winnipeg Free Press*, 14 June 1902.

36 Ibid., 14 June 1902.

37 "Jewish Farmers Are Numerous in Canada," *Winnipeg Free Press*, 23 November 1912.

38 Ibid.

39 Gertrude W. Dubrovsky, *The Land Was Theirs: Jewish Farmers in the Garden State* (Tuscaloosa: University of Alabama Press, 1992), 38.

40 Howard Gontovnick, "From Colony to Community: Ste Sophie, Quebec," Canadian Jewish Studies 9 (2001), 190–209.

41 Lavender and Steinberg, *Jewish Farmers of the Catskills*, 26.

42 Dubrovsky, *The Land Was Theirs*, 135.

43 Ibid., 135.

44 Lavender and Steinberg, *Jewish Farmers of the Catskills*, 41.

45 Ibid., 41.

46 Ibid., 42.

47 Robert P. Amyot and Lee Sigelman, "Jews without Judaism? Assimilation and Jewish Identity in the United States," *Social Science Quarterly* 77, no. 1 (March 1996): 177–89 (quote at 177).

48 See Nathan Glazer, *American Judaism* (Chicago: University of Chicago Press, 1958).

49 Amyot and Sigelman, "Jews without Judaism?," 186.

50 Ibid., 187.

51 Charme Stuart, Bethamie Horowitz, Tali Hyman, and Jeffrey S. Kress, "Jewish Identities in Action: An Exploration of Models, Metaphors, and Methods," *Journal of Jewish Education* 74, no. 2 (2008): 115–43 (quote at 115).

52 Ibid., 117.

FIVE

Bacon, Beans, and a Fine Dish of "Ditto" Commonalities in Early Jewish Life and Religiosity along the Pacific West Coast

Lillooet Nördlinger McDonnell

The discovery of gold in California in 1848 turned that soon-to-be state into an "Eldorado"[1] – a golden land of possibilities. San Francisco, North America's first major Pacific port, soon became the main hub of settlement along the west coast, and many Jewish merchants settled in that burgeoning "instant city" and invested in its economic and social future.[2] Then in the late 1850s and early 1860s, gold rushes along the Fraser Canyon and in the Cariboo launched an era of mass immigration to what is now the province of British Columbia. As Jewish pioneer Frank Sylvester noted in his diary, "the first arrivals [to Victoria, Vancouver Island] from California and elsewhere in 1858, came ... really for two purposes only: trading and mining."[3] British Columbia's early settlers were a mix of Britons, Americans, Canadians, Europeans, and Asians, and like their Californian counterparts were adventurous fortune seekers prepared for frontier life. Among the throng of gold rush era migrants to British Columbia were more than two hundred Jews, who settled in Victoria.[4]

The region was a colonial frontier – an extension of British society, guided by British forms of authority and cultural norms and standards, rather than an extension of the American West, where lawlessness prevailed in the early years. By geographic necessity, British Columbia's gold rush settlers had to pass through San Francisco before arriving on Vancouver Island and making their way to the goldfields on the British Columbia mainland.[5] The steady stream of migrants by way of California and the maintenance of north–south trade links greatly influenced the social and cultural flavour of Victoria, especially its Jewish community. So it is not surprising that Victoria's new Jewish community had an abundance of family and business ties in San Francisco.

British and Canadian influence was prominent in the area, and it continued to strengthen after British Columbia entered Confederation in 1871. This chapter asks: What influence did the Americans have on Jewish religious and cultural practices in British Columbia during the late colonial and early Confederation years? The discussion will pay particular attention to the cultural links between the early Jewish community in Victoria and its American counterpart in San Francisco. To explore this question, we turn to the life and experiences of one man, Frank Sylvester, an early Jewish settler in Victoria with family ties to San Francisco. Sylvester advocated strongly against reforms to Jewish religious tradition and synagogue practices, yet when out on the gold trail, his daily meals consisted of the not very kosher combination of bacon and beans. As we will see, Jews on the west coast in the mid-nineteenth century, in both Canada and the United States, were forced to reconcile their religious lives with their often integrated public lives.

The Early Life of Frank Sylvester

Frank Sylvester was born Francis Joseph Silberstein in Liverpool, England, on 20 December 1842, to Eula Sarah Pulvermacher (1807–55) and Heyman (a.k.a. Heinrich) Silberstein (1805–83), of Prussia.[6] The Pulvermachers were against their daughter Eula's marriage to Heyman, "a poor but honest tailor."[7] Eula and Heyman had eight children, although only three would survive into adulthood.[8] The Silbersteins immigrated to England in the mid-1830s.[9] Once settled in Liverpool, they worked as labourers to support their children: Rebecca (1831–88) and Rachel (1833–81), both born in Prussia, and Aaron (1837–43), Harriet (1839–50), and Frank (1842–1908), all born in Liverpool.[10] In 1843 the family set sail for America aboard the SS *Europe*, arriving in New York on 22 June 1843. Baby Frank – by then one and a half years old – and the rest of the Silberstein family were among the thousands of immigrants who crossed the Atlantic in search of a new home and greater opportunities in North America.[11]

The Anglicization of Jewish and other foreign-sounding names was common in the mid-nineteenth century. By 1850, the family had changed their name from Silberstein to Sylvester; Heyman became known as Henry, and Eula was registered as Julia. The New York census notes that Henry Sylvester continued to work as a tailor, and it is possible that his wife helped in these endeavours, as was common among Jewish workers in New York City's growing garment industry. Rebecca and Rachel soon married, reducing the financial burden on their parents. Around 1850, Rebecca married Martin Prag, a Jewish immigrant from Poland, who at that time worked as a tinsmith;[12] around 1855, Rachel married Henry M. Cohen, a pawnbroker from Prussia. Each daughter named her first son George Washington.[13] By virtue of having come to the United States as an infant, Frank Sylvester became a naturalized American citizen – unlike the rest of his family, who were considered alien residents of the United States. Indeed, Frank and his young nephew George W. Prag (1849–88), were the only American members of the Sylvester household in 1855.[14]

After Eula's untimely death in 1855, Henry made sure his son Frank accompanied him to *shul* (synagogue) every day for nearly a year, where together they recited *Kaddish*, the mourner's prayer, in Eula's memory.[15] Once this mourning period was over, Henry decided to take a chance at a better life. In 1856, father and son left the crowded tenements of New York City and crossed the continent in search of prosperity. The Sylvesters' journey by stagecoach was likely arduous and not without peril.[16] Before the American transcontinental railroad was completed in 1869, it could take up to a year to reach the Pacific coast from New York.[17] The pair eventually reunited with Rebecca and Rachel and their families in San Francisco.[18]

Like many families on the west coast, Martin Prag had entered the wholesale business, opening Austin & Prag, Stove and Tin Ware Dealers, in 1850.[19] Taking full advantage of the arrival of his young unemployed brother-in-law, he started a satellite store in Shasta, California. Opening branch stores was a strong impetus for mobility; it was common for men to have their brothers, cousins, and other extended kin clerk for them until they were ready to run branch stores of their own.[20] San Francisco provided the personnel and supplies for the region's merchandising networks as well as for its emerging Jewish communities. As the networks of brothers, cousins, and *landsleit* (fellow Jews from the same district or town) founded new stores in remote outposts, they established Jewish organizations and institutions tied to San Francisco.[21]

The store in Shasta foundered, but Frank Sylvester was determined to succeed. So with the help of his brother-in-law, he set sail for Victoria in 1858, where he was one of the first fifty Jewish arrivals on the island.[22] He intended to open a hardware store there and perhaps try his hand at mining.[23] Unable at first to sell merchandise in Victoria, he ventured into the goldfields, where merchandising proved more successful than in Victoria. Between 1861 and 1864, he travelled between San Francisco, Victoria, and the goldfields, on average four times per year, selling goods to the miners. He also set up a shop in Victoria and participated in the life of the town,[24] where he earned a respected place for himself in the burgeoning Jewish community and in the community at large.

As gold prospects declined, Sylvester began to spend more time in Victoria. He settled there permanently in 1864 after being hired as an accountant at the auctioneering firm of J.P. Davies & Co.[25] The firm's proprietor, Judah Phillip Davies (known as J.P. to friends and family), was originally from England, but he had spent time in Australia and California before arriving in Victoria in 1863 with his wife, Miriam (a.k.a. Maria) and their six children, including two daughters, Elizabeth and Cecelia Davies, who were a few years Sylvester's junior. Davies was an acculturated Jew, well accustomed to the hardships of a frontier that aspired to establish a thriving bourgeois society, complete with all the accoutrements of a functioning Jewish community. Within a short time, Sylvester proved himself a reliable employee as well as a loyal friend to the Davies family. The sudden death of the recently married Elizabeth Davies Schultz in 1866 strengthened the bond between Sylvester and Cecelia Davies, and soon after, a courtship began.

That same year, Sylvester was shipwrecked off the coast of California while returning to Victoria after a supply run. Shipwrecks were common off California's coast in those days, partly due to severe weather and faulty equipment, and the delays could be interminable.[26] Sylvester's ship, an old Hudson's Bay Company paddle steamer, the *Labouchere*, struck Point El Rayes starboard. The crew and a handful of other men, Sylvester among them, managed to get all of the women, children, and other passengers onto three lifeboats. They then set about building a raft with whatever supplies they could find – basically, anything that could float. By early morning, the *Labouchere* had sunk six and a half kilometres offshore. Three men drowned; however, Sylvester and the rest of the crew were rescued by a passing sailboat. All that Sylvester lost was his boots.[27]

In 1866, Sylvester received his first Christmas present from a fellow Jew. The event was significant enough for him to note in his journal: "On Christmas I received a nice silver match box from Hoffman with the letters F.S. cut on the front. This is the first present I have ever received at Christmas."[28] That same year, Sylvester attended his first mass on Christmas Eve. The services apparently were not to his liking, although he seemed to have

Figure 5.1: Frank Sylvester (1842–1908), Victoria, British Columbia, ca. 1900. Collection: Congregation Emanu-El fonds. Jewish Museum and Archives of British Columbia, L.18501.

enjoyed the Latin singing. On 24 December 1866, he wrote, "I went to High Mass at Church till one. Large numbers were present. The singing was very nice. There was a ceremony of Latin prayers rendered by three priests in yellow coats. The ceremony, to my eyes is very ridiculous looking ... The Priests also distribute Holy Wafers which are eagerly sought after by devout Catholics."[29] Such associations were atypical for traditional Jews in Eastern Europe. The fact that Frank so willingly associated with the non-Jewish sectors of Victoria society and that they so willingly included him reflects the symbiotic relationship that existed between the two groups. Cecelia Davies and Frank Sylvester married in 1869 and went on to raise five daughters and three sons: Elizabeth Eula (1869–1937), Louise Marion (1871–1955), William Benjamin (1874–1931), Clarence Bertram (1876–1933), Mabel Violet (1878–1945), Jesse Percival (1880–1945), Rachel Valentine (1884–1975), and Rebecca Florence (1889–1979).[30]

Early Jews in San Francisco and Victoria

Jewish immigration to North America often brings to mind the waves of Eastern European Jews – greenhorns – who arrived in the late nineteenth century and crowded into the Lower East Side in Manhattan, the "Main" in Montreal, or the "Ward" in Toronto. These Jews worked as peddlers and petty traders, spoke faltering English, and faced discrimination in housing and employment; it often took a generation or more for them to ameliorate their circumstances.[31] On the west coast, circumstances both resembled and deviated from those on the east. Many of the Jews who came to the west coast were from German-, French-, and Polish-speaking lands, with a sprinkling of Sephardic Jews as well as Jews from czarist Russia, the Caribbean, and South Africa. Some of these Jews had undergone *Bildung* (Germanization through education) or had experienced formal emancipation in their home countries; notwithstanding this, they continued to face discrimination in continental Europe, which crippled their chances of social mobility. They escaped by immigrating to England or elsewhere. The promise of gold lured some to California. A few of these early Pacific Jews came as miners, but most came as merchants who catered to the miners' needs.

Prominent Jews in California included Adolph Sutro, an engineer from Prussia, who at one point owned one-twelfth of the land in San Francisco and became its mayor in 1894; Levi Strauss of Bavaria, who popularized riveted canvas work pants with reinforced seams (a.k.a. Levi's jeans); and Isaias Wolf Hellman, also of Bavaria, who was California's most prominent financier.[32] California's Jews quickly became key figures in the state's new towns and cities. They erected permanent brick buildings, supplied merchandise, became creditors, and were prominent civic and political leaders. For example, Abraham Labatt, a Sephardic Jew from South Carolina, was selected as San Francisco's first alderman; Emanuel Linoberg was elected to the first town council of Sonora; and Los Angeles elected Morris L. Goodman as a councilman.[33]

By 1852 nearly a quarter of a million people had passed through San Francisco en route to the nearby goldfields.[34] Despite its remote location on "the edge of the world," San Francisco thrived as a result of its coastal location and its role in the commercial boom brought on by the American Civil War (1861–65), during which it supplied wool, wheat, and gold to the Union.[35] In 1850, the American Jewish population was around 50,000; by 1860, 150,000; by 1880, 280,000.[36] In San Francisco in 1849 there were around 50 Jews; twenty years later, 16,000, or somewhere between 7 and 8 percent of the city's inhabitants.[37] By 1870, San Francisco had surpassed Cincinnati, Ohio, as the largest western Jewish community.

Like their counterparts in California, most of Victoria's Jewish pioneers established permanent supply businesses in Victoria, with only a minority venturing out into the mining regions during the summer months.[38] These people, too, were of various cultural backgrounds – including Jews from Prussia, Russia, Poland, and Bavaria, and of Sephardic background.[39] These immigrants were fluent in English, familiar with British and American culture, had a penchant for trade (and economic success), and were determined to build a community. Some, like J.P. and Miriam Davies, were British-born and arrived on Vancouver Island after spending significant time in California. Others, like Frank Sylvester, had lived in New York City before going west to seek their fortunes in the gold rush and connect with family business networks.

Other immigrants included Alexander Aaron Phillips, the first Jew known to have to set foot on British Columbian soil.[40] Originally from England, Phillips had spent time in Australia and California before venturing north to Vancouver Island, where he opened the island's first cider house, Pioneer Syrup, Soda & Cider Works, and became a founding member of various voluntary associations. He eventually married his distant cousin from San Francisco and went on to have eleven children.[41] It was thanks to Phillips's initiative that much of the region, including Washington State, was supplied with Passover *matzot* during those early gold rush years.[42] Other early Jewish settlers in Victoria exhibited similar characteristics and crossed Jewish and non-Jewish boundaries. There was Lewis Davis, owner of the Star and Garter Hotel, who provided Victoria's Jews with a temporary house of worship until 1863, when the island's first synagogue, Congregation Emanu-El, was built. There was also Lewis Lewis, a dry goods merchant and a member of the Masons and the Odd Fellows, who provided money for Victoria's first Jewish cemetery. Another Mason, a Jew of Polish origin named Abraham Blackman, arrived via Stockton, California, and worked as an ironmonger and hardware dealer while founding the Victoria Hebrew Benevolent Society (Khevra Kadisha) and serving as the first treasurer of Congregation Emanu-El as well as its first cantor for the High Holidays.[43]

The Oppenheimer brothers, originally from Bavaria, settled in New Orleans and then San Francisco before arriving in Victoria in 1858–59.

They eventually began a chain of supply warehouses throughout the Cariboo and helped build a section of the Cariboo Wagon Road. The Oppenheimers were involved in establishing and supplying volunteer fire brigades throughout the region. One brother, David, became the second mayor of Vancouver in 1888. Other Jewish businessmen became involved in politics. Selim Franklin served as a member of the Legislative Assembly of Vancouver Island from 1860 to 1866; his brother Lumley Franklin was elected mayor of Victoria in 1866; and Henry Nathan became the first Jew elected to the Canadian Parliament, serving from 1871 to 1874.[44] In 1878, J.P. Davies ran for the House of Commons as a Liberal-Conservative candidate in the Victoria riding, but lost.[45]

Like San Francisco's early Jews, Victoria's Jews comprised a merchant class, who included petty traders, retail storekeepers, and saloon proprietors, and a more elite group of businessmen, who included large-scale wholesalers, commission merchants, auctioneers, and land agents. The latter group included J.P. Davies, Frank Sylvester, and the Franklin and Oppenheimer brothers.[46] Located as they were in a relatively isolated setting, by necessity Victoria's early Jews interacted to a high degree with general society, and in their capacity as merchants they worked alongside their non-Jewish counterparts to develop Victoria, both socially and economically. They joined local voluntary and fraternal associations such as the fire brigade, hospital boards, Masonic lodges, and Odd Fellows societies. As noted, several became involved in governance at the colonial, municipal, and later provincial levels.[47] Despite the socio-economic hierarchy that existed among Victoria's Jewish merchant class, overlapping family business and communal ties enhanced communal cohesion. At the same time, seasonal visits between San Francisco and Victoria quickly bonded Jews together in a solid community.[48] These communal foundations enabled Jewish immigrants to maintain some cultural and religious traditions while negotiating their place in a pluralistic frontier society.

The Fraser River gold rush of 1858 had brought more than 20,000 new residents to Victoria nearly overnight.[49] By the time of the second gold rush of 1863, Victoria was a small city, where there were more tents than buildings and only a handful of Jews. Between 1858 and 1863 the Jewish population grew to 242, fluctuating between 4 and 4.8 percent of Victoria's total population (see Table 5.1).[50] Victoria began losing its status as the Canadian west coast's leading commercial centre in 1866, when the two colonies of Vancouver Island and mainland British Columbia amalgamated, ultimately joining Confederation in 1871.[51] With the end of Victoria's free port status and declining gold discoveries, the number of immigrants fell significantly; Victoria's Jewish population slowly declined as the economy drifted into

Table 5.1: Total Jewish population in British Columbia, 1858–1871

Year	Total #	Households #	Single #	Families #	Children #
1858	50	32	19	13	6
1859	99	60	33	27	12
1860	149	76	34	42	31
1861	167	76	35	43	34
1862	217	78	49	57	54
1863	242	106	54	65	58
1864	221	119	29	67	58
1865	208	96	28	60	60
1866	191	88	27	56	52
1867	177	83	24	61	51
1868	144	85	15	43	43
1869	134	58	17	38	41
1870	118	45	12	33	40
1871	93	34	8	26	34

Source: Christine Boas Wisenthal, "Insiders and Outsiders: Two Waves of Jewish Settlement in British Columbia, 1858–1914" (M.A. thesis, UBC, 1987), 19.
Note: Table includes total Jewish population, total number of Jews living in households, total number of single Jewish residents, total number of Jewish families, and total number of Jewish children.

Table 5.2: Jewish population of British Columbia, 1871–1931

Year	1871	1881	1891	1901	1911	1921	1931
BC	100	104*	277*	554*	1,384*	1696	2743
Canada total	1,333*	2,455	6,503*	16,717	75,838	126,201	156,726

Source: Wisenthal, "Insiders and Outsiders," 20.
Note: * = Jews by religion

recession. By 1871 there were only ninety-three Jews in Victoria – less than 3 percent of its population.[52] When the Canadian Pacific Railway crossed the Rockies, terminating at Port Moody in 1887, Victoria ceased to be a destination for Jews arriving on Canada's Pacific coast. At that point, Vancouver began its commercial domination of the province.[53] Most of British Columbia's Jews eventually moved to the mainland, but they continued to live in Victoria, and throughout the nineteenth century they strongly resembled their counterparts in San Francisco.

Evolving American Jewish Traditions of the Nineteenth Century: minhag American

As historian Jonathan D. Sarna has observed, by the nineteenth century, American Jewry was diverse and pluralistic, open to dissention in the synagogue and to individualist choices when it came to religious practices.[54] In essence, nineteenth-century American Jews sought ways to be both Jewish and American. One could argue that American Jews were in the midst of carving out their own traditional standards, as Jews of Europe and the Middle East had done before with their various *minhagim* (rites/customs), such as *minhag Polin, minhag Ashkenaz, minhag Sepharad,* and *minhag Romania.* In the context of this discussion, the term *minhag American* refers to the evolving traditions of American Jews during the nineteenth century, including divisions between traditionalist and reformist elements. Indeed, the *minhag American* partly accounts for the variability of Jewish religiosity in nineteenth-century Victoria.

The term *minhag American* should not be confused with the title of Rabbi Isaac Meyer Wise's *siddur* (prayer book), *Minhag America: The Daily Prayers for American Israelites,* originally published in 1857 in German/Hebrew and English/Hebrew. The book is also referred to as *Minhag Amerika* or *Minhag Amerikah.* The *siddur* was formatted like a traditional prayer book but included major reforms such as the elimination of the call to return to the land of Israel to rebuild the Holy Temple.[55] Rabbi Wise was a moderate Reform rabbi who argued for a synthesis of traditions that would supersede Sephardic, Ashkenazi, and Polish traditions. His *siddur* was widely used throughout the 1860s and 1870s by congregations across the United States. However, his *siddur* was not quite the unifier that he envisioned. Instead, divisions arose between traditionalists and reformists as the century wore on.[56]

Regardless of their origins or inclinations towards tradition, nineteenth-century North American Jewry displayed unique traits that did not exist in Europe. As a result, early Jewish identity on the Pacific coast moved in a multiplicity of directions.[57] According to historian Jeanne Abrams, the early Jewish population of the American west was "composed of both traditionalists and reformers who cared enough about their Jewish roots to join together to establish the institutions so necessary for the preservation of Jewish life."[58] The famed Jewish traveller Israel Benjamin "recorded the existence of active Jewish religious communities in California's mining camps and ... Sacramento,"[59] but except when it came to the High Holidays, he noted a lack of religious observance throughout the year.[60] In San Francisco, Benjamin also observed that *shochtim* (ritual slaughterers) formed a visible part of the community.[61] Still, laxity existed with regard to Jewish dietary laws, or *kashrut*, even in San Francisco.[62]

Until the 1870s, there was a sense that one of the main goals of American Jewish communities – whether they were traditionally inclined or not – was to conform to American modes of conduct.[63] Thus, Jewishness on the west coast had yet to define its boundaries. For that reason, adjustments and reforms were made to traditional religious practices, and this in turn fostered a high degree of integration and religious flexibility. Indeed, the diverse nature of west coast Jewry was felt from San Diego to Victoria. "With San Francisco as its hub, Jews built social, religious, and business networks that flourished up and down the coast. Clergy achieved … recognition for their modern views, and Jews participated actively in civic and ecumenical life."[64] A distinctive feature of American Jewish history during this era was the absence of educated religious leaders. The lack of ordained rabbis in America persisted until the 1840s, and even then only a few arrived. Because religion in eighteenth-century North America was a private rather than a communal affair, even when traditional rabbis arrived in the nineteenth century, they found that the will of the laity dominated the congregations. Rabbis could either go along with popular demands for change to traditional rites or find other congregations to mentor.[65] Lay leadership in effect dominated Jewish communal infrastructure.[66] Although many Jewish immigrants were accustomed to traditional life and aspired to maintain it, the study or analysis of sacred texts and commentary played little or no role in their daily lives. They were not trained scholars infused with the desire to maintain a traditional *kahal* in a different society, or with knowledge of how to do so.[67] Indeed, religious behaviour in America was dominated by the prevailing American philosophy that religion was a matter of personal choice rather than communal control. Therefore, once established in roles of religious leadership, Jewish laity perceived itself to have the power to implement changes.[68]

By the 1860s and 1870s, the US economy was booming, thanks in part to the American Civil War, and optimism prevailed. This confidence was reflected in the discourse between liberal Jews and Protestants, who spoke warmly of universalism.[69] Rabbi Isaac Mayer Wise, known for his reformist tendencies, predicted that "within fifty years Judaism's teachings would be common property of the American people."[70] Most American Jews chose to adapt some Jewish traditions to American culture but not others, and fell somewhere in between traditionalist and reforming tendencies.[71] By the 1860s and 1870s, many congregations across the United States had adopted Wise's *Minhag America*, which, as noted earlier, was formatted like a traditional *siddur* but included major reforms.[72]

As the nineteenth century progressed, congregations across America continued to push for changes. Common changes taking place included a shortened worship service, the addition of sermons and vernacular readings, mixed seating (first introduced in eighteenth-century American churches as a way of promoting the sanctity of the family in the face of increasing industrialization),[73] organ music, and the adoption of non-orthodox liturgies, such as Rabbi Wise's *siddur*. And the push for change was not limited to reformists. Even traditionalist-leaning congregations made modifications. Sabbath observance was respected in varying degrees. For example, some merchants opened their doors only on Saturday afternoons in order to attend Sabbath services in the morning.[74] Although traditionalist rabbis may not have condoned such practices, they did rationalize other unconventional practices.[75] These modifications were intended to attract younger Jews to synagogue, make non-Jewish friends and visitors feel welcome (thereby improving Jews' public image), and create a formal and grand atmosphere for worship.[76] However, changes like these also had unexpected results. Rabbis became the wardens of the faith, permitting congregants to freely and openly abandon religious practices if they so chose.[77]

Gold rush Jewry in San Francisco was not immune from the whims of lay leaders or the social pressure to fragment, reform, or abandon religious practices. In 1849, Lewis Franklin advertised in one of San Francisco's local newspapers that High Holiday services would be held in his wood-framed, canvas-covered store on Jackson Street. Jewish men who sold dry goods in the region's mining camps answered the notice. Franklin hosted around thirty Jews for Rosh Hashanah, with an additional twenty at Yom Kippur.[78] Franklin, the great-grandson of a rabbi from Breslau, had left Liverpool in the 1840s and settled in Baltimore before making his way to San Francisco. Once there, he realized how easy it was for Jews to ignore religious obligations, and he recognized the need to establish a permanent synagogue where the region's Jews would uphold Jewish law and keep the sabbath.[79] He noted: "How clearly apparent it is that Interest, Wealth, [and] Gold, are the stumbling blocks to the tranquility of the mind, and the rejoicing of the soul. How fleeting and deceptive are the blessings which attend this acquisition of gold."[80] Franklin's pleas were heeded, and San Francisco Jews banded together to establish committees to raise funds for a synagogue, import a *mazot* baker, and bring in a *shochet*. When disagreements erupted over whether to hire a German or a Polish applicant, two congregations were formed: Emanu-El (1850) and Sherith Israel (1851).[81]

As Sarna notes, by the time of the American Civil War, in major cities across the United States, no single synagogue represented the community as a whole. Indeed, synagogues often symbolized and promoted fragmentation.[82] As Sarna puts it, the American Jewish community mirrored the federalist pattern; that is to say, American Jewry was diverse, free, democratic, and unified.[83] There were several differences in San Francisco's two synagogues from the outset. Sherith Israel members tended to come from England, Posen, and Poland, while Emanu-El's members came from the Rhineland and France, although both congregations also included a number of American-born Sephardi.[84] Both congregations introduced reforms, although Sherith Israel did so in a more restrained way.

Sherith Israel followed Polish *minhagim*, emphasized decorum, practised "enlightened orthodoxy" as observed in England, hired clergy from England, and the English language dominated.[85] Sherith Israel's first rabbi, the London-born Henry A. Henry, had been educated and involved in Jewish as well as non-Jewish communal organizations. He was fully ready to integrate into the wider community, and he presented himself that way.[86] In contrast, Emanu-El's first rabbi, Julius Eckman, spoke English but had been educated in Germany, and the congregation followed German *minhagim*, with the language of sermon discourse in German.[87] Eckman insisted on traditional Jewish practice, which put him at odds with segments of his congregation. Being from Germany, he did, however, support reforms such as the introduction of a choir and an organ.

Like many congregations in the United States, Emanu-El's membership was in constant flux, and the laity felt confident in questioning the hired religious authority as well as questioning which observances best fit with American life. They often hired a series of rabbis until they found one who matched their desires.[88] In 1864 the congregation became known as Temple Emanu-El when it abandoned German *minhagim* and adopted "a moderate Reform prayer book ... which included prayers in German and created a more performance style service."[89] Those who disagreed with this method of worship started another congregation, Ohabai Shalome (Lovers of Peace), which followed German *minhagim* but allowed for family seating, a choir, and English sermons.[90]

Despite the innovations, some areas of Jewish practice remained constant. For example, the customs surrounding the burial of the dead remained relatively unchanged. In the United States, as in Europe, there were separate burial societies for men and women. Often known as the Khevra Kadisha (literally, "Sacred Society"), the Hebrew Benevolent Association, or the Ladies Hebrew Association, these associations were established on a voluntary basis to perform the prescribed rituals surrounding burial of the dead, and to care for the sick and needy.[91] No financial rewards were offered in exchange for membership, and initiation fees were quite high; but at the same time, membership in such organizations often placed members in positions of influence and power within the community. The burial society was the first Jewish communal organization to be established; typically one or two years after Jews arrived in a new region. These associations, especially the ladies' associations, also raised funds on behalf of the communal treasury, by holding balls, theatrical events, and picnics. It was the Hebrew Benevolent Association that secured a cemetery, established a social network and a treasury, and held routine religious services in members' homes.[92] Besides providing burial needs, the benevolent associations took care of ailing members of the Jewish community. All Jews agreed that the poor needed to be cared for, regardless of religious affiliation. Indeed, Jews had a long tradition of taking care of the ailing members of their communities, be it in the form of orphanages, stipends for widows, dowries for poor brides, distribution of free *matzot*, or interest-free loans, all in the name of *tsedaka* (justice). As the name implies, *tsedaka* was not done purely out of the goodness of one's heart; it was also a religious obligation to be fulfilled.

This desire to fulfill the obligation of charity giving, or *tsedaka*, corresponded to an era of volunteerism in the nineteenth-century United States, which shaped Jewish philanthropic activities.[93] Nineteenth-century Americans, Jews included, were a nation of joiners – joiners of voluntary associations and members of clubs, societies, and fraternal organizations. Jewish Americans established their own associations, such as the B'nai Brith and the Young Men's Hebrew Association (YMHA). Lacking taxes to support their communities, these organizations often performed *tsedaka*. As in other American charitable associations, Jewish women played a significant role in collecting funds for charitable organizations, something that was institutionally impossible within the traditional communities of Europe. In America, women's auxiliary associations were often the main fundraisers for building synagogues and other major communal ventures. Women also founded and organized the Jewish Sunday school movement. Women attended synagogue services more regularly than they had in Europe, and more often than not, it was women's faces that the rabbi saw on a Saturday morning, while the men were working. As women became more involved in synagogue life, mixed seating came to the forefront of community discussions.[94] As Jews emulated American methods for conducting charity, the concept of *tsedaka* became strongly associated with the idea of doing good deeds rather the traditional concept of doing justice.[95]

Ultimately, American Jews sought ways to be both Jewish and American. When nineteenth-century American Jews created new traditions, it was in order to harmonize Judaism with American life.[96] The organizational principles that allowed for the formation of homogenous European Jewish communities, dominated by rabbinical authorities, were not possible to duplicate in America. In the United States, individual effort played an equal and sometimes greater role than religious tradition in shaping Jewish practices.[97] Correspondingly, Jews in the United States were more predisposed to greater assimilation with American society.

Communal Development among Victoria's Jews

In many ways, the pattern of early Jewish communal development in the Crown colony of Vancouver Island mimicked the development of Jewish communities in the nineteenth-century United States, especially in terms of the degree to which communal institutions and practices were inclined to integrate with society at large. Many of Victoria's first Jewish arrivals in 1858 were single men of much the same European origin and background as their American counterparts. They were eager for adventure, in search of their fortunes, and ready to make their mark away from the watchful eyes of their siblings in California.[98] They quickly established the rudiments of a Jewish community, which consisted of informal gatherings in homes and/ or businesses. By 1859 the Hebrew Benevolent Society had been formed and was providing charity to needy Jewish immigrants. The society also acquired a 1.5-acre plot of land beyond the northeastern edge of the city for a Jewish burial ground. The Jewish cemetery was consecrated in February 1860.[99] As women and families arrived, Victoria's Jewish community began to take root. The ladies' auxiliary of the Hebrew Benevolent Society was formed and was instrumental in raising funds on behalf of the community, including funds to construct Congregation Emanu-El, Vancouver Island's first synagogue. As the rudiments of Jewish life were established, traditional Jewish notions of charity in the form of *gmilot-hesed* (benevolent kindness) and *tsedaka* both inspired and informed the involvement of Victoria's early Jews in the greater community.[100]

Synagogue Life: Victoria's Congregation Emanu-El

On 2 June 1863, the Jewish community laid the first cornerstones of a synagogue. As with the opening ceremonies for other North American Jewish congregations, distinguished guests attended the opening ceremony for Congregation Emanu-El, including the mayor of Victoria and the chief justice of the colony, members of the St. Andrews Society, the Germania Sing Verein (Choral Society), the French Benevolent Society, and members of the Masonic lodge.[101] Several of the congregation's members were also active members of Vancouver Island's Masonic lodges. For that reason, two cornerstones were laid, one by the Masons and the other by members of the congregation.[102] Abraham Hoffman, first secretary to Congregation Emanu-El, in his inaugural address at the ceremony, spoke of the congregation as one day attaining "the magnitude of a mighty institution, a shrine for the destitute, a school for our youth and the blessing of those that seek the house of God in prayer, [and] might in the turmoil, troubles and anxieties sometimes cast a lingering look upon the religion that our forefathers upheld so faithfully."[103]

Congregation Emanu-El's synagogue was deemed officially ready for use on 22 November 1863. Its construction had cost the community $9,196.60. Non-Jews had donated 70 percent of the contributions to the building fund. The remaining contributions came from Jews all over the colonies of Vancouver Island and British Columbia, as well as San Francisco and Great Britain. Despite the generous donations, the Jewish community of Victoria found itself in debt.[104] The accumulated community debt inspired the women to unite their efforts and form Victoria's Hebrew Ladies' Benevolent Society (HLBS). The Hebrew Ladies became known for their popular annual balls and their successful fundraising.

Although Victoria's early Jewish settlers had quickly rallied their efforts to build a synagogue, strict religious observance was another matter entirely. Some of Victoria's Jews did not follow religious doctrine strictly. Like their American counterparts, some successful entrepreneurs kept their businesses open on Saturdays. It is difficult to imagine that those who often socialized with non-Jews through community-wide social organizations would have adhered to dietary laws when dining outside their own homes. It is known that Jews like Frank Sylvester, who staunchly supported orthodox practices in the community, abandoned many of them when away from home.[105] Sylvester's pioneering activities on the gold trails gave him the reputation of an adventurer. Although he observed the High Holidays and associated with fellow Jews, and overall was an avid participant in Jewish life in Victoria, when out in the field, he was far from observant.[106] He is said to have "mixed freely" with the young men of the region, so freely in fact that he sometimes completely abandoned his religiosity. In writing about his travels, he once described the daily non-kosher meals on the road: "Our bill of fare was not much varied – for breakfast we had bacon and beans. For dinner beans and bacon and for supper a fine dish of 'ditto' ..."[107]

In early November 1863, the community's first rabbi, Reverend Marcus R. Cohen, complained that the synagogue arrangements were unsatisfactory.[108] He was referring to the fact that the congregation lacked a proper schedule for Sabbath and Holiday services. Reverend Cohen argued that this kept people from attending synagogue services. He believed that without a proper foundation, the community's children would suffer from lack of religious grounding in Jewish heritage, or *yiddishkeit*. He believed it was crucial that they spend time in the synagogue, because "the present age demands of us some improvement in our religious affairs and unless some steps are taken in the matter I fear that all your labour ... in erecting so noble an edifice ... will prove 'labour in vain.'"[109] Efforts were made to rectify the situation. In fact, congregants entered into a nearly continuous debate on how to "improve" synagogue life, be it through innovation or adherence to tradition.

Irrespective of Cohen's comments, synagogue membership became the principal means by which Victoria's Jews affirmed their religious and ethnic identity. Even Jews who had abandoned traditions, especially those in isolated locales, were able to nominally attach themselves to Congregation Emanu-El. Observing *kashrut* at home was another way for Victoria's Jews to express their Jewish identity, since kosher meat was available from relatively early on, as were Passover *matzot*, which were manufactured in Victoria for Jews throughout the Pacific Northwest.[110] Essentially, Victoria's Jewish community emphasized its Jewishness through religious observance of life cycle events, supported by a communal infrastructure comprised of Jewish benevolent societies. Victoria's Jewish community can best be described as a blend of traditional adherence and pragmatic abandonment.

Congregation Emanu-El received its first Torah scrolls from Temple Emanu-El in San Francisco, and in reciprocation Victoria's Jewish community named their synagogue after the one in San Francisco.[111] The congregation's prayer books were also imported from the United States, as opposed to England, where the prayer books of earlier Jewish communities in eastern Canada had come from. Victoria's Congregation Emanu-El used the prayer book *Tefilot Yisrael* (Prayers of Israel), published in New York by Henry Frank in 1856. It was said that every Jewish family in the United States was in possession of this *siddur*.[112] Considering the social ties of Victoria's Jews to San Francisco, it is understandable that Victoria's early Jewish immigrants – an aspiring group of entrepreneurs – named their own synagogue after the most prestigious Jewish congregation in the Pacific Northwest, especially given that they received their own Torah scrolls and other assistance from there.

San Francisco's Temple Emanu-El was a testament to Jewish success on the west coast. Grand and distinctive, the building was one of the city's first visible landmarks on the urban skyline. As was typical of North American synagogues at that time, this house of worship had features reminiscent of a medieval Gothic cathedral, but it was also replete with Jewish symbols. Temple Emanu-El's physical prominence also signified its leading status, and its congregants included members of the region's wealthy families, including the Sloss, Gerstle, Schwabacher, and Hellman families. The business and family networks of these members extended throughout the Pacific Northwest, and as such, congregations like Emanu-El in Victoria benefited from the financial support of San Francisco's Jewish community.

As previously mentioned, American Jewish experience of the nineteenth century was characterized by a grappling with tradition. The extent to which a congregation reformed its practices varied from congregation to congregation. Like its American neighbours to the south, Congregation Emanu-El in Victoria faced pressure to reform, albeit several decades later. In 1885, a motion was brought forward to introduce instrumental music into religious services. Some members of the congregation had collected $200 for the express purpose of purchasing an organ. Some congregants, Frank Sylvester among them, dismissed the proposition. In fact, choirs and organs were quite popular in the Reform movement at that time. The matter resurfaced again in May 1891, when a businessman named Henry Emanuel Levy purchased a small organ and offered it to the congregation. The congregation accepted the offer, and the instrument was installed.

Correspondingly, 1891 is the year that the Victoria congregation welcomed the arrival of Reverend Dr. Solomon Philo, formerly affiliated with the Reform movement's Hebrew Union College of Cincinnati. Although rifts developed between the congregants and their new rabbi, at the end of his first year in Victoria his contract was renewed for an additional two years. After much controversy, Reverend Philo's term in Victoria came to end in 1894, and he went on to found the Reform Congregation Emanu-El of Vancouver.[113] During the same period, orthodox Sherith Israel of San Francisco drifted away from traditional *minhagim*. Beginning in 1870, the congregation allowed families to sit together instead of separating men and women. In June 1890 the congregation purchased an organ, just in time for the High Holidays.[114] Sherith Israel officially joined the Reform Movement in 1903.

British Columbian Jews during the mid-nineteenth century were closely connected to Jewish communities along the Pacific west coast. Owing to direct links to San Francisco and the experience of all of Victoria's early Jews in the United States, the nature of Judaism in Victoria can only be understood in terms of the events taking place within American Jewry. The term *minhag American* has been used to describe the religious practices of Victoria's Jews, not because Victoria's Jewry subscribed to a particular form of American Judaism, but because all that they experienced religiously could be characterized by the American Jewish experience of the nineteenth century. It was this foundation in the *minhag American* that connected Vancouver Island's (and, later, British Columbia's) Jews with their Californian and west coast counterparts. American society clearly influenced early British Columbian Jewry.

Concluding Remarks

Frank Sylvester is often lauded as a typical Jewish pioneer, and it seems he was also a God-fearing one. On 31 December 1866, he wrote: "I thank God I have been permitted till the present to live in health and happiness and trust that He will, in His infinite mercy decree that I may be permitted to continue in health and happiness."[115] Sylvester's adherence to traditional Jewish practices was likely an extension of his respect for orthodoxy. As mentioned earlier, he led the opposition committee against the installation of an organ in Congregation Emanu-El, a practice associated with Reform congregations. However, this loyalty to tradition is perhaps surprising in light of his leniency towards Jewish observances within his personal life and home. His wife, Cecelia Davies Sylvester, was very similar to Frank, in that both integrated into Jewish and non-Jewish sectors of Victoria. Still, there can be no doubt that Frank Sylvester's primary identity was that of a Jew.

Jews were not merely tolerated as a minority in Victoria, but accepted as equals into the general community as business associates, members of voluntary associations, and politicians. Jews expressed their cultural and religious identity while contributing to the development of Victoria's wider community. Furthermore, like their American counterparts, Victoria's Jews became preoccupied "with ethics and moral improvement rather than the traditional pursuit of learning,"[116] thereby creating a localized "civil Judaism."[117] As such, they actively joined community-wide voluntary organizations in the name of improving economic, social, and cultural conditions in the newly settled colony. They became members of Masonic lodges, the Independent Order of Odd Fellows, the Vancouver Island Chamber of Commerce, the Victoria Board of Trade, volunteer fire brigades, and hospital and orphanage boards. More ambitious Jews vied for elected political positions.[118]

Frank Sylvester's propensities for community involvement led him to join many of Victoria's voluntary associations.[119] He was a member of the Ancient Order of United Workmen, the Ancient Order of Oriental Humility, the Olympic Baseball Club, and the Sing Verein. Like his father-in-law and other Victoria Jews, Frank Sylvester was also a member of the Masonic and Odd Fellow lodges. A capable businessman who spoke several languages, he was elected secretary and board member to the financial committee of the Tiger Company, the local fire brigade, and in his later years he held the post of secretary to the British Columbia Historical Society.[120] And he was equally recognized in Victoria's general community as well as the Jewish community for his entrepreneurship, his generosity, and his commitment to community service.

Early Jewish settlers to British Columbia were steeped in a Jewish culture characterized by the *minhag American*, which sought to harmonize Jewish life with American life. Heavily influenced by social and religious trends in the United States, Victoria's colonial and early provincial Jewish community is best described as having traditional tendencies. For the most part, early Jewish settlers were flexibly observant Jews – like Frank Sylvester – who fought to maintain affiliations with traditional Judaism in their institutions. They may have aspired to tradition, but always in tandem with the inevitabilities of living in a colonial frontier society in which one crossed Jewish and non-Jewish boundaries on a daily basis.

Notes

1   Frank Sylvester, "Old Time Reminiscences of B.C.," Frank and Cecilia Sylvester family fonds, University of Victoria Archives, AR 281.

2   Ellen Eisenberg, Ava F. Kahn, and William Toll, *Jews of the Pacific Coast: Reinventing Community on America's Edge* (Seattle: University of Washington Press, 2009), 26.

3   Frank Sylvester, "The Douglas Route From Victoria to Lillooet," Frank and Cecilia Sylvester family fonds, University of Victoria Archives, 1908, AR281 Acc. No. 1988-071 1.4.

4   Cyril Leonoff, "Introduction," *Pioneer Jews of British Columbia, Western States Jewish History*: XXX VII, 3 and 4; *The Scribe*: XXV, 1 and 2 (2005/5765): 23.

5   Jean Barman, *The West beyond the West: A History of British Columbia*, 3rd ed. (Toronto: University of Toronto Press, 2007), 15.

6   British Vital Records Index, Liverpool, October–December 1842; 1897 Census Victoria from Joan Modrall, "Old Roots New Shoots: All We Know of the Harris/Davies/Light/Sylvester/Brooker/Taylor Families-Family History," Frank and Cecilia Sylvester Series, University of Victoria, AR281, Acc. no. 2008-028 1.8: 102, 134.

7   The Pulvermachers had already lost one daughter to intermarriage, an act they considered tantamount to the death of their child. Modrall, "Old Roots New Shoots," 102.

8   Ibid.," 103.

9   The family name of Silberstein was also spelled Silverston and Silverstein. Ibid., 101.

10 Harriet Sylvester, who was registered on the ship manifest of 1843, is presumed to have died between 1843 and 1850, quite possibly as a result of the stressful voyage across the Atlantic. New York County, NY, *NY 131 [132]*, (New York City, 13 August 1850), Ward 10.

11 Lillooet Nördlinger McDonnell to James P. Alsina, correspondence, 9 December 2008.

12 New York County NY, *NY 131 [132]*, (New York City, 13 August 1850), Ward 10.

13 New York County, *New York City, Manhattan* (5th Electoral District, Dwelling #5, Family #5, 4 June 1855), 14th Ward.

14 Ibid.

15 Modrall, "Old Roots New Shoots," 103.

16 Cyril Leonoff, *Pioneers, Pedlars, and Prayer Shawls: The Jewish Communities in British Columbia and the Yukon* (Victoria: Sono Nis Press, 1978), 16.

17 Eisenberg, Kahn, and Toll, *Jews of the Pacific Coast*, 22.

18 In the early 1860s, Rachel and Henry Cohen moved to Victoria and opened a men's clothing store on the south side of Yates Street. The business was unsuccessful, and the family moved to Reno, Nevada. Modrall, "Old Roots New Shoots," 106.

19 Martin Prag was related to Conrad Prag (1831–83), another '49er merchant and a founding member of San Francisco's and Salt Lake City's Jewish communities. Conrad Prag's wife, Mary Goldsmith Prag (1846–1935, herself the daughter of San Francisco *shochet* Isaac Goldsmith), gave birth to two children, Florence (1866–1948) and Jessie (1869–1879). In 1921, Goldsmith Prag was named the first Jewish member of the San Francisco Board of Education, where she served until her death. Her daughter, Florence Prag, married Congressman Julius Kahn. Upon his death, Prag Kahn succeeded him, becoming the first Jewish woman to sit in the US Congress. Ava F. Kahn, "Mary Goldsmith Prag," *Jewish Women: A Comprehensive Encyclopaedia*, http://jwa.org/encyclopedia/article/prag-mary-goldsmith#bibliography. Martin Prag also shared a connection to John Sullivan Deas (ca. 1838–1880), who has been described as a mulatto. Martin Prag had previously employed Deas (as a tinsmith) in San Francisco. Deas may have come to Vancouver Island around 1862 to help Frank Sylvester with the hardware business. He soon established his own business, known as Birmingham House, in Victoria, and eventually opened salmon canneries on the Fraser and Columbia Rivers. H. Keith Ralston, "John Sullivan Deas: A Black Entrepreneur in British Columbia Salmon Canning," *BC Studies* 32 (Winter 1976–77): 64–77.

20 Eisenberg, Kahn, and Toll, *Jews of the Pacific Coast*, 29–30.

21 Ibid., 29-30.

22 The first Jew to arrive on British territory in the Pacific North West was Adolf Friedman in 1845. He settled first in Tacoma, then part of Hudson's Bay Company territory. He supplied goods to pioneer fishermen. He later moved to Victoria to marry Masha Stusser, a cousin. Friedman, originally from Latvia, sailed to North America via Cape Horn with thirty-five Scandinavian soldiers from Port Libau. Leonoff, *Pioneers, Pedlars, and Prayer Shawls*, 12.

23 Modrall, "Old Roots New Shoots," 107.

24 Ibid., 116.

25 "Sudden death of well-known citizen" (miscellaneous photos, sketches, and programs, University of Victoria, 1934), AR 281, Acc. no. 2005-020: sec. 1.9. Frank worked for J.P. Davies & Co. until the death of his father-in-law in 1879, at which point Joshua Davies cut Frank's wages from $150 to $75 a month and Frank left abruptly. Afterwards, Frank worked for his son's company, Sylvester Feed & Co. Modrall, "Old Roots New Shoots," 32, 130–31.

26 Eisenberg, Kahn, and Toll, *Jews of the Pacific Coast*, 24.

27 Geoffrey Castle, "Shipwrecked," *Pioneer Jews of British Columbia*, *Western States Jewish History* 37, nos. 3–4; *The Scribe* 25, nos. 1–2 (2005/5765): 155,158, 161.

28 Sylvester, "A trip to the Cariboo in 1864," 128.

29 Ibid., 127.

30 Modrall, "Old Roots New Shoots," 134, 150–59.

31 Frances Dinkelspiel, *Towers of Gold: How One Jewish Immigrant Named Isaias Hellman Created California* (New York: St. Martin's Griffin, 2008), 4–5.

32 Ibid., 2–5.

33 Eisenberg, Kahn, and Toll, *Jews of the Pacific Coast*, 21.

34 Steven Mark Dobbs, "Jewish Community," *Encyclopaedia of San Francisco*, http://www.sfhistoryencyclopedia.com/articles/j/jews.html.

35 Eisenberg, Kahn, and Toll, *Jews of the Pacific Coast*, 25.

36 Dinkelspiel, *Towers of Gold*, 19.

37 Eisenberg, Kahn, and Toll, *Jews of the Pacific Coast*, 25.

38 Christine Boas Wisenthal, "Insiders and Outsiders: Two Waves of Jewish Settlement in British Columbia, 1858–1914," M.A. thesis, University of British Columbia, 1987, 30.

39 Ava F. Kahn and Ellen Eisenberg, "Western Reality: Jewish Diversity during the 'German' Period," *American Jewish History* 92, no. 4 (2007): 457.

40 Ibid., 457.

41 "A. Phillips Soda Works Bottle" (Vancouver: Jewish Historical Museum and Archives, 2007), http://www.jewishmuseum.ca/node/239.

42 L. Nördlinger McDonnell, "In the Company of Gentiles: Exploring Jewish Integration in BC, 1858–1971," Ph.D. diss., University of Ottawa, 2011, 394.

43 Ibid., 392–95.

44 Ibid., 61.

45 Modrall, "Old Roots New Shoots," 23; Arthur Daniel Hart, *The Jew in Canada: A Complete Record of Canadian Jewry from the Days of the French Régime to the Present Time* (Toronto: Jewish Publications, 1926), 575.

46 Boas Wisenthal, "Insiders and Outsiders," 14. The Oppenheimer brothers, originally from Saar, Germany, settled in New Orleans and San Francisco before arriving in Victoria in 1858–59. Brothers Godfrey and Charles started a supply business, in Victoria and Yale; later, when joined by brothers David and Isaac, the brothers began a chain of supply warehouses throughout the Cariboo. Charles was contracted to build a section of the Cariboo Wagon Road. David and Isaac opened an import wholesale business in 1882. In 1886 they moved to the newly incorporated city of New Westminster. The Oppenheimers were involved in establishing and supplying volunteer fire brigades in Yale and elsewhere. All were Masons. David Oppenheimer became the second mayor of Vancouver. Leonoff, *Pioneers, Pedlars, and Prayer Shawls*, 88.

47 Boas Wisenthal, "Insiders and Outsiders," 61. It is known that in 1863, four Jews listed themselves with the Chamber of Commerce: E. Sutro, N. Koshland, S. Goldstone, and J. Rueff.

48 Supply trips to San Francisco were made by businessmen who often also had family connections there. Boas Wisenthal, "Insiders and Outsiders," 14.

49 British Columbia Archives, Royal British Columbia Museum (2013), http://www.bcarchives.gov.bc.ca/exhibits/timemach/galler04/frames/beginning.htm.

50 Boas Wisenthal, "Insiders and Outsiders," 14.

51 Tina Merrill Loo, *Making Law, Order, and Authority in British Columbia, 1821–1871* (Toronto: University of Toronto Press, 1994), 15.

52 Boas Wisenthal, "Insiders and Outsiders," 14.

53 The first generation of Jewish settlers to Vancouver witnessed the railway boom in the city, as well as a depression in the mid-1890s, which was followed by the economic revival sparked by the Klondike Gold Rush of 1898 to 1901. During the early decades of the twentieth century, Vancouver's economy continued to expand in tandem with that of the Prairie Provinces and the British Columbia interior.

54 Jonathon Sarna, *American Judaism: A History* (New Haven: Yale University Press, 2004), 59–60.

55 Hasia R. Diner, *A Time for Gathering: The Second Migration, 1820–1880* (Baltimore: Johns Hopkins University Press, 1992), 122.

56 Isaac Mayer Wise, "Rejoinder to Talmid's Thoughts on Deuteronomy 30:6 (1)," *The Occident* 5 (1847): 109

57 Ibid., 1–2, 51.

58 Jeanne E. Abrams, *Jewish Women Pioneering the Frontier Trail: A History in the American West* (New York: NYU Press, 2006), 92.

59 Ibid., 87.

60 Israel J. Benjamin, *Three Years in America, 1859–1862*, vol. 1 (New York: Arno Press, 1975), 235–36; from Abrams, *Jewish Women Pioneering the Frontier Trail*, 87.

61 Benjamin, *Three Years in America*, 235–36; from Abrams, *Jewish Women Pioneering the Frontier Trail*, 87.

62 Abrams, *Jewish Women Pioneering the Frontier Trail*, 87.

63 Ibid., 15.

64 Eisenberg, Kahn, and Toll, *Jews of the Pacific Coast*, 45–46.

65 Diner, *A Time for Gathering*, 3.

66 Naomi W. Cohen, *Encounter with Emancipation: The German Jews in the United States, 1830–1914* (Philadelphia: Jewish Publication Society of America, 1984), 39.

67 Diner, *A Time for Gathering*, 3.

68 Ibid., 3.

69 Sarna, *American Judaism*, 124.

70 Ibid., 124.

71 Diner, *A Time for Gathering*, 116.

72 Ibid., 122.

73 Sarna, *American Judaism*, 124.

74 Diner, *A Time for Gathering*, 138. Other Jews organized themselves along the lines of Bohemian, Lithuanian, or Russian *khevre*.

75 Isaac Leeser, the cantor for Philadelphia's Orthodox *shul* of Mikveh Israel and a major opponent of the Reform movement, introduced innovations in his own *shul*. Leeser faced his congregants like a Protestant preacher; he promoted weekly sermons, the use of the catechism for children, and English translations of the Bible and prayers. He also encouraged women to establish Sunday schools, which until that point had been a mainly Protestant phenomenon. Like his Reform co-religionists, Leeser used the Torah rather than the Talmud to justify his actions. Orthodox Rabbi Bernard Illowy, who served in New York's Shaar Tsedek, as well as Orthodox congregations in St. Louis, Cincinnati, and New Orleans, sanctioned the confirmation ceremony. Even Victoria's own rabbi, Reverend Dr. M.R. Cohen (b. 1827), originally from Poland, delivered his sermons in English, not Yiddish. Allan Klenman, "British Columbia's First Rabbi," *Scribe* 11 (March 1982): 5–7. In 1873, Harlem's Congregation Hand-In-Hand considered itself Orthodox while advocating mixed seating. Diner, *A Time for Gathering*, 122.

76 Sarna, *American Judaism*, 125–26.

77 Ibid., 125–26.

78 Eisenberg, Kahn, and Toll, *Jews of the Pacific Coast*, 26.

79 Ibid., 26.

80 Lewis A. Franklin, "Sermon, 1850," *Asmonean*, 15 November 1850: 30–31; from Eisenberg, Kahn, and Toll, *Jews of the Pacific Coast*, 26.

81 Eisenberg, Kahn, and Toll, *Jews of the Pacific Coast*, 26.

82 Sarna, *American Judaism*, 59–60.

83 Ibid., 59–60.

84 Eisenberg, Kahn, and Toll, *Jews of the Pacific Coast,* 27.

85 Ibid., 27.

86 Ibid., 27.

87 Ibid., 27.

88 Ibid., 27.

89 Ibid., 28.

90 Ibid., 28. Associations such as the *Mevaker Holim* and *Bikur Holim* were specifically designated to care for the ill.

91 Diner, *A Time for Gathering,* 96.

92 Ibid., 96.

93 Ibid., 104.

94 Ironically, it was the men who argued in favour of or against issues such as mixed seating. Ibid., 120.

95 Ibid., 104.

96 Ibid., 123.

97 Ibid., 120.

98 Abrams, *Jewish Women Pioneering the Frontier Trail,* 5.

99 This parcel of land would remain the only Jewish cemetery in the province until Mayor David Oppenheimer arranged for a separate section of the Mountain View cemetery to be allotted to the Jewish community of Vancouver. Cyril – "The Rise of Jewish Life and Religion in BC, 1858–1948," *The Scribe* 28 (2008): 50.

100 Abrams, *Jewish Women Pioneering the Frontier Trail,* 8.

101 Kahn and Eisenberg, "Western Reality," 469.

102 Cyril Leonoff, "The Hebrew Ladies of Victoria, Vancouver Island," *Pioneer Jews of British Columbia, Western States Jewish History (WSJH)* 37, nos. 3–4; *The Scribe*: 25, nos. 1–2 (2005/5765): 26.

103 Gerald Tulchinsky, "The Canadian Jewish Experience: A Distinct Personality Emerges," in *From Immigration to Integration: The Canadian Jewish Experience – A Millennium Edition,* ed. Frank Dimant and Ruth Klein (Toronto: B'nai Brith Canada, 2001), 57. PABC File 7b, documents Re: Hebrew synagogue Emmanuel 1862–63. Abraham Hoffman to the Board of Trustees and members of the congregation Emmanuelle, 22 November 1862.

104 Accumulated debt was for $5,152, plus interest. Boas Wisenthal, "Insiders and Outsiders," 111; Leonoff, *Pioneers, Pedlars, and Prayer Shawls,* 26.

105 Boas Wisenthal, "Insiders and Outsiders," 119.

106 Ibid., 108.

107 Frank Sylvester, "A trip to the Cariboo in 1864," Frank and Cecelia Sylvester Series, 1.11 Historical Manuscripts, University of Victoria, 1873–1908, Acc. no. 1998-071; Modrall, "Old Roots New Shoots," 109.

108 Tulchinsky, "The Canadian Jewish Experience: A Distinct Personality Emerges," 58. The term "Reverend" was used by rabbis from Britain and Canada.

109 Tulchinsky, "The Canadian Jewish Experience," 58.

110 Boas Wisenthal, "Insiders and Outsiders," 108.

111 According to local lore, the first Torah scrolls Victoria's Jewish community received were sent by San Francisco's Emanu-El synagogue. Rabbi Harry Brechner Congregation Emanu-El, Victoria, British Columbia 11-01-2009.

112 *Tefilot Yisrael Prayers of Israel* (New York: Henry Frank, 1856). Henry Frank was the first Bavarian publisher and printer who published Jewish theological books in Hebrew with German translations. His books were used in all the theological schools and colleges throughout Bavaria. When he immigrated to New York in 1848, he continued to publish Hebrew texts, but instead of German, English translations were provided. His work, *Tefilot Yisrael Prayers of Israel,* "soon found its way into all Jewish families of the United States." Samuel R. Wells, "Henry Frank: The First Hebrew Publisher in the United States," *American Phrenological Journal* 49 (1869): 161.

113 For example, Rev. Philo did not wear a *kipah* when teaching Hebrew school and asked the children to remove their head coverings as well. Leonoff, *Pioneers, Pedlars, and Prayer Shawls,* 48.

114 Kahn and Eisenberg, "Western Reality," 456.

115 Sylvester, "A trip to the Cariboo in 1864," 128.

116 Susan L. Tananbaum, "Philanthropy and Identity: Gender and ethnicity in London," *Journal of Social History* 30 (June 1997): 937–61.

117 Jonathon Woocher, "*Civil Judaism,*" in the United States, (Philadelphia: Center for Jewish Community Studies, 1978); from Susan M. Chambré, "Parallel Power Structures, Invisible Careers, and the Changing Nature of American Jewish Women's Philanthropy," *Journal of Jewish Communal Service* 76, no. 3 (Spring 2000): 182.

118 Boas Wisenthal, "Insiders and Outsiders," 111.

119 Ibid., 130.

120 Ibid., 130–33.

SIX

They Who Control the Time
The Orthodox Alliance of Abraham De Sola and Jacques Judah Lyons and the Nineteenth-Century Jewish Calendar

Zev Eleff

On 7 July 1853, newspaper editor Robert Lyon announced plans to produce a Jewish calendar for North American Jews.[1] The publication proposed by Jacques Judah Lyons of New York would serve as an "Almenack, extending over a period of fifty years."[2] Lyons served as minister of Shearith Israel of New York, the first Jewish congregation founded in North America.[3] The newspaperman provided ample room for what he deemed a most worthy project. Lyons lived in Manhattan but preferred to worship in the German-style congregations rather than fumble with Shearith Israel's unfamiliar Portuguese rite. Still, he was a rare advocate of the ministry and its activities in a mostly anticlerical American Jewish community.[4] Consequently, he happily anticipated that the new fifty-year lunar calendar "will show in a clear and comprehensive method the period when the whole of the Festivals occur, with the Parashot and Hapthorot for each Sabbath, and much other useful and interesting information."

Lyons was no doubt excited to see the newspaper's announcement for his calendar. He must have been just as stunned, however, to find an advertisement for a similar project in that very same edition.[5] According to this other short notice, Abraham De Sola, minister of Montreal's Sephardic congregation, was calling for subscriptions for his own "Jewish Calendar for Fifty Years." De Sola's reference work promised to offer "an essay on the Jewish Calendar, various important tables, and a large amount of Chronological and other information."[6] To avoid duplication of their efforts, the two men reasoned "to unite in one publication."[7] The results of their joint effort produced a calendar with months to spare before the Jewish New Year (5615) in 1854. North American Jews greeted Lyons and De Sola's *Jewish Calendar for Fifty Years* with quick enthusiasm. It would remain in demand until the final decades of the nineteenth century, despite the availability of other Jewish calendars on the continent.[8] The work commanded an immediate readership because there was a considerable market among the nearly 100,000 Jews of the United States, and the 500 or so Israelites of Canada.[9]

At mid-century, North American Jews possessed just a few calendars and almanacs. Moreover, the available calendars presented intercalation tables that were difficult to interpret and that often contained very noticeable errors.[10] For instance, Moses Lopez of Rhode Island published a North American Jewish calendar in 1806. His was a book-length work that offered 130 pages of tables that provided information for some Jewish holidays but omitted data for other festivals.[11] By the 1850s, there were only a limited number of copies of Lopez's work, making it "inaccessible" to most North American Jews.[12] As well, his tables extended only to 1859 and would soon be obsolete for those fortunate enough to own a copy of the calendar. In addition to Lopez's calendar, several Jewish and general newspapers printed yearly calendars that plotted the Jewish holidays on the Gregorian calendar. These were easier to work with than Lopez's tables but were of little help to Jews requiring a more extensive calendar.

This situation made the 177-page Lyons–De Sola publication a much-needed reference book for North American Jewry. Their calendar included a lengthy essay on the Jewish intercalation system and a directory of seventy-three Jewish communities scattered across the continent. Yet Lyons and De Sola intended to do much more with their work. In many respects, the two Jewish ministers anticipated what a historian has recently noticed about European Judaism: that "calendars, along with the almanacs and yearbooks that evolved out of them, emerged as literary and culture omnibuses in the nineteenth century."[13] The calendar as a conduit of Jewish culture is a subject that has recently received scholarly attention, as has the field of visual and material history. The particular culture that the Sephardic clergymen sought to propagate was one of religious orthodoxy and traditional synagogue adherence. This was certainly a marked difference from the Lopez calendar, which, according to one scholar, demonstrated a "desire of Jews to function as independent religious actors, without having to rely on the synagogue."[14] In contrast, the Sephardic ministers sought to create a reference work that would reinforce Orthodox Jewish life and weaken the momentum of religious reform that was then under way in the New World. While traditionalist leaders of German congregations possessed similar goals, the 1854 endeavour was essentially different because of the nature of the Sephardic communities the authors led. The expectations of their Portuguese congregations compelled them to be more subtle and imaginative than their Ashkenazic counterparts.[15]

Neither De Sola nor Lyons lacked orthodox convictions or the knowledge to enter the arena of religious polemic. Upon Lyons's death in 1877, one writer recalled him as a "staunch pillar of Orthodox Judaism, and amid all the changes that have occurred in American Judaism he steadfastly adhered to the ritual and ceremonies of the Portuguese Minhag."[16] Likewise, the well-known Sabato Morais of Philadelphia remembered his friend as someone who persevered in a "country of compromises."[17] Another writer described how Lyons "oppos[ed] with all [his] power and influence the inroads made upon the ancient Jewish ritualism by the new Reform teachers."[18] As for Lyons's intellectual abilities, it was the consensus that his "attainments as a Hebrew scholar" were "considerable."[19] This is all the more significant given that the Surinam-born minister never received formal rabbinic training before his appointment as *hazzan* of Surinam's Congregation Neve Shalome at the age of twenty.[20]

Unlike his colleague in New York, De Sola rarely encountered opposition to his Orthodox viewpoint. Overall, Canadian Christianity – deeply influenced by its conservative Catholic and Anglican origins – was far more traditional than American varieties.[21] The same was true of Judaism north of the United States. The first Reform congregation in Montreal was not founded until several months after De Sola's death in 1882, nearly sixty years after the first Jewish reform effort in America.[22] Before this, religious "radicals" in Europe would have quickly found that America offered them more agreeable comrades than did the women and men of De Sola's community. Thus, the Montreal minister's traditionalism went mostly uncontested in Canada. He garnered a reputation for himself as the leading spokesman of Judaism and, in the words of English Chief Rabbi Nathan Adler, "reflect[ed] lustre on himself and upon Orthodox Judaism in general."[23]

An elite regimen of religious training more than prepared the native of England. His father, David Aaron De Sola, was the "much respected" leader of London's Portuguese community, for many years serving as senior minister of the Bevis Marks synagogue.[24] The father's fame and religious commitment ultimately influenced the son to pursue a career in the ministry.[25] The younger De Sola earned formal ordination at Jews' College in London. There, he studied principally under Louis Loewe, who was very fond of De Sola and who submitted a stellar recommendation when his pupil applied for a position across the Atlantic:

> I beg to state that Mr. Abraham De Sola has been for some time under my tuition. The subject of his studies has been the Talmud, the Commentary of Abarbenel to the Tora, and the "Cuzari" by Rabbi Yehooda Halevi.

> I have also particularly examined him in Hebrew Grammar, the Torah, "Shulchan Arooch," "Halachoth Tephilah," and feel much pleasure in stating that I was perfectly satisfied.

> I have found him throughout an attentive and assiduous student, and consider him well qualified for the office of Hazan, to which he aspires.[26]

Certainly, Lyons and De Sola positioned themselves as staunchly Orthodox and possessed the intellectual capacity to defend their common view of Judaism. De Sola, in particular, went to great lengths to assert himself as an intellectual leader and as a conduit between the American and Canadian Jewish communities. For instance, he delivered lectures in Canadian colleges and wrote many articles in the New York Jewish press. In 1873, he travelled to Washington, D.C., to open Congress with a prayer. Why, then, did they leave it to German Orthodox ministers like Samuel Mayer Isaacs and Morris J. Raphall to defend traditional Judaism?[27] In all likelihood, the Spanish and Portuguese religious culture prevented them from engaging in open conflict; thus, they looked for another mode of expression.

There was much that was similar between the two congregations. For instance, both retained great fidelity to Sephardic rites and culture even though by the nineteenth century most congregants actually claimed an Ashkenazic background. Of course, there were also important differences between the Portuguese communities in New York and Montreal. Lyons's congregation was far more established and boasted more members than did De Sola's. The Montreal synagogue continually struggled to retain members and raise funds for De Sola's salary. As late as 1861, the Montreal clergyman acknowledged receipt of a letter informing him that the congregation could "not any longer be able to pay me the same amount of salary." He "regretted the necessity" but nevertheless affirmed his dedication to the synagogue.[28] Even so, the religious dynamic was very similar in New York and Montreal (in fact, both congregations went by the name "Shearith Israel"). These congregations and their members differed from their Ashkenazic counterparts, as well as from the other Sephardic congregations in the New World. Inside the synagogue, both congregations did their earnest best to emulate the Portuguese customs developed in London. Worshippers in New York and Montreal used the prayer book edited by David Aaron De Sola (Abraham's father) rather than the American version produced by Philadelphian Isaac Leeser.[29] Similarly, children in the congregations' Hebrew schools studied from Abraham De Sola's volume of catechisms rather than more popular American alternatives.[30]

The New York and Montreal synagogues also shared a bond of religious laxity. It was an open secret that most of the Portuguese Jews in North America ignored religious observance outside the synagogue. While there is little doubt that German congregations in the United States also harboured their share of religious miscreants, it seems to have been far less overwhelming in those Ashkenazic communities. As for the Sephardic Jews of North America, the road to religious non-observance had been well paved by the beginning of the nineteenth century, decades before large numbers of German Jews arrived on the continent. There exist numerous accounts of Sephardic Jews in America who intermarried with Christians, ate forbidden foods, and desecrated the Sabbath.[31]

The other noticeable phenomenon linked to the Portuguese Jews was that despite their behaviour outside the synagogue, they insisted on traditional services inside it.[32] In these communities, reforms to rituals were rarely ever considered. Moreover, while few members were penalized by North America's Sephardic congregations for religious infractions committed outside the synagogue walls during the nineteenth century, we do find instances as late as 1858 when members were "excluded from the synagogue" after they were found "guilty of disorderly and improper conduct in the synagogue."[33]

Especially in New York, adherents to the Portuguese rite eschewed anything that appeared to accommodate Ashkenazic or modern practices. Quite religiously schizophrenic, these women and men were content to compromise on most everything pertaining to their religion except for the synagogue rituals. In 1852, a writer observed this when he characterized the Portuguese congregations as a fully separate "party" from the varieties of Ashkenazic communities: "They call themselves orthodox, not indeed as much in private life as in the Synagogue. In private life they have almost totally yielded to the country and its customs, habits, views, language, practices, and in many respects also, to its mode of living. They have forgotten the Spanish and almost generally also the Hebrew language, in which respect there is but a few honorable exceptions."[34]

This was also true for Canadian Jews. Among other observations, a Polish Jew in Montreal described how his more affluent Sephardic neighbours "will not hesitate to continue a most orthodox violation of the Sabbath."[35] Despite some very public displays of religious flouting, Canada's Portuguese Jews remained dedicated to their worship. "The old fanatics, as well as some of the new," continued that same Eastern European writer, "prefer the old synagogue where the services are quiet and orderly." These accusations elicited a response from a lay leader of the Sephardic congregation. While the respondent capably deflected some of the writer's claims, he admitted defeat when it came to the Sephardic community's rampant non-observance.[36]

Acceptance of this sort of "Synagogue Judaism" allowed Sephardic Jews to come to terms with conditions in the New World. It also insulated them from other North American Jews. While relegating religious life to the synagogue, the Portuguese Jews exercised caution when associating with co-religionists whose rituals and rites differed from their own. Cooperation with Ashkenazic synagogues occurred, but it seemed to bring about unease and tension.[37] Also, Portuguese Jews refrained from public debate about synagogue ritual and religious observance. The case of the German Jews of North America was quite the opposite. "Whoever takes the Jewish American periodicals in his hands, reads now a series of other articles, than he formerly used to," wrote one observer. "Controversies on the most different religious subjects; debates upon all the important questions of the day; queries and answers of the most skeptical and most conservative character, fill the columns, and the so called orthodox party as well, as the so styled reformers, are busy, in looking in their armories for the weapons, to be used in the ensuing contest."[38] On the whole, it was the German element that lined up on this religious battlefield.

Sephardic Jews, by contrast, were fully uninterested in entering into this debate. In all probability, engaging it at all would have forced uncomfortable introspection of their behaviour. To avoid this, the Sephardic Jews tried to ignore the North American Jewish press; few of them subscribed to the Jewish weekly newspapers.[39] If they read anything at all, wrote De Sola of his Montreal community, it was far more likely to be the *Jewish Chronicle* of London, which served as a link to the Sephardic community of Great Britain.[40] The same was true of New York, where "the *Jewish Chronicle* is much admired" and "its arrival is eagerly looked for."[41]

The Spanish and Portuguese emphasis on the synagogue placed great demands on the clergy. In some sense, De Sola and Lyons functioned as professional Jews. Their congregations had hired them to lead services and lead unquestionably Orthodox lives inside the synagogue as well as outside it. The Sephardic lay leaders also expected their ministers to stay clear of the "unbecoming" debates among the Ashkenazic Jews of North America. For precisely this reason, Lyons and De Sola, despite their traditionalist proclivities, recused themselves from this kind of public discussion on reform and religious progress. On occasion they printed sermons in the newspapers, but the content was always anodyne.[42]

Lyons and De Sola's calendar, therefore, afforded the editors a unique opportunity to advocate for traditional Jewish practice and to undercut ritual reforms that were spreading throughout the continent. Perhaps it would go so far as to deny those reforms any legitimacy, in a manner that suited their community members. From the perspective of De Sola, this occasion meant entering into a debate that rarely took place in religiously conservative Canada. It also afforded him the chance to stymie any reform attempt in Montreal, where traditional Judaism still held sway. Unless completely divorced from their religion, Jews gravitated to their calendars for one reason or another, whether or not they were punctilious in their observance of each and every festival, pious in abstaining from food on every customary fast day, or hardly passable in their commemoration of *yahrzeit* (anniversary of death) of a relative. Nearly every Jew who observed his or her faith in some fashion required access to a calendar. They relied on it to function, no matter how they practised religion. Accordingly, the Orthodox orientation of Lyons and De Sola's calendar reinforced the ministers' traditional agendas.

Perhaps most important of all was that their calendar displayed immense scholarship. Lyons and De Sola spared no effort to demonstrate their competency in traditional rabbinic literature and in modern works by Jewish and Christian Hebraic scholars. Fully aware that North America hosted more highly literate reform clergy than traditionalist ones at that moment, in their introductory essay – aptly titled "The Jewish Calendar" – they made sure to inject dozens of Biblical, Talmudic, and Kabbalistic references. That their rationale relied on the authority of the Talmud and later halakhic codes was no small matter. Time and again, Lyons and De Sola explained the intricacies of calendar intercalations and the astronomy of the Jewish yearly cycle by drawing on traditional sources, most notably Yosef Karo's *Shulhan Arukh* and the writings of the "great Maimonides."[43] Although Kabbalistic sources were not nearly as impressive to the German Jews of North America, full discussion of Zoharic and constellational symbolism was standard fare when presenting the Spanish and Portuguese outlook on the subject.[44]

In the text of Lyons and De Sola's calendar, readers found a schedule of holidays and ritual events that accommodated the customs of both Sephardic and Ashkenazic Jews. Portuguese adherents were no doubt happy to find that their religious habits and ways were often emphasized over those of their counterparts, as in the case of the autumn Hoshanah Rabbah holiday, described as follows: "It is observed with heart-stirring and special solemnity by the Portuguese Jews."[45] Still, Lyons and De Sola were fair to the German Jews when they wrote about the nocturnal penitential prayers that preceded the coming New Year: "Prayers are commenced from the first of the month, according to the Portuguese Custom; but by the German, one week before Rosh Hashanah."[46]

For all of these aspects, the calendar was very well received. Newspaper editor Robert Lyon, by and large a conservative in his religious outlook, surmised "the work is creditable to their learning and standing, and will supply an absolute want."[47] Another newspaper editor, this one more progressive than Lyons, conveyed the same favourable review: "The authors show therein not only a vast erudition on the subject, but also the precious art of concise style. It contains all necessary to be known on the subject, in a few pages."[48] Finally, another commentator, this one far more familiar with the Portuguese community than the previous two, fully agreed that the calendar was of splendid design and content. He further prayed, "the reverend authors may be amply remunerated for their exertions in serving the Jewish public."[49] Yet all three reviewers missed the editors' truest intention, which was to emphasize the traditional Jewish year with all of its rituals and practices as they related to the synagogue. The calendar implicitly combatted the ritual reforms that were spreading across the continent. Major renovation of Jewish ritual in North America did not commence until the post–Civil War period. However, the first wave of debate took place just as De Sola and Lyons published their calendar. Two particular ritual reforms discussed throughout North America's Jewish communities were more relevant to the Lyons–De Sola work than others that took hold in subsequent decades: the abolishment of the second day of the Jewish festivals, and the reintroduction of the triennial cycle for the weekly reading of the Torah.

The significance of these ritual changes cannot be overstated. Orthodox leaders had little trouble defending themselves against radical reformers who sought to eliminate the kosher diet and other practices explicitly mentioned in Scripture. Likewise, many traditionalists welcomed the opportunity to debate those who denied Jewish dogma, such as the belief in the Messiah and the Resurrection of the Dead, two religious planks that, thanks to Maimonides, were deeply entrenched in Jewish dogma at the time.[50] Orthodox leaders also felt comfortable arguing for the continuance of less straightforward aspects of Jewish law, such as separate seating in the synagogue, on the basis of a biblical proscription.[51] Other controversies made religiously conservative Jews more uneasy. These subjects more often than not revolved around the authority of rabbinic tradition. Reform elements criticized their Orthodox opponents' supposed closed-mindedness. Some progressives could not understand why they should be bound by the opinions recounted in the Talmud and the subsequent rabbinic literature.[52] When other rabbinic opinions could be found, it made little sense to stand unequivocally by one strand of the tradition while other authentic practices – ones offered up long ago – deserved reconsideration. Two of the most rehearsed forms of this debate centred on the observance of the second day of Jewish festivals and the weekly Sabbath Torah reading cycle.

The Bible requires observance of just one day of the Jewish holidays. Yet at the time that the Jewish court dispatched messengers to inform distant communities of the new lunar month, according to the Babylonian Talmud (Beitzah 4b and Rosh Hashanah 22b), those faraway Jews not yet informed by the court's agents would observe two days of the festival out of doubt regarding which day witnesses testified to the appearance of the new moon. Although later generations declared the new month based on calculations instead of relying on testimonies, Jewish communities in the Diaspora retained the two-day stringency out of respect for the "customs of our forefathers." Taking issue with its lack of biblical basis, nineteenth-century reformers in Europe and America undertook to abolish the practice in their congregations.

Reformers in Westphalia were the first to abrogate the second festival day, in 1807. At the outset, the decision developed only mild traction. By the 1840s, though, the issue served as one of the primary fulcrums of Jewish reform in Great Britain and Central Europe. As the issue impacted ritual and liturgy for the first and biblically ordained festival day, liberals and conservatives waged fierce battles over the matter. Progressive thinkers contended that the Talmudic custom should not serve as the final word, while more Orthodox leaders defended the practice, claiming it to be integral to a sacred religious tradition.[53] The polemic quickly migrated to North America. Across the Atlantic in 1843, Charleston's Beth Elohim was the first congregation to do away with the practice in the New World.[54] The Charleston holiday reform garnered much criticism in the national Jewish press as well as coverage overseas, and partly as a result, it did not immediately spread beyond South Carolina. Nevertheless, Charleston's affront to tradition carried significant long-term weight. In 1848, a Reform response to British Chief Rabbi Nathan Adler's condemnation of the festival change drew strength from the Charleston reformers.[55] No doubt, both De Sola and Lyons took notice of this. More urgently, back in North America, an increasing number of congregations eventually followed Charleston's lead. The same year that Lyons and De Sola's calendar appeared, the more progressive Isaac Mayer Wise of Cincinnati predicted that within a decade, even the "conservatives will be no more opposed ... to the abolition of the second holidays."[56]

The *Jewish Calendar for Fifty Years* put forward no argument for why a second day should remain embedded in the Jewish year. In fact, the only subtle comment appeared in a discussion of the New Year, in which the editors simply offered the "Second Day of Rosh Hashanah, observed with the strictness of the first."[57] But through their silence, Lyons and De Sola made perhaps an even stronger argument for retaining the second festival day tradition. While liberal thinkers made the case that the holiday should be removed on the grounds of rabbinic authority, Lyons and De Sola changed the line of argument altogether. Instead of debating the modern force of ancient rabbinic authority, the editors rested their claim on the authority of the Jewish calendar itself. Looked at this way, an attempt to dispense with the second festival day was not a matter of contrasting biblical and rabbinic laws. Rather, according to Lyons and De Sola, the matter sat at the centre of one of the most fundamental features of Jewish life: the calendar. For centuries, the Jewish calendar had served both as a means of keeping time of religious obligations and the primary method for a Jew to connect with co-religionists. Throughout the Diaspora, Jewish communities maintained calendars to remind their members of each and every moment that religion called upon them to ritualize and publicly observe their faith. Especially in later centuries, when printing costs decreased, calendars, along with prayer books, emerged as domestic icons for all things Jewish. What is more, the Jewish calendar, like any other variety, relies on its interrelated parts to comprise the greater whole. One date may be rendered meaningless if one preceding calculation or event is incorrect or deleted. Therefore, removal of any piece of the calendar, De Sola and Lyons would have argued, was an assault on Jewish life and culture.

The change from the annual to the triennial cycle was far less problematic from the standpoint of Jewish law since it had precedent dating back to a Palestinian custom from the Talmudic and the immediate post-Talmudic periods.[58] American reformers like Max Lilienthal took full advantage of this. Writing on the expanded cycle, Lilienthal argued, "the reform is no innovation at all, but only a retrocession of the service to its primitive origin."[59] Marshalling several sources to support his view, he asserted that his citations argued for a "verdict of the true and learned Orthodoxy." Lilienthal surely recognized that his was the rhetoric of a polemicist and not a historian. The annual cycle had been an undisputed staple in the synagogue for centuries. Back in Bavaria, where Lilienthal had trained in one of the region's most religiously traditional and intellectually exceptional orthodox academies, few would have countenanced such a change in practice. In fact, mainstream traditionalists throughout Europe adhered to the annual cycle. And while the matter was raised in Europe during the middle decades of the century, it received rather mixed support.[60]

The situation in North America differed. Not too long ago, one historian of American Judaism probably overstated his point when he suggested that the major difference between reformers in Europe and North America was that in the latter, "Jewish reformism emerged out of the desire not to change the established social and political order but to join it."[61] However, he was correct that religious progressives in America, influenced by their Christian counterparts, sought out ritual augmentations that might improve synagogue decorum.[62] For moderate reformers, the thought was that shortening prayer services in the synagogue, particularly on the Sabbath and holidays, could improve the overall dynamic of that sacred space. A return to the triennial cycle would afford more time to complete the recitation of the Torah; it would also reduce the time needed during any single week. The Lyons–De Sola calendar included the various weekly portions set along the annual reading cycle to prevent the spread of this reform. Its corresponding Torah portion marked each week. Naturally, no defence for the annual cycle was to be found in the work. Rather than lobby for its custom over the triennial cycle, De Sola and Lyons thought it best to incorporate their tradition into the calendar, hoping that the calendric system would speak for itself.

Of course, at its core the Lyons–De Sola calendar was a schedule for North American congregations. The dates provided in the work indicated to Jews when they were expected to be present in the synagogue and what liturgical business would be conducted there on that particular day. So it was not out of place for the editors to append a lengthy directory of seventy-three Jewish communities in the United States and Canada. Most entries provided basic information. The listing identified times for services, the names of the religious functionaries and lay president, and any auxiliary institutions such as burial societies and Hebrew schools attached to the synagogue. In most cases, Lyons and De Sola identified whether a congregation's liturgical custom matched the Bohemian, German, Dutch, Polish, or Portuguese rite. Notably, the profiles of a few congregations did not include this information. For example, in the entries for Charleston's radical Reform Congregation Beth Elohim and New York's liberal Temple Emanu-El, no liturgical foundation was provided.[63] The omission was not accidental. As was their way, Lyons and De Sola were careful not to enter into any explicit polemic. It was important to them as Spanish and Portuguese leaders to refrain from this sort of controversy. So despite their calendar's stance against religious reform, its editors were careful not to levy any overt charges against progressive congregations. They simply hoped that North American Jews, even the ones in Charleston, would accept their calendar and conform to its systems.

In her study of Jewish calendars, historian Elisheva Carlebach offered a sharp insight into the culture of these timekeeping devices. "Calendars situated the users in a particular year within a particular chronological system," she asserted. "This seemingly, stable, dependable, and predictable aspect of the calendar, in which one numbered year invariably followed the next, served as a grid on which to plot the entire sweep of past events."[64] Lyons and De Sola were more interested in the present and future, however. These staunchly Orthodox exponents viewed the growing number of reformers in North America as a threat. Obedience to their calendar kept Jews coming to the synagogue. Moreover, calendars represented a valuable and very accessible "religious text" for thousands of North American Jews who could not access more advanced rabbinic writings. Despite whatever traditions they forsook outside of that space, North American Jews could maintain their religious identities so long as they retained their fidelity to the traditional synagogue. This was the creed of the Portuguese Jews of North America. Surely, both Lyons and De Sola hoped that their Sephardic congregants as well as all other Jews on the continent would increase their observance in all facets of Jewish life. However, their experiences as leaders of Portuguese congregations had taught them that the synagogue and its religious culture were most important. Unlike other Orthodox champions, these two men argued not from the standpoint of rabbinic authority but from the dependable tradition of Jewish time and place.

Notes

1 On Robert Lyon, see Barbara Straus Reed, "United, Not Absorption: Robert Lyon and the Asmonean: The Origins of the First English-Language Jewish Weekly in the United States," *American Journalism* 7 (Spring 1990), 77–95.
2 "Jewish Calendar," *The Asmonean* (8 July 1853), 98.
3 On the date of its founding, see Leo Hershkowitz, "The Mill Street Synagogue Reconsidered," *American Jewish Historical Quarterly* 53 (June 1964), 404–10.
4 On Lyon's views, see "The Cleveland Beth Din," *The Asmonean*, 21 May 1852, 36. Isaac Leeser described American Jewry's general feelings toward the ministry as "a great aversion to priestly domination." See "Union for the Sake of Judaism," *The Occident* (August 1845): 220–21.
5 Jacques J. Lyons and Abraham De Sola, *A Jewish Calendar for Fifty Years* (Montreal: John Loveli, 1854), 2.
6 "Jewish Calendar for Fifty Years," *The Asmonean*, 8 July 1853, 100.
7 Lyons and De Sola, *A Jewish Calendar*, 2. Lyons and De Sola were old friends. In fact, they first met in 1846 when De Sola arrived in North America. De Sola stayed for some

time at Lyons's residence. See Evelyn Miller, "The 'Learned Hazan' of Montreal: Reverend Abraham de Sola, LL.D.: 1825–1882," *American Sephardi* 7-8 (1975): 24. See also Richard Menkis, "'In This Great, Happy and Enlightened Colony': Abraham De Sola on Jews, Judaism, and Emancipation in Victorian Montreal," in *L'antisémitisme Éclairé*, ed. Ilana Y. Zinguer and Sam W. Bloom (Leiden: Brill, 2003), 313–31.

8 Herman Phillips to Abraham De Sola, 22 March 1880, reel 220, Abraham De Sola Papers, McGill University, Montreal. There is some indication that De Sola was preparing a revised calendar in the early 1870s. See Samuel Mayer Isaacs to Abraham De Sola, 17 April 1871, reel 128, Abraham De Sola Papers, McGill University, Montreal.

9 More precise population numbers are difficult to ascertain. See Jonathan D. Sarna, *American Judaism: A History* (New Haven: Yale University Press, 2004), 375; and Louis Rosenberg, *Canada's Jews: A Social and Economic Study of Jews in Canada in the 1930s* (Montreal and Kingston: McGill–Queen's University Press, 1993), 10.

10 See Jonathan D. Sarna, "An Eighteenth Century Hebrew *Lu'ah* from Pennsylvania," *American Jewish Archives Journal* 57 (2005): 25–27.

11 Michael Satlow, "Two Copies of a Printed Early American Jewish Calendar in Providence," *Rhode Island Jewish Historical Society Notes* 15 (November 2009), 416–27.

12 "A Jewish Calendar for Fifty Years," *The Occident*, September 1854, 320.

13 Elisheva Carlebach, *Palaces of Time: Jewish Calendar and Culture in Early Modern Europe* (Cambridge, MA: Harvard University Press, 2011), 210–11.

14 Michael Satlow, "Jewish Time in Early-Nineteenth-Century America: A Study of Moses Lopez's Calendar," *American Jewish Archives Journal* 65 (2013): 13.

15 On the early connections between the Congregation Shearith Israel of New York and Montreal's Congregation Shearith Israel, see Jay M. Eidelman, "Kissing Cousins: The Early History of Congregations Shearith Israel of New York and Montreal," in *Not Written in Stone: Jews, Constitutions, and Constitutionalism in Canada*, ed. Daniel J. Elazar, Michael Brown, and Ira Robinson (Ottawa: University of Ottawa Press, 2003), 71–83.

16 Julian Werner, "Death of Rev. Jacques J. Lyons," *The American Israelite*, 31 August 1877, 5.

17 A Eulogy at the Funeral of J.J. Lyons, n.d., Sabato Morais Papers, box 12, FF 11, Herbert D. Katz Center for Judaic Studies at University of Pennsylvania, Philadelphia.

18 "Julius D. Lyons," *American Israelite*, 17 August 1877, 6.

19 Werner, "Death of Rev. Jacques J. Lyons," 5.

20 David and Tamar de Sola Pool, *An Old Faith in the New World: Portrait of Shearith Israel, 1654–1954* (New York: Columbia University Press, 1955), 178–79.

21 Mark A. Noll, "'Christian America' and 'Christian Canada,'" in *The Cambridge History of Christianity: World Christianities, c. 1815–c.1914*, ed. Sheridan Gilley and Brian Stanley (Cambridge: Cambridge University Press, 2006), 373–77.

22 Michael Brown, "The Beginnings of Reform Judaism in Canada," *Jewish Social Studies* 34 (October 1972): 323. By way of comparison, a group of Jews in Charleston founded the Reformed Society of Israelites in 1824. Although the society did not last long, its legacy influenced the initial reforms at Charleston's Beth Elohim. See William James Hagy, *This Happy Land: The Jews of Colonial and Antebellum Charleston* (Tuscaloosa: University of Alabama Press, 1993), 236–70.

23 Nathan Adler to Abraham De Sola, 4 March 1872, reel 189, Abraham De Sola Papers, McGill University, Montreal.

24 "An Anglo-Jewish Minister Opening a Sitting of the American Congress," *Jewish Chronicle*, 9 February 1872, 8.

25 David Aaron De Sola published dozens of works, none of them very polemical. One of those, the six-volume *Translation of the Forms of Prayer According to the Custom of the*

Spanish and Portuguese Jews, was the most widely used prayer book by Sephardic Jews in North America. Moreover, that 1836 work also contained a Jewish calendar, a feature that the younger De Sola later characterized as "a labor of no slight character." See Abraham De Sola, "Biography of David Aaron De Sola," *The Occident*, June 1864, 11.

26 Abraham De Sola, "To the Members of the Congregation 'Mikveh Israel,' Philadelphia," 29 May 1850, FF 20–269, Arnold and Deanne Kaplan Collection of Early American Judaica, University of Pennsylvania, Philadelphia.

27 To be sure, Isaac Leeser (although German-born) and Sabato Morais were leaders of Philadelphia's Spanish and Portuguese Jewish community who played prominent roles in nineteenth-century polemics. Yet both ministers hardly felt bound by their pulpit roles and constantly sought identities that stretched far beyond the synagogue. See Lance J. Sussman, *Isaac Leeser and the Making of American Judaism* (Detroit: Wayne State University Press, 1995), 105–54; and Arthur Kiron, "Golden Ages, Promised Lands: The Victorian Rabbinic Humanism of Sabato Morais," Ph.D. diss., Columbia University, 1999, 265–317. That the Sephardic community in Philadelphia developed differently than the Portuguese communities elsewhere in America is an interesting topic in its own right. See Lance J. Sussman, "Isaac Leeser and the 'Philadelphia Pattern,'" in *When Philadelphia Was the Capital of Jewish America*, ed. Murray Friedman (Philadelphia: Balch Institute Press, 1993), 22–33.

28 Abraham De Sola to A.H. David, 4 June 1861, reel 51, Abraham De Sola Papers, McGill University, Montreal.

29 Pool, *An Old Faith in the New World*, 84.

30 Jacques Judah Lyons to Abraham De Sola, 12 September 1862, reel 53, Abraham De Sola Papers, McGill University, Montreal. On American Jewish catechisms, see Jonathan D. Sarna, "'God Loves an Infant's Praise': Cultural Borrowing and Cultural Resistance in Two Nineteenth-Century American Jewish Sunday-School Texts," *Jewish History* 27 (March 2013), 73–89. Publication of De Sola's prayer book received fierce response from competitors. See Isaac Leeser, "The Jewish Child's First Catechism of Bible History," *The Occident*, September 1853, 321–25; and Abraham De Sola, "Rev. Mr. De Sola's Rejoinder," *The Occident,* November 1853, 413-19; and December 1853, 469–76.

31 See Hyman B. Grinstein, "The American Synagogue and Laxity of Religious Observance, 1750–1850," M.A. thesis, Columbia University, 1936, 2–15; and E. Digby Baltzell, "The Development of a Jewish Upper Class in Philadelphia, 1782–1940," in *The Jews: Social Patterns of an American Group*, ed. Marshall Sklare (Glencoe: The Free Press, 1958), 276–80. On attempts to push intermarried Jewish men out of the synagogue, see "Query on the Burial of Persons Married to Gentiles from the Trustees Answered," 1843, box 2, folder 102, Jacques Judah Lyons Collection, American Jewish Historical Society, New York; and Extract from K.K. Shearith Israel Minutes, FF 20-219, Arnold and Deanne Kaplan Collection.

32 The one major exception to this was in Charleston. On this, see Allan Tarshish, "The Charleston Organ Case," *American Jewish Historical Quarterly* 54 (June 1965): 411–49.

33 Robert L. Kravitz, "Congregational History: The Congregation Mickve Israel (Philadelphia), 1850–1875," term paper, Hebrew Union College, 1971, 15. The paper is listed as call number "SC-6463" at the American Jewish Archives, Cincinnati.

34 "The Parties," *The Asmonean*, 20 December 1852, 90.

35 "Montreal," *The Israelite*, 15 October 1858, 114.

36 Abraham Hoffnung, Letter to the Editor, *The Israelite*, 19 November 1858, 157.

37   See Israel Goldstein, *A Century of Judaism in New York: B'nai Jeshurun, 1825–1925* (New York: Congregation B'nai Jeshurun, 1930), 133–37.

38   Max Lilienthal, "Religious Controversies," *The Israelite*, 29 September 1854, 92.

39   See "Montreal," *The Israelite*, 15 October 1858, 114.

40   Abraham De Sola to Isaac Leeser, 22 November 1859, Gershwind-Bennett Isaac Leeser Digital Repository of the University of Pennsylvania, http://ubuwebser.cajs.upenn.edu/documentDisplay.php?id=LSDCBx2FF6_41.

41   "New York," *Jewish Chronicle*, 21 March 1851, 190. See also "The London Jewish Chronicle and the Asmonean," *The Asmonean*, 11 April 1851, 196.

42   It was not until the early 1870s that De Sola considered writing for the Orthodox *Jewish Messenger* of New York, and even then his material was non-confrontational. See Samuel Mayer Isaacs to Abraham De sola, 7 January 1869, 70; Samuel Mayer Isaacs to Abraham De Sola, 23 December 1870, reel 111, Abraham De Sola Papers, McGill University, Montreal.

43   See, for example, Lyons and De Sola, *A Jewish Calendar*, 4, 6, 17.

44   For an example of American Ashkenazic Jewish caution toward kabbalistic sources, see "Kabbalah and Philosophy," *The Asmonean*, 8 June 1854, 62–63. One rare exception to this rule was Isidor Kalisch, who translated several kabbalistic works into English. See Samuel Kalisch, "Rabbi Isidor: Kalisch: A Memoir," in *Studies in Ancient and Modern Judaism: Selected Writings of Rabbi Isidor Kalisch*, ed. Samuel Kalisch (New York: George Dobsevage, 1928), 1–60.

45   Lyons and De Sola, *A Jewish Calendar*, 28.

46   Ibid., 33.

47   "Reviews," *The Asmonean*, 11 August 1854, 132.

48   "A Jewish Calendar for Fifty Years," *The Israelite*, 8 September 1854, 69.

49   "A Jewish Calendar for Fifty Years," *The Occident*, September 1854, 320.

50   On the reception of Maimonides's principles of faith, see Marc B. Shapiro, *The Limits of Orthodox Theology: Maimonides' Thirteen Principles Reappraised* (Oxford: Littman Library of Jewish Civilization, 2004), 1–37.

51   On this issue, see Jonathan D. Sarna, "The Debate over Mixed Seating in the American Synagogue," in *The American Synagogue: A Sanctuary Transformed*, ed. Jack Wertheimer (Cambridge: Cambridge University Press, 1987), 363–94.

52   See, for example, Isaac M. Wise, "Principles of Judaism," *The Occident*, January 1851, 495.

53   Jacob Katz, *Divine Law in Human Hands: Case Studies in Halakhic Flexibility* (Jerusalem: Magnes Press, 1998), 265–80.

54   On Charleston's reform, see Tarshish, "The Charleston Organ Case," 433.

55   "Dr. Adler's Sermon on the Yom Tov Sheni, or Double Festivals," *Jewish Chronicle*, 19 May 1848, 541.

56   "The Second Period of American Jewish History," *The Israelite*, 4 August 1854, 28. See also "Jewish Authorities on Reform," *The Occident*, September 1854, 288–95; and "The Second Holy-Days," *The Israelite*, 29 September 1854, 93.

57   Lyons and De Sola, *A Jewish Calendar*, 27.

58   See Lionel E. Moses, "Is There an Authentic Triennial Cycle of Torah Reading?," in *Responsa 1980–1990: The Committee on Jewish Law and Standards of the Conservative Movement*, ed. David J. Fine (New York: Rabbinical Assembly, 2005), 77–128.

59   L.D., "May the Torah be Read in Three Years, instead of in One Year," *The Asmonean*, 21 July 1854, 109. It was common knowledge that Lilienthal published under the pseudonym

"L.D" (the initials of "Dr. Lilienthal" in reverse). See "Jewish Ministry," *The Asmonean*, 3 November 1854, 22. See also Bruce L. Ruben, *Max Lilienthal: The Making of an American Rabbinate* (Detroit: Wayne State University Press, 2011), 116.

60 See Michael A. Meyer, *Response to Modernity: A History of the Reform Movement in Judaism* (Oxford: Oxford University Press, 1988), 189; and David Phillipson, *The Reform Movement in Judaism* (New York: Macmillan, 1907), 426n1.

61 Leon A. Jick, *The Americanization of the Synagogue, 1820–1870* (Hanover: Brandeis University Press, 1976), 81.

62 On Christian decorum reform, see Richard L. Bushman, *The Refinement of America: Persons, Houses, Cities* (New York: A.A. Knopf, 1992), 313–52. For an early complaint against the noisy and disorganized American synagogue, see "Rev. Dr. Raphall," *The Asmonean*, 9 November 1849, 21.

63 Lyons and De Sola, *A Jewish Calendar*, 150, 163.

64 Carlebach, *Palaces of Time*, 189.

SEVEN

Finding a Rabbi for Quebec City
The Interplay Between an American Yeshiva and a Canadian Congregation

Ira Robinson

A major problem, encountered numerous times in the history of organized Jewish religious life in Canada, has been where to obtain rabbinic leadership. No matter what the religious orientation of a given Canadian Jewish congregation, its spiritual leadership has almost inevitably come from outside Canada. As Morton Weinfeld has stated: "Judaism in Canada is a branch plant operation. Reform, Conservative, and Reconstructionist Judaism in Canada are all completely dependent on their American counterparts for infrastructural support, and, more importantly, for the major rabbinic seminaries. These rabbis in Canada must be trained in the United States. There are some Ultra-Orthodox rabbinic seminaries in Canada, but the larger, Modern Orthodox institutions such as Yeshiva University are south of the border. The majority of pulpit rabbis in Canada have historically been American."[1]

This means that Judaism in Canada has frequently been subject to Judaic ideas and movements originating elsewhere. While Weinfeld may be on solid footing with respect to the twentieth century, in the nineteenth century the first Canadian rabbis came from Europe, especially England.[2]

At the turn of the twentieth century, Eastern European immigrant Jewish communities in Canada were supplied with imported rabbinical leaders trained in Eastern Europe.[3] These European rabbis were integrated into the existing North American rabbinical networks and the rabbinical associations created to represent them and their interests. The names these rabbinic organizations adopted, such as the *Agudas ha-Rabbonim d'Artzos ha-Beris ve-Kanada*, reflected from the beginning a rabbinic presence in Canada.[4] By the mid-twentieth century, however, most Canadian rabbis were indeed being trained in the United States, which necessarily gave American Jewry considerable influence in the development of Judaism in Canada.[5] Several attempts over the years to establish rabbinical training institutions in Canada have not succeeded in measurably satisfying the Canadian Jewish demand for spiritual leadership.[6]

Thus the process whereby American rabbis become spiritual leaders of Canadian synagogues is worth investigating in the context of any examination of the commonalities and distinctness of Canadian and American Jewries. Rabbinic placement is an interesting example of both the connections and the disconnections experienced by Jews in communities and countries with close and lasting ties. This chapter will illustrate the relationship between rabbinical institutions in the United States and congregations in Canada as it played out in the mid-twentieth century by using the specific example of Congregation Bais Israel-Oheb Sholom of Quebec City, Quebec (hereafter the Congregation) and the Rabbi Isaac Elchanan Theological Seminary of Yeshiva University in New York City (hereafter the Yeshiva). This relationship was conducted between the 1930s and the 1960s. The chapter will thus examine in detail the ways in which several newly ordained American Orthodox rabbis were placed as spiritual leaders in a Canadian city whose majority French Canadian language and culture make it perhaps the most distinctive of Canadian cities from the perspective of Americans.

We begin our consideration of the three decades of relationship between the Congregation and the Yeshiva with Moshe Rosman's observation on rabbinical exchanges between the Jewish communities of Poland and Germany in the early modern period: "Regional ... differences should not, however, obscure the many traditions, institutions, and cultural constructs that the Jews of the sub-regions had in common, as well as the many types of familial, social, cultural, economic, political, intellectual, and religious affinity between them ... Rabbis born in Germany might be trained in Poland and then serve in either place. In general rabbis moved easily from positions in Polish cities to ones in German communities and back again, implying that their cultural acuity did not require much adjustment when crossing the political borders."[7]

In that case, commonalities predominated. We will see how similar relations were at work in the sub-regions of North America defined as the United States and Canada in the twentieth century.

The Congregation

Our chronological story begins in the mid-1930s with the Quebec City congregation. Eastern European immigrant Jews founded it in 1898, and it constituted the only synagogue in the city, which had a Jewish population of some five hundred in the 1931 Canadian census.[8] The synagogue was Orthodox, as were nearly all the synagogues founded by turn-of-the-century immigrants in North America.[9] From its foundation to the 1930s, its spiritual leadership, like that of many smaller Canadian Jewish communities of the era, was not rabbinic in the strict sense of the term.[10] The Congregation was led by Jews who possessed the qualifications of *shochet* (kosher slaughterer), cantor (prayer leader), and Hebrew teacher. Often these various qualifications were united in one person. While these men undoubtedly possessed knowledge of the rabbinic tradition greater than that of the other members of the congregation, they had not earned the formal title of rabbi and did not enjoy the status of rabbis. They were most commonly given the title of Reverend, which had been adopted in the English-speaking world to denote a Jewish religious functionary who did not have formal rabbinic qualifications.[11] Thus when the Congregation needed a formal rabbinic ruling on an issue in *halakha* (Judaic law), it needed to call upon a qualified rabbi from the nearest large Jewish community, Montreal.[12] However, in the mid-1930s the Quebec City congregation made a most important decision. In 1934, it hired a spiritual leader, Rabbi Bernard Mednick, who possessed formal Orthodox rabbinic credentials and had been trained in an American institution, the Yeshiva.[13]

This was an important departure for the Congregation in several respects. Most important, it was upgrading its spiritual leadership from *shochet*/cantor to rabbi. Doing this meant that the Congregation wished to advertise its progress in means (it could financially support a rabbi as well as a *shochet*/cantor). In a certain way, the Congregation was also declaring its independence of the Montreal rabbinate. By choosing an American-trained as opposed to a European-trained rabbi as its spiritual leader, it was also making an important cultural statement. It was letting the world at large know that it was thinking of the religious future of the community's children, who were being educated in the English Protestant schools of Quebec City. It was securing a rabbinic leader who possessed not only the traditional rabbinic education that qualified him to be an Orthodox rabbi, but also the ability to impart that knowledge in the language of the North

American Jewish future – English. As congregational President O. Miller wrote to the Yeshiva's Rabbi Morris Finer in 1945, after Rabbi Mednick had left for another rabbinic position in Union City, New Jersey: "We are interested in engaging a modern, young Rabbi who possesses a fluent knowledge of both English and Jewish [Yiddish]."[14]

The Yeshiva

For the Yeshiva, the Congregation represented both an opportunity and a challenge. The major attraction of the Congregation for the Yeshiva was the fairly strict Orthodox nature of the congregation. While, as has been said, the vast majority of synagogues founded by Eastern European Jewish immigrants at the turn of the twentieth century were at least nominally "Orthodox," by the 1930s, many of them had compromised strict Orthodox practices by having men and women seated together and not separated by a *mechitsa* (partition). For the Yeshiva, this reality was problematic in the extreme. It significantly reduced the number of synagogues in which its graduates could serve with good conscience. In the first half of the twentieth century there were, however, so few strictly Orthodox congregations available that wanted to hire the sort of English-speaking Orthodox rabbi the Yeshiva ordained that the Yeshiva's graduates often, with the formal objections but the tacit acquiescence of the Yeshiva's officials, accepted pulpits in such congregations.[15] As Victor Geller states, in that era "there was no more vexing problem facing the Orthodox community" than synagogue seating.[16] Even as late as 1963, towards the end of the era covered in this article, the Yeshiva's placement service reported that, of thirty-eight rabbinical placements made, only twenty were in synagogues with *mechitsot*.[17]

Because the Quebec City congregation's synagogue was built to satisfy the strictest Orthodox standards of separation of men and women, the Yeshiva's officials could recommend it as a pulpit for their rabbinic graduates without a moment's moral hesitation. Thus the Yeshiva's Rabbi Morris Finer assured Abraham Halbfinger, who had experienced problems in his post as rabbi in a New England town because his congregation refused to institute separate seating in the synagogue[18]: "I can tell you without hesitation that Quebec offers a splendid opportunity and that you will find this post most congenial."[19]

Quebec City also had a major drawback in the eyes of the Yeshiva's placement officials. The challenge of the Quebec City congregation, in the eyes of the Yeshiva, was its location far from New York. In the mid-twentieth century as today, North American Orthodoxy, while it had spread across the North American continent, was very much centred in the New York

City area, and many of the Yeshiva's graduates, as a result of the New York orientation of American Orthodoxy, often hesitated to serve congregations far from the city with its well-developed religious, educational, and *kashrut* infrastructure that made Orthodox Jewish life livable.[20] Thus the Yeshiva's placement director, Rabbi Finer, commented in a memorandum on a possible candidate for the Quebec City post, "He is unenthusiastic; would prefer post closer to New York."[21] This was a challenge that the Yeshiva was all too familiar with, and that it attempted to combat with its "Community Service Bureau," initiated formally in 1944, that was designed to help foster a viable Orthodox life in isolated communities.[22] On balance, therefore, the Quebec City Congregation represented a challenge that the Yeshiva was eager to tackle.

It was clear to all parties that the Yeshiva was in competition for rabbinical positions with graduates of other rabbinical seminaries, particularly the Jewish Theological Seminary. Thus congregational officer Maurice Pollack made certain to mention in a 1952 letter to Rabbi Finer that "When Mr. [O.] Miller and I were in New York, we interviewed another rabbi who might suit, only we want to give the preference to a Rabbi from your Yeshiva."[23]

Rabbinic Qualifications

It is worthy of note that the Yeshiva never sought to "sell" its rabbis to the Congregation in terms of their advanced Talmudic learning, although this was, of course, the main education they received in the Yeshiva. Instead, the Yeshiva tended to emphasize the rabbinical candidates' social skills, as well as those of their wives. Rabbi Finer thus wrote congregational officer O. Miller in 1953 that Rabbi Bernard Walfish, then being considered for hire, was "a wonderful 'mixer' socially."[24] Finer described Walfish to congregational officer Maurice Pollack in this way: "He is not only a very warm and charming person but is also extremely capable and conscientious with an excellent scholastic background. Moreover, you will find that your new rebbetzin is also a very sweet and charming person whom the community is going to like immensely."[25]

The rebbetzin was a very important factor in the decision-making process, as Rabbi Finer wrote to Bernard Walfish: "The only reason that Mr. Pollack suggested that your wife accompany you to Quebec City is that he wanted to have all the parties present so that a decision might be reached immediately. Evidently, they did have a candidate there who first came up by himself and then told them that he would not be in a position to make a decision unless his wife saw the community. They then arranged for her to come up but finally did not take this man."[26]

Crossing the Border

As it happens, the first Yeshiva-ordained rabbi to serve in Quebec City, Rabbi Bernard Mednick, was a Canadian. This meant that Yeshiva officials had to worry about his legal status as a foreign student in the United States and his ability to cross the border between Canada and the United States. Thus the RIETS Registrar, Samuel L. Sar, wrote on 18 June 1937: "We respectfully request the immigration authorities to grant [Bernard Mednick] a visa to cross the border into America thus giving him the opportunity to complete his course in our institution upon completion of which he will be entitled to full ordination."[27]

All the other Yeshiva rabbis who served in Quebec City were US citizens, and the issue was the reverse – the legality of the presence of Americans working in Canada. Thus, on 24 March 1950, Rabbi Joshua Epstein wrote to the Yeshiva's Rabbi Abraham Avrech: "[The] American Consulate in Quebec ... require[s] a letter from the firm in the states which has sent me to Canada. The Consulate told me that I am under that classification, because the school has sent me. Please send me a letter to that effect, so that I can be registered with the local American consulate. Unless I have that registration, I can loose [*sic*] my citizenship."[28]

An Outlying Community

The rabbis sent to Quebec City by the Yeshiva were generally young men, at or near the beginning of their careers. Their youth and relative inexperience was sometimes an issue. In 1957, Rabbi Finer had to reassure congregational official I. Abramson, who was worried about Rabbi Norbert Weinberg's youth, "that chronological age is in itself not the measure of maturity."[29] Another rabbi, Abraham Halbfinger, was described thus to the Congregation: "Although a young man, Rabbi Halbfinger is a person of maturity, ability, and possesses a fine personality."[30] As we will see, there were many reasons why the Yeshiva considered placing young rabbis in Quebec City, which it considered a "smaller community,"[31] as an appropriate placement strategy.

A large part of the equation was that the Quebec City Congregation was not the sort of place the Yeshiva's rabbis wished to stay long, in large part because they considered it to be an "outlying community."[32] In 1944, Rabbi Mednick expressed himself in this way to the Yeshiva: "At present, after over seven years of service in Quebec, I feel that it is inadvisable [*sic*], to the point of urgency, that I get myself another position."[33] In another letter written later that year, Mednick spoke longingly of obtaining "a position in a larger Jewish community, such as New York, Boston, or Baltimore, where I could settle down permanently."[34]

Rabbi Joshua Epstein similarly expressed his feeling that he had stayed too long in Quebec City in a letter to Rabbi Abraham Avrech of the Yeshiva's Community Service Division, dated 9 February 1951. Among the points he made in that letter were the smallness of the Quebec City Jewish community and the distance between Quebec City and the nearest major Jewish community, Montreal. These two factors combined to make his social life with "people of my own religious upbringing" next to impossible. Avrech promptly responded to reassure Epstein: "It is not our intention to let you remain in Quebec for any length of time. The original intent in placing you was to get you some experience and maturity in the pulpit."[35]

Rabbi Bernard Walfish expressed his inability to stay permanently in Quebec City in terms of his children's education in the following 1956 letter to Rabbi Finer:

> I would be willing to stay on for another year or two. Except for one important factor – my son. Sending him to school in Quebec (he started this year) poses a very serious problem to us. He has to go to a Protestant school and as you can imagine, he is constantly under a Christian influence. Besides that his Jewish education would not be the kind I would want him to receive if he went to our Talmud Torah ... I would like a position where I can bring my children up in a Jewish fashion ... and where I can expect a certain degree of permanency.[36]

The Quebec City Ambiance

In the mid-twentieth century, the Jewish community of Quebec City conducted its business primarily in English and Yiddish.[37] Nonetheless, the fact that Quebec City had a francophone majority was not lost on the Yeshiva. The Yeshiva's Rabbi Finer apparently knew some French himself as he opened a 1954 letter to Rabbi Walfish with "Comment ça va?"[38] However, the French-language ability of rabbinical candidates for the Quebec City post never seems to have been a matter of serious consideration. In only one case did Rabbi Finer mention a possible candidate for the post who possessed some knowledge of French ("qui parle français").[39] The francophone nature of Quebec City did have a certain negative impact on Rabbi Joshua Epstein. In his 1951 letter expressing his desire to leave Quebec, one of the points he made was that because the city's university, Laval, was French-speaking, he was unable to further advance his studies.[40]

Another issue in the correspondence between the Quebec City rabbis and their Yeshiva involved contact between them and local non-Jewish clergy. Rabbi Walfish in 1954 announced a class in the Congregation's Adult Institute on "Comparative Religions" in connection with which he had invited a Roman Catholic *abbé* to speak on "the basic principales [*sic*] and practices of Catholicism."[41] As he expressed it in a letter to his congregants: "This course was included in our curriculum so that all of us may gain a better knowledge of what our Christian friends and neighbors believe. It is my firm belief that through this knowledge we will not only further the cause of brotherhood and friendship amongst the different denominations of our city, but we will also begin to realize and understand that Judaism is the foundation of all other religions."[42]

While Rabbi Walfish's invitation reflected the ongoing and developing interfaith dialogue in Quebec City between its rabbis and both Protestant and Catholic clergy,[43] it absolutely horrified Walfish's contacts at the Yeshiva, who were wary of interfaith dialogue in general, and particularly on the part of an inexperienced rabbi.[44] As the Yeshiva's Rabbi Finer put it: "Seeing the notice only reinforces my instinctive negative reaction toward this type of course ... There is enough to teach about Judaism without extending gratuitous invitations to missionaries."[45]

Level of Congregational Judaic Knowledge

From the correspondence in the Yeshiva University Archives we learn much about the level of Judaic knowledge present among the members of the Quebec City congregation. In the early 1950s, Rabbi Joshua Epstein wrote that he was going to conduct "a community Seder for all those who could benefit thereby, and believe me there are a lot of them."[46] This clearly implies that a large number of his congregants did not possess sufficient Judaic knowledge to conduct the traditional Seder ritual on their own in their homes. In another letter, Rabbi Epstein indicated that he had made efforts so that "every woman in Quebec today knows how to read Hebrew and follow the services.[47] All men who formerly were unfamiliar with our service have been introduced to it and are on their way to be well-acquainted with it."[48] Thus a considerable number of his congregants were substantially unfamiliar with the Judaic liturgy.

Even those who grew up in Quebec City who had acquired a considerable amount of Judaic knowledge were unable to truly enter the ranks of the educated Orthodox, because Talmud, the essential ingredient in the advanced Orthodox curriculum, was entirely missing in Quebec City. Thus one young man from Quebec City, Neil Gilman, who wished to go to the Yeshiva, was told that "because he is twenty-one years old and has not learned any Talmud ... there was no class for him." He matriculated instead at the Jewish Theological Seminary and was to become one of the more distinguished members of the Seminary's faculty.[49]

Fundraising for the Yeshiva

As early as 1951, congregational officer O. Miller was assured by Rabbi Finer that Dr. Samuel Belkin, the president of the Yeshiva, "has a particularly deep interest in the welfare of your Jewish community."[50] When Bernard Walfish was selected as Quebec City's rabbi in 1953, Rabbi Finer similarly signalled to him the Yeshiva's special interest in the Congregation as well as the reason why: "From the Yeshiva's point of view, we are interested in having a good man in Quebec City, particularly because of Mr. Pollack."[51] Maurice Pollack, who owned Quebec City's largest department store, was a very wealthy man and a "big giver" to the Yeshiva. In 1954, Finer informed Walfish, Pollack had given $5,000 to the Yeshiva, and the Yeshiva hoped for similar donations in the future.[52] Indeed, that same year, Rabbi Finer informed Rabbi Walfish that Pollack had given the institution a donation of the considerable sum of $25,000 "to improve the Pollack Library" at the Yeshiva.[53]

Maurice Pollack was not the only person of wealth in the Quebec City community who was being groomed for a large donation. As Rabbi Walfish wrote Rabbi Finer in 1954: "Next week Max Clarfield, one of the wealthiest men in the community, is going to be in New York with his wife. I have been trying to cultivate him so that he will give something substantial to Yeshivah ... He certainly is a prospect. He is a generous man and he loves to be made important."[54]

In 1956, Walfish spoke of the possibility of an annual fundraising event in Quebec City for the Yeshiva that could raise from three to five thousand dollars.[55] He well understood that the Yeshiva was concerned to keep on Maurice Pollack's good side. Rabbi Walfish was actually concerned that his move to a new rabbinate might even be held up because of this situation. As he wrote to Rabbi Finer: "En passant, as we say in Quebec, how is the position situation? Do I have a chance this year or have I already been relegated to the role of martyr for the cause of Mr. Pollack?"[56]

Rabbi Walfish's successor in Quebec City, Rabbi Norbert Weinberg, was hand-picked by the Yeshiva leadership at the very top, which would likely not have been the case with rabbinical placement in other small, faraway communities. As congregational official I. Abramson was told in 1957: "We have been holding Rabbi [Norbert Weinberg] in reserve for Quebec City for the past few months ... and I want you to know that Dr. Belkin himself was involved in the selection."[57] Belkin, the Yeshiva president, came personally to Quebec City, a considerable distance from New York, in February 1960 for a consultation on Quebec's community problems together with Rabbis Finer and Walfish.[58] Once again, this constituted very special treatment for the Quebec City congregation.

The Intermarriage Crisis

As Michael Brown points out, intermarriage became an important issue in Canadian Jewry in the twentieth century, and one of the primary areas where this issue found expression was in the synagogue. Brown notes that the issue was addressed in Canadian synagogue constitutions as early as the 1930s, a time when intermarriage affected only a few Jews. He further finds that by the 1960s, some Canadian Orthodox congregations had tightened their membership guidelines so as not to appear to condone intermarriage. This included calling for the expulsion of members who intermarried.[59]

The Quebec City Congregation, throughout its history, had apparently never accepted as members Jewish men who intermarried. In 1960, however, "two persons, members of prominent families in the community, who had married non Jewish women applied for membership and, because of the pressure brought by their families, were admitted into membership."[60] The controversy this action generated split the congregation, and it is of the utmost importance for us to note that Maurice Pollack became the main protagonist of the side that bitterly opposed accepting one of the inter-married men as a member. The Yeshiva's Morris Finer, in his summary of the issue, states that Pollack "took a strong stand against this, not entirely on ideological grounds but rather because of some of the personalities involved."[61]

On 14 September 1960, the congregational leadership that had originally accepted the intermarried man as a member, in a possible gesture of compromise, amended the Congregation's by-laws to the effect "that any new applicant married outside the Jewish faith cannot be accepted."[62] However, this amendment, which effectively grandfathered the original inter-married member, was rejected outright by Pollack.

The Congregation's rabbi, Abraham Halbfinger, was caught in the middle of this quarrel, and as the official upholder of Judaic law in the community, he appealed to the Yeshiva for guidance on how to deal with this apparent flagrant breach of Judaic law and custom. On 20 February 1961, Rabbi Abraham Halbfinger wrote Rabbi Walfish, who had become an official at the Yeshiva, asking him to "write me as soon as possible regarding the decisions of Rabbi Weinberg,[63] as well as your own opinion. On what halakhic point is M. Salmanowitz entitled to an Aliyah and also to membership?"[64]

In July 1961 the matter came to a crisis. From the Yeshiva's perspective, the Congregation had overridden the religious decision of Rabbi Halbfinger by accepting the intermarried man as a member. Yeshiva officials Finer and Walfish both met with Halbfinger to try to sort the matter out. They were, however, constrained in their possible actions by their ties to Maurice Pollack. Thus Rabbi Finer took care to contact Pollack, who informed him "that the community should be 'punished' for its behavior towards the rabbi." A congregational meeting at which Rabbi Halbfinger could state his position was suggested.[65] On 4 July 1961, Pollack sent a telegram to Finer: "Suggestion for general meeting with Rabbi Halbfinger and Rabbi Walfish good and believe would clear up matters satisfactorily."[66]

After these preliminaries, on 6 July 1961, Rabbi Halbfinger wrote to congregational President Jack Rosenheck, asserting his rabbinic authority: "I must take exception to the statement about the Board's actions, for in any matter of a Religious nature, which involves Jewish law, it is the Rabbi of the congregation, and only he, who can make the decision."[67] The Congregation's leaders' response to this demand did not satisfy Halbfinger, who resigned, leaving the Congregation without a rabbi. Although no one knew it at the time, Halbfinger would be the last Yeshiva-trained rabbi to officiate in Quebec City.

In the fall of 1961, Pollack wrote to the Yeshiva's Rabbi Walfish that at a recent synagogue meeting, which he had not attended because it was controlled by the other faction in the synagogue, when someone asked "what they were going to do for a rabbi," Congregational officer Sydney Lazarovitz replied "that the 'Yeshiva have black-balled us and refused to give us a rabbi." Pollack wrote further that he had consulted with Rabbi Bernard Mednick, who "told me honestly that there is no use figuring on a rabbi from the Yeshiva because we have already had three or four rabbis and they have had to leave because here they do not want to have a rabbi unless he will do what they want in religious matters, they do not want to listen to the rabbi."[68]

In another letter to the Yeshiva's Rabbi Finer, Pollack expressed himself forcefully on the subject: "I would ask you, naturally I have not the right to recommend I am only expressing my wish, do not give Quebec a rabbi because he will be badly treated."[69] Finer replied on 25 December 1961, assuring Pollack that "whatever we do in Quebec City will have your prior consent."[70]

This understanding between Maurice Pollack and the Yeshiva that the Yeshiva should refuse to send the Congregation a new rabbi was reiterated a couple of years later. Pollack wrote Finer on 28 June 1963:

I am not telling you what to do, only I am giving you my opinion, you should give him the same answer as Rabbi Walfish gave them at a meeting when he was in Quebec, until such time as they make a change that men who are married to gentile girls and have gentile children who are being brought up as Catholics, these men should not be allowed to be members of our congregation, they could come to Synagogue and have seats, but should not be members, and until such time as this change is made you will not have any dealings with them.[71]

A year later, the Yeshiva's Rabbi Walfish reassured Pollack that if the Congregation contacted the Yeshiva in the future, the institution would "be guided by your advice."[72]

The Disintegration of the Quebec City Community

The intermarried membership crisis seems to have precipitated a drastic decline in the institutional integrity of the Quebec City congregation. It did manage to hire a rabbi with no connection to the Yeshiva, who proved to be not really satisfactory.[73] In September 1964, Pollack described to Rabbi Walfish how far the Jewish community's institutional infrastructure had broken down: "At the present time our community is down that [*sic*] it could not be worse; we have no rabbi, no Shoichet, and no Jewish butcher."[74]

On 19 July 1965, congregational officer Ernest Gilman once again appealed to Yeshiva official Rabbi Herbert C. Dobrinsky to recommend a rabbi for the community.[75] As Gilman put it:

This is of the utmost urgency, as for the last three years we have had no spiritual leadership to speak of, and the situation is now critical.

We have recently reorganized this community under a new executive who are most anxious to have orthodox leadership, and we feel that a graduate Rabbi from your Yeshiva would stimulate and revive our community.[76]

In an internal memorandum dated the same day, Dobrinsky, originally a Canadian, noted that he had also received a telephone call from Gilman, stating that the rabbi they had for the past two years had not been satisfactory and begging the Yeshiva to send someone whom they were "willing to pay $9,000 or even more." Rabbi Dobrinsky noted in the memorandum that "we must check with Mr. Pollack ... to see how he feels about our referral of candidates."[77] Pollack thus still possessed an effective veto with respect to the Yeshiva's response to the Congregation.

Gilman followed his appeal with a 22 July letter to Rabbi Dobrinsky reiterating the Orthodoxy of the Congregation and stating that a new bylaw had been passed by the Congregation's board stating that "any member who marries outside the faith automatically loses his membership in our synagogue."[78] Gilman also had a telephone conversation with the Yeshiva's M. Finer on 23 July. In this conversation, he argued that there are "many congregations in Montreal and elsewhere who have such [intermarried] people among their membership and yet there is no discrimination against them, they have Orthodox rabbis from Yeshiva and elsewhere."[79]

The new bylaw was obviously designed for compromise on the outstanding issue between the Yeshiva and the Congregation, but the Yeshiva continued its hard line towards the Congregation, because Mr. Pollack would not assent to any compromise on the issue. Rabbi Finer, in a memorandum of 26 July, indicated that he was stalling Gilman because he needed to consult with Dr. Belkin, who was currently trying to iron out a dispute ("sichsuch") concerning a major contribution to the Yeshiva by Pollack, and therefore Dr. Belkin "did not want to antagonize" him.[80] Rabbi Finer summed up the situation as it appeared to him at the time in a memorandum dated 29 July 1965: "Largely because of Mr. Pollack and his strong stand (although we might have reached the same policy decision anyway) we refused to recommend any rabbis to this congregation ... I checked with Mr. Pollack ... His attitude is still adamant. He feels we should not recommend a rabbi under these circumstances ... Meanwhile I checked with Dr. Belkin. He felt that Mr. Pollack was being a little unreasonable but, at the same time, we should not try to offend him."

On 2 August 1965, Rabbi Dobrinsky regretfully concluded his memorandum on the Quebec City affair in the following way: "It is indeed a pity that our efforts to assist this congregation have been stymied by Mr. Pollack who has insisted on this procedure which we are not certain is completely correct in that the community has now made amends by ruling that those who intermarry will lose membership. By the same token for us to recognize the status of those who have intermarried and to allow them to remain in the congregation would be tantamount to our agreement to this."[81]

Conclusion

For nearly three decades, the Congregation and the Yeshiva had maintained a relationship that was of mutual benefit. The Congregation received competent English-speaking Orthodox rabbinic guidance, and the Yeshiva was able to place its graduates in a position that did not require them to compromise with their Orthodox principles concerning women's place in the house of worship. As the relationship between the Congregation and the Yeshiva developed, its limitations became clear. Quebec City could not offer the Yeshiva's rabbis the social, religious, and educational environment that could persuade them to make Quebec City their permanent home.

The ending of the relationship between the Yeshiva and the Congregation in Quebec City demonstrates quite clearly that the Yeshiva's commitment to its large donor, Maurice Pollack, effectively tied its hands, and that it became an unwilling partisan in an intra-congregational struggle, even against its better judgment. The decline of the Quebec City Congregation that started in the 1960s was the product of many factors, most especially the overall decline of the anglophone community in Quebec City. Had the crisis over intermarried members, which brought with it the cessation of the relationship between the Yeshiva and the Congregation, not arisen, this process of Jewish community disintegration would most likely still have occurred. However, there is room to speculate that the communal rupture that caused the cessation of relations between the Congregation and the Yeshiva served to exacerbate and perhaps precipitate the conditions leading to the Congregation's ultimate decline.

Notes

1　Morton Weinfeld, *Like Everyone Else, but Different: The Paradoxical Success of Canadian Jews* (Toronto: McClelland and Stewart, 2001), 300.

2　Richard Menkis, "'In this Great, Happy and Enlightened Colony': Abraham de Sola on Jews, Judaism and Emancipation in Victorian Montreal," in *L'antisémitisme éclairé: Inclusion et exclusion depuis l'Époque des Lumières jusqu'à l'affaire Dreyfus*, ed. Ilana Y. Zinguer and Sam W. Bloom (Leiden: Brill, 2003), 313–31.

3　Ira Robinson, *Rabbis and Their Community: Studies in the Immigrant Orthodox Rabbinate in Montreal, 1896–1930* (Calgary: University of Calgary Press, 2007), 1–19.

4　Jeffrey Gurock, *American Jewish Orthodoxy in Historical Perspective* (Hoboken: KTAV, 1996), 7–8. Cf. Gurock, *Orthodox Jews in America* (Bloomington: Indiana University Press, 2009); and Victor Geller, *Orthodoxy Awakens: The Belkin Era and Yeshiva University* (Jerusalem: Urim, 2003).

5　On American Judaism, see Jonathan Sarna, *American Judaism: a New History* (New Haven: Yale University Press, 2004).

6　There were several attempts to create Canadian *yeshivot*, which in an official sense advertised themselves as rabbinical training institutions and even granted a few rabbinic ordinations. One of these was the Rabbinical College of Canada, founded in Montreal in 1941. See its Wikipedia article: http://en.wikipedia.org/wiki/Rabbinical_College_of_Canada. On a contemporary attempt to create a rabbinic training institution in Toronto, the Canadian Yeshiva and Rabbinical School, see http://www.cdnyeshiva.org.

7　Moshe Rosman, "Jewish History Across Borders," in *Rethinking European Jewish History*, ed. Jeremy Cohen and Moshe Rosman (Oxford: Littman Library of Jewish Civilization, 2009), 24–25.

8　This chapter confines itself to a discussion of the rabbinic issues of the Quebec City congregation. For a comprehensive study of the history and development of that congregation, see Ira Robinson, "'No Litvaks Need Apply': Judaism in Quebec City," in Pierre

Ancti and Simon Jacobs, eds., *Les Juifs de Québec: Quatre cents ans d'histoire* (Québec: Presses de l'Université du Québec, 2015), 21–34.

9 Gurock, *American Jewish Orthodoxy*, 63–102; Robinson, *Rabbis and Their Community*, 69–70.

10 An example of this phenomenon is Rev. Hyman Goldstick of Calgary, Alberta, who led the Jewish congregation in that city on the basis of his qualifications as a *sho̱het*.

11 Robinson, *Rabbis and Their Community*, 73, 85.

12 "An Ofener Brief zu di Keneder Rabbonim," *Keneder Adler* [Montreal], 5 June 1910; "An Antfer fun ho-Rav Zvi Ha-Kohen," *Keneder Adler*, 8 June 1910.

13 On the *yeshiva*, see Gurock, *The Men and Women of Yeshiva: Higher Education, Orthodoxy, and American Judaism* (New York: Columbia University Press, 1988); Aaron Rothkoff, *Bernard Revel – Builder of American Jewish Orthodoxy* (Philadelphia: Jewish Publication Society, 1972); Gilbert Klaperman, *The Story of Yeshiva University, the First Jewish University in America* (New York: Macmillan, 1969); Geller, *Orthodoxy Awakens*.

14 O. Miller to Morris Finer, 18 July 1945. This document and all subsequent archival documents presented in this article are taken from the Yeshiva University Archives [YUA]. I would like to thank the archivist, Ms. Shulamit Berger, for her help and cooperation. YUA/Rabbinic Placement Records-Communities/Box 92/Quebec-Quebec City 1945 -1956/2.

15 Gurock, *The Men and Women of Yeshiva*, 124.

16 Geller, *Orthodoxy Awakens*, 224–26.

17 Ibid., 250.

18 Morris Finer, memorandum, 4 March 1960. YUA/Rabbinic Placement Records-People Files/Halbfinger, Abraham.

19 Morris Finer to Abraham Halbfinger, 3 March 1960. YUA/Rabbinic Placement Records-People Files/Halbfinger, Abraham.

20 Geller, *Orthodoxy Awakens*, 121.

21 Morris Finer, memorandum, 4 March 1960. YUA/Rabbinic Placement Records-People Files/Halbfinger, Abraham.

22 Gurock, *The Men and Women of Yeshiva*, 145.

23 Maurice Pollack to Morris Finer, 4 February 1952. YUA/Rabbinical Placement Records-Communities/Box 92/Quebec-Quebec City 1945–1956/2 YUA/Rabbinical Placement Records-Communities/Box 92/Quebec-Quebec City 1945-1956/2.

24 24 August 1951. YUA/Rabbinic Placement Records-Communities/Box 92/Quebec-Quebec City 1945-1956/2.

25 4 March 1953. YUA/Rabbinical Placement Records-Communities/Box 92/Quebec-Quebec City 1945-1956/2. Cf. Morris Finer to Maurice Pollack, 17 February 1953. YUA/Rabbinic Placement Records-People Files/Walfish, Bernard.

26 Morris Finer to Bernard Walfish, 17 February 1953. YUA/Rabbinic Placement Records-People Files/Walfish, Bernard.

27 YUA/Samuel Sar/Box 10/M.

28 YUA/Rabbinic Placement Records-People Files/Epstein, Joshua.

29 Morris Finer to Maurice Pollack, 20 June 1957. YUA/Rabbinic Placement Records-Communities/Box 92/Quebec-Quebec City 1957/3.

30 M. Finer to Maurice Pollack, 3 March 1960. YUA/Rabbinic Placement Records-Communities/Box 92/Quebec-Quebec City 1957/1.

31 Norbert Weinberg to M. Finer, 6 March 1959. YUA/Rabbinic Placement Records-Communities/Box 92/Quebec-Quebec City 1957/3.

32 Abraham Halbfinger to Morris Finer, 25 April 1961. YUA/Rabbinic Placement Records-People Files/Halbfinger, Abraham.

33 Bernard Mednick to E. Marcus, 28 June 1944. YUA/Rabbinic Placement Records-People File/Mednick, Bernard.

34 Bernard Mednick to M. Finer, 20 August 1944. YUA/Rabbinic Placement Records-People File/Mednick, Bernard.

35 Abraham Avrech to Joshua Epstein, 20 February 1951. YUA/Rabbinic Placement Records-People Files/Epstein, Joshua.

36 Rabbi Bernard Walfish to Morris Finer, 9 January 1956. YUA/Rabbinic Placement Records/People Files/Walfish, Bernard.

37 Robinson, "'No Litvaks Need Apply.'"

38 24 February 1954. YUA/Rabbinic Placement Records/People Files/Walfish, Bernard.

39 Morris Finer to Maurice Pollack, 3 July 1952. YUA/Rabbinical Placement Records-Communities/Box 92/Quebec-Quebec City 1945-1956/2.

40 Joshua Epstein to Abraham Avrech, 9 February 1951. YUA/Rabbinic Placement Records-Communities/Box 92/Quebec-Quebec City 1945-1956/2.

41 Bernard Walfish, letter to Congregation, 5 November 1954. YUA/Rabbinic Placement Records/People Files/Walfish, Bernard.

42 Bernard Walfish to Congregation, 5 November 1954. YUA/Rabbinic Placement Records/People Files/Walfish, Bernard.

43 Rabbi Norbert Weinberg was similarly active in this area. Cf. Robinson, "'No Litvaks Need Apply,'" nn71–72, 74.

44 On the wary attitude of the *yeshiva* towards such dialogue, see Joseph B. Soloveitchik, "Confrontation," *Tradition* 6, no. 2 (1964). http://www.bc.edu/dam/files/research_sites/cjl/texts/cjrelations/resources/articles/soloveitchik.

45 M. Finer to Bernard Walfish, 12 November 1954. YUA/Rabbinic Placement Records/People Files/Walfish, Bernard.

46 Undated. Probably 1950 or 1951. YUA/Rabbinic Placement Records-People Files/Epstein, Joshua.

47 This refers to the ability to read the sounds made by the Hebrew letters and words in the prayer book.

48 Joshua Epstein to Abraham Avrech, 8 February 1951. YUA/Rabbinic Placement Records-Communities/Box 92/Quebec-Quebec City 1945-1956/2.

49 Bernard Walfish to Morris Finer, 17 November 1955. YUA/Rabbinic Placement Records/People Files/Walfish, Bernard.

50 Morris Finer to O. Miller, 7 September 1951. YUA/Rabbinic Placement Records/Box 92/Quebec-Quebec City 1945-1956/2.

51 Morris Finer to Bernard Walfish, 17 February 1953. YUA/Rabbinic Placement Records/People Files/Walfish, Bernard.

52 24 February 1954. YUA/Rabbinic Placement Records/People Files/Walfish, Bernard.

53 28 December 1954. YUA/Rabbinic Placement Records/People Files/Walfish, Bernard.

54 23 December 1954. YUA/Rabbinic Placement Records/People Files/Walfish, Bernard.

55 Rabbi Bernard Walfish to M. Finer, 9 January 1956. YUA/Rabbinic Placement Records/People Files/Walfish, Bernard.

56 Bernard Walfish to Morris Finer, 17 November 1955. YUA/Rabbinic Placement Records/People Files/Walfish, Bernard.

57 Morris Finer to I. Abramson, 20 June 1957. YUA/Rabbinic Placement Records-Communities/Box 92/Quebec-Quebec City 1957/1.

58 Maurice Pollack to Dr. Samuel Belkin, 19 February 1960. YUA/Rabbinic Placement Records-Communities/Box 92/Quebec-Quebec City/1957/1.

59 Michael Brown, "Signs of the Times: Changing Notions of Citizenship, Governance, and Authority as Reflected in Synagogue Constitutions," in *Not Written in Stone: Canadian Jews, Constitutions and Constitutionalism in Canada*, ed. Dr. Belkiniel Elazar, Michael Brown, and Ira Robinson (Ottawa: University of Ottawa Press, 2003), 92–93.

60 Morris Finer, memorandum, 29 July 1965. YUA/Rabbinic Placement Records-Communities/Box 92/Quebec-Quebec City/1957/1.

61 Finer, memorandum, 29 July 1965. YUA/Rabbinic Placement Records-Communities/Box 92/Quebec-Quebec City/1957/1.

62 "By-Laws of Beth Israel Ohev Sholom of Quebec," 1. YUA/Rabbinic Placement Records-Communities/Box 92/Quebec City, Canada/3.

63 On Rabbi Yechiel Weinberg and his influence, see Marc B. Shapiro, *Between the Yeshiva World and Modern Orthodoxy: The Life and Works of Rabbi Jehiel Jacob Wienberg* (London: Littman Library of Jewish Civilization, 1999).

64 Abraham Halbfinger to Bernard Walfish, 20 February 1961. YUA/Rabbinic Placement Files-People Files/Halbfinger, Abraham.

65 Morris Finer, memorandum, 6 July 1961. YUA/Rabbinic Placement Files-People Files/Halbfinger, Abraham.

66 YUA/Rabbinic Placement Records-Communities/Box 92/Quebec-Quebec City 1957/1.

67 Abraham Halbfinger to Jack Rosenheck, 6 July 1961. YUA/Rabbinic Placement Records-People Files/Halbfinger, Abraham.

68 Maurice Pollack to Bernard Walfish, 24 November 1961. YUA/Rabbinical Placement Records-Communities/Box 92/Quebec City, Canada 3.

69 Maurice Pollack to Morris Finer, 11 December 1961. YUA/Rabbinic Placement Records-Communities/Box 92/Quebec City, Canada, 3.

70 Morris Finer to Maurice Pollack, 25 December 1961. YUA/Rabbinic Placement Records-Communities/Box 92/Quebec City, Canada 3.

71 Maurice Pollack to M. Finer, 28 June 1963. YUA/Rabbinic Placement Records-Communities/Box 92/Quebec City, Canada, 3.

72 Bernard Walfish to Maurice Pollack, 4 September 1964. YUA/Rabbinic Placement Records-Communities/Box 92/Quebec City, Canada, 3.

73 Herbert Dobrinsky, memorandum of 10 August 1962. YUA/Rabbinic Placement Records-Communities/Box 92/Quebec City, Canada, 3.

74 Maurice Pollack to Bernard Walfish, 14 September 1964. YUA/Rabbinic Placement Records-Communities/Box 92/Quebec City, Canada, 3.

75 Rabbi Herbert C. Dobrinsky was the Assistant Director of Yeshiva University's Community Services Division. He was born in Montreal and had previously been Rabbi of the Beth Israel Synagogue in Halifax. "Montreal Native Appointed to Yeshiva University Post," *Canadian Jewish Chronicle*, 5 October 1962, http://news.google.com/newspapers?nid=883&dat=19621005&id=ZOJOAAAAIBAJ&sjid=Z0wDAAAAIBAJ&pg=4683,3776855.

76 Ernest Gilman to Rabbi Herbert Dobrinsky, 19 July 1965. YUA/Rabbinic Placement Records-Communities/Box 92/Quebec-Quebec City 1957/1.

77 Herbert Dobrinsky, memorandum, 19 July 1965. YUA/Rabbinic Placement Records-Communities/Box 92/Quebec-Quebec City 1957/1.

78 Ernest Gilman to Herbert Dobrinsky, 22 July 1965. YUA/Rabbinic Placement Records-Communities/Box 92/Quebec-Quebec City 1957/1.

79 Morris Finer, memorandum, 29 July 1965. YUA/Rabbinic Placement Records-Communities/Box 92/Quebec-Quebec City 1957/1.

80 Morris Finer, memorandum, 26 July 1965. YUA/Rabbinic Placement Records-Communities/Box 92/Quebec-Quebec City 1957/1.

81 Herbert Dobrinsky, memorandum, 2 August 1965. YUA/Rabbinic Placement Records-Communities/Box 92/Quebec-Quebec City 1957/1.

EIGHT

"Chasing the Cure" on Both Sides of the Border
Early Jewish Tuberculosis Sanatoriums in Denver and Montreal

Jeanne Abrams

Tuberculosis, commonly known as "consumption," the "White Plague," or simply "TB," held the appalling distinction of being the leading cause of death in late-nineteenth- and early-twentieth-century North America. For centuries, no single accepted standard for tuberculosis treatment prevailed, and until Robert Koch's discovery of the *tubercle bacillus* in 1882, most physicians surmised that the disease was hereditary and best treated in a favourable climate. Although the Canadian medical establishment quickly accepted Koch's findings, American doctors debated their legitimacy for many years. However, by the last decades of the nineteenth century, as germ theory developed and fear of contagion spread, physicians and public health officials in both countries increasingly viewed the sanatorium as the best place to aid victims and as the optimum way to isolate them from the general population. By the turn of the century, sanatorium care dominated efforts to treat tuberculosis in both the United States and Canada.[1]

After Dr. Edward Trudeau opened his pioneer sanatorium in 1886 at Saranac Lake, New York, in the heart of the Adirondack Mountains, it became a model for TB treatment on both sides of the border. Canada's first TB sanatorium opened in 1897 on the shores of Lake Muskoka near Gravenhurst, Ontario. By 1925, there were more than five hundred TB sanatoriums in the United States alone; Canada, with its smaller population, had 61 by 1938. In the absence of a "magic bullet" medication, nearly all sanatoriums relied primarily on the triad of fresh air, enforced rest alternating with moderate exercise, and large quantities of nutritious food to treat the disease, especially to strengthen and build resistance in TB victims to prevent relapses. Sanatoriums provided close medical supervision and enforced isolation and strict rules governing patient life to prevent the spread of infection.

The National Jewish Hospital for Consumptives (NJH) and the Jewish Consumptives' Relief Society (JCRS) in Denver along with the Mount Sinai Sanatorium in Montreal provided the most advanced medical treatment available at the time to an increasing number of predominantly poor, Eastern European, Jewish immigrant consumptives, who migrated in large numbers to America beginning in the late 1880s and to Canada in the early 1900s in search of economic opportunities and to escape persecution in Russia. That tidal wave of immigration intersected with the rise of the North American tuberculosis movement and the proliferation of tuberculosis sanatoriums. In both Denver and Montreal, by the first decades of the twentieth century the number of Jewish tuberculosis victims, most of them members of the working class who had contracted the disease after their arrival in North America, had reached epidemic proportions. Confronted with the daunting prospect of contagion, the local Jewish communities made TB care a focus of philanthropic concern and responsibility.

This chapter will compare the manner in which these three American and Canadian TB institutions were founded, funded, and populated, and how patient treatment was carried out. It will also explore to what degree each sanatorium was a "Jewish" institution and whether regional differences or class affiliations trumped ethnic and religious commonalities. The demographic influence of the three sanatoriums on local Jewish population trends will also be examined. Since Mount Sinai was the *only* Jewish Canadian sanatorium, some of the patients from locations other than Montreal who entered the institution eventually settled in nearby Montreal permanently.[2] However, the vast majority of Jewish Eastern European immigrants were attracted to Montreal for economic reasons rather than in search of better health. Montreal was at that time the centre of Canada's garment industry, and like New York, its numerous factories, many of them owned by established Jews, provided jobs for many newcomers. Labouring in congested factories was often linked to pulmonary tuberculosis, nicknamed "the tailor's disease," which increasingly was recognized as a disease of the working poor.

Figure 8.1: Exterior of Mount Sinai Sanatorium and grounds, Montreal, ca. 1930s. Courtesy Canadian Jewish Congress Charities Committee National Archives.

Figure 8.2: Nurse taking temperature of male tuberculosis patient on the verandah of National Jewish Hospital for Consumptives, Denver, Colorado, 1907. Open-air therapy was a cornerstone of TB treatment at the turn of the century. Courtesy Beck Archives, Special Collections, University Libraries, University of Denver.

In stark contrast, Denver was home to very little manufacturing in the early twentieth century, but the promise of a cure for tuberculosis in one of the many local sanatoriums attracted tens of thousands of people to the city between the 1880s and 1930s. TB had a profound demographic influence on Denver's population growth, particularly that of its Jewish community. According to one early report, by 1925 as much as 60 percent of Colorado's population had migrated to the state, either directly or indirectly, for treatment of tuberculosis. This figure may have even been higher with regard to Denver's Jewish population.[3]

In Denver, many Russian Jewish consumptives who were able to bring their illness under control settled there permanently, and relatives and *landsleit* often followed. They helped grow the Denver Jewish community exponentially and at the same time made significant contributions to the philanthropic, cultural, political, commercial, and religious life of the larger community. For example, Eastern European Jewish women immigrants were the prime movers behind the Denver Sheltering Home for Jewish Children, which opened in 1907 to aid the children of tuberculosis victims, and it attracted the support of Denver's Jews from all strata of society. The Sheltering Home eventually evolved into the world-renowned Jewish National Home for Asthmatic Children.[4]

Many physicians considered high altitude and fresh mountain air an especially healthful environment for consumptives. Denver, near the foothills of the American Rockies, and Sainte-Agathe-des-Monts, in the Laurentian Mountains, 100 kilometres northwest of Montreal (about a two-hour train trip in the early years), fit the "prescription" perfectly. By 1896, Colorado was being flatteringly referred to as "the World's Sanatorium"; likewise, in the early twentieth century the Laurentian Mountains attracted many Canadian tuberculosis victims seeking informal healing. In both locations, TB sufferers were "chasing the cure."[5] Many of them found lodgings in private homes or boarding houses, but usually without proper medical supervision.

The small but largely acculturated and affluent German-Jewish Reform community brought the sanatorium movement to Denver in 1899, when it opened NJH. During its first year, the sanatorium treated 149 patients: 121 men and 28 women.[6] It was followed in September 1904 by a second nationally based Denver Jewish sanatorium, the JCRS, organized by Eastern European immigrants. By the end of the year, twenty patients had been treated and housed in fifteen wooden tent-cottages; within a short time the JCRS was treating as many patients as NJH.[7]

In Canada, in 1909, a former two-storey farmhouse in Prefontaine near Sainte-Agathe-des-Monts, donated by the Paris-based Jewish Colonization

Association, was converted into a small cabin with a capacity to treat twelve Jewish tuberculosis patients. However, it was clearly inadequate to address the growing number of Jewish victims of consumption affected by the TB epidemic in Montreal and other Canadian cities and towns. That same year, the Montreal Jewish community, whose leaders believed wholeheartedly in the efficacy of sanatorium care, began planning for the Mount Sinai Sanatorium.[8] As an early Admissions Committee chairman maintained, "there is no substitute for sanatorium treatment and any one unfortunately so afflicted should not hesitate to enter a sanatorium." Mount Sinai opened in 1912 in Sainte-Agathe on a 160-acre tract of land. It featured a new permanent building with a capacity of forty beds. It treated eighty-three patients in 1913, its first full year of operation.[9] Like the NJH and the JCRS, in effect Mount Sinai was a "national" institution since a significant proportion of Canadian Jewry at the time lived in Montreal, and as noted, Mount Sinai was the only Jewish sanatorium in the country.

All three institutions were founded by Jews to provide aid and relief, primarily to their indigent co-religionists, although both NJH and the JCRS were formally non-sectarian and the Mount Sinai administration asserted that it treated patients "irrespective of creed, nationality."[10] It is highly significant that care at the three Jewish institutions was provided free of charge. Nearly all contemporary sanatoriums, even those philanthropic undertakings provided by ethnic and religious groups, generally offered just a fraction of "charity" beds, and the majority of patients were charged at least a modest sum to help offset expenses.[11] That said, NJH's famous motto, "None May Enter Who Can Pay – None Can Pay Who Enter," applied to both the JCRS and Mount Sinai. Mount Sinai, however, actively encouraged contributions from the friends and family members of patients.[12] Without question, genuine altruism and Jewish tradition, which placed great emphasis on responsibility for the sick and indigent, influenced the establishment of NJH, the JCRS, and Mount Sinai as free sanatoriums.

At the same time, tensions in both the United States and Canada between the earlier established Jewish community and the Eastern European newcomers, who arrived in large numbers between 1880 and the mid-1920s, played out in the three sanatoriums in this study. In contrast to the JCRS, which arose from very humble beginnings, initiated by a small group of immigrant working-class tradesmen, NJH and Mount Sinai were founded and largely funded by already established middle- and upper-class Jews in their respective cities, who often operated from a sense of *noblesse oblige*. It should be noted, however, that the acculturated Jewish establishment families in Montreal were by this time more diverse than the predominantly German Jewish elite in the United States. For most of the nineteenth century, Jewish immigrants to Canada had come mainly by way of Great Britain. They first included Jews of Sephardic origin, then later on, of Polish, Lithuanian, and Prussian origins. Although the Sephardic Jewish population was very small, Montreal's first synagogue, Shearith Israel (Spanish and Portuguese), established in 1768, followed Sephardic rites in its prayer services despite the Ashkenazic background of many of its congregants.[13]

The opening of those two sanatoriums also reflected the desire of their founders to demonstrate that Jews not only "took care of their own" but also were loyal citizens who took seriously their duty to the broader community. As historian Naomi Cohen has observed in *Encounter with Emancipation*, at the time German Jews throughout America, and by extension their elite counterparts in Canada (largely of English rather than German origin), believed that philanthropy and charity were twin expressions of the strong civic responsibility of the Jew in society at large. Moreover, as members of a rising middle class, Jews in both countries hoped to enhance their position in general society "by chalking up an impressive record in philanthropy."[14] Of course, Jewish philanthropy in North America during that era often paralleled charitable activities among their gentile peers in broader society, but it also exhibited particular Jewish distinctions. For millennia, Jewish tradition had obligated both men and women to fulfill the concepts of *tsedakah*, according to which charity was an act of righteousness and justice, and *gemilut chasadim*, acts of loving-kindness. Jewish values stressed the giving of both time and money.[15]

Indeed, the founders of Mount Sinai Sanatorium would undoubtedly have been pleased to learn that it would later be described as the "jewel in the crown of Jewish philanthropy in Montreal."[16] Historian Irving Abella confirms this outlook with regard to the Canadian Jewish community: "But Jewish philanthropy extended far beyond their own poor. As early as the first years of this century [the twentieth] the Jewish community contributed handsomely to non-Jewish institutions ... Montreal Jewry were in the forefront of much of the city's charitable work."[17] However, as historian Ira Robinson has observed, this may have been a more accurate description of the Montreal Jewish community in the late nineteenth rather than the early twentieth century. By 1931, at least one prominent local rabbi had criticized the Jewish community for not lending enough financial support to McGill University and the two Montreal gentile-based general hospitals, from which it had benefited.[18]

Denver and Montreal provide a rich source of comparison because their early Jewish communities exhibited some similarities as well as significant differences. After New France (which would eventually become the province of Quebec) formally came under British control in 1763, Jews were permitted to settle in the region, and before long some had become success-ful merchants and pillars of their local communities, even though the Jew-ish community remained tiny for most of the nineteenth century. Although Denver's Jewish community was not founded until a century later, in 1859, when fortune seekers arrived in Colorado in droves to seek their fortunes in gold, Jews served as important merchant suppliers there. In both cities, most Jews were engaged in commerce. Still, the Jewish population in each location was only around five hundred before the Eastern European influx of the mid-1880s. That influx began as a trickle; in Montreal, the real surge did not come until after 1900. Before their arrival, English-speaking estab-lished, acculturated Jews predominated in both locations. But in the case of Montreal, by the 1860s and 1870s the Jewish community already included a rising number of Polish Jews of very modest means, and early on institu-tions were established to assist indigent Jews.[19]

The Jewish population in Denver and Montreal grew rapidly through the first decades of the twentieth century, augmented by newcomers from Russia. Denver's Jewish population had risen to about 17,000 by 1927; in the larger urban centre of Montreal, the Jewish community grew even more dramatically, by 1931 numbering close to 58,000.[20] For the most part, Jews in both cities were well integrated in the early years, and some became respected, pivotal members of their general communities, sometimes even entering the upper ranks of society.

In Montreal, for example, tobacco magnate Mortimer Davis, the son of English and German-Jewish immigrants, became a leading Canadian busi-nessman and philanthropist and was ultimately knighted by King George V in 1916 – the first Canadian Jew to receive that honour. Davis also became a leading figure in the Montreal Jewish community and a primary funder and founder of the Mount Sinai Sanatorium when it opened in 1912.[21] Promi-nent Montreal Jewish clothing manufacturer Mark Workman served as the early Mount Sinai Sanatorium president. It is noteworthy that both Davis and Workman became members of the "uptown" Reform congregation Emanu-El, where Workman's son-in-law Nathan Gordon served as rabbi for a decade beginning in 1907. Gordon also appears to have worked on behalf of Mount Sinai.[22] Like so many members of the Jewish elite at the time, Davis and Workman likely believed that because of their affluence and privileged status, it was their duty to help take care of the poor, the needy, and the sick. Both also provided strong financial and moral sup-port to the creation in 1917 of a Federation of Jewish Charities in Montreal, which they felt would consolidate philanthropic work and fundraising and make it more efficient. Unsurprisingly, their largesse gave them a major role in deciding charitable allocations. Davis and Workman were named the federation's first two honorary presidents, positions they held for many years.[23]

Similarly, in Colorado, Frances Wisebart Jacobs, the wife of Bavarian-born Jewish merchant Abraham Jacobs, became an icon of philanthropy, and came to be known as Denver's "Mother of Charities." She moved comfortably in the growing city's elite social circles, was a member of the Reform Temple Emanuel, and, together with a Protestant minister and a Catholic priest, organized a federation of Denver charities that was the forerunner of the Community Chest, which later evolved into the modern, national American United Way. She also founded Denver's first free kindergarten and was the primary impetus behind the founding of NJH.[24] Davis, Workman, and Jacobs all worked diligently to found local Jewish sanatoriums that would be able to return ill consumptives back to their families and society in restored health.

Let us now turn to patient life and treatment. Fresh air was considered essential to tuberculosis treatment at all three sanatoriums, and patients at NJH, the JCRS, and Mount Sinai spent many hours outdoors in all seasons, often despite extreme heat or cold. They were often dispatched to open sun porches or verandas, and at the early JCRS, patients even resided in tent-cottages, where windows, doors, and roofs could be opened to maximize access to fresh air. Early on, long-time JCRS president Dr. Philip Hillkowitz extolled the virtues of Colorado's climate: "The benefits of open air life in tents are … well known to everybody … The mild Colorado climate renders the tents habitable all the year around. Even during one of our cold spells when the temperature dropped to 16 degrees below zero, additional blankets made the patients fairly comfortable."[25]

Similarly, William Friedman, the rabbi of the Denver Reform congregation Temple Emanuel, who was a central force in Denver's general community and a founder of NJH, observed in 1905 that "the patients are out of doors practically all day and many sleep out of doors at night with the exception of the short winter season."[26] This was confirmed by Shana Korngold, the sister of future Israeli Prime Minister Golda Meir, who was a patient at NJH in 1907 and then at the JCRS. She later recalled that "even on the coldest night did the sick ones, well wrapped up, sleep outside."[27]

At Canada's Mount Sinai, patients were encouraged to remain outside in the open air as much as possible. For example, the institution's 1922 annual report featured photographs of patients wearing coats and caps and wrapped in blankets, and reclining in rows on porch lounge chairs. One picture depicted a lone patient seated in an Adirondack chair on a veranda overlooking the beautiful mountain vista surrounding Mount Sinai and bore the caption "Another Bid for Life."[28] As time passed, open-air treat-

Figure 8.3: Patients undergoing heliotherapy on the veranda of the Texas Building at the Jewish Consumptives' Relief Society (JCRS) sanatorium, Denver, Colorado, 1930s. Courtesy Beck Archives, Special Collections, University Libraries, University of Denver.

ment was modified to more reasonable expectations, and heliotherapy became popular at all three institutions. In the 1920s and 1930s, it was a common sight to see patients lying outdoors in beds or recliners to soak up the "healthful" rays of the sun. Enforced periods of rest were also built into the sanatorium schedule.

If fresh air and rest were the foundations of sanatorium therapy, nutritious food in generous amounts formed the building blocks. In 1905, Russian-born Dr. Charles Spivak, the "guiding genius" and founder of the JCRS declared, "milk, eggs, and meat are the main factors in battling with the disease."[29] Spivak served as the executive secretary (chief administrator, as we would term it today) of the institution from its opening in 1904 until his death in 1927. Certainly, the food bills at NJH, the JCRS, and Mount Sinai reflected the centrality of those items in the patient diet. For example, at NJH in 1900, when the institution housed 149 patients, the bill for eggs alone reached $240 for a single month – a considerable sum at the time.[30] At Mount Sinai Sanatorium for the year 1917, when 72 TB patients were treated, the disbursement for butter and eggs was $2,808 and that for meat, $3,280.[31]

It is also interesting that NJH, the JCRS, and Mount Sinai all sponsored farms to provide patients with extra nutrition in the form of fresh milk, eggs, and vegetables. Providing their own food products helped reduce sanatorium food costs, and the surplus could sometimes be sold to the local community. Louis Salomon, the president of Mount Sinai in 1927, was proud to report the erection of a new chicken house, underwritten by the Nathanson family of Montreal, which "enables us not only to supply the patients plentifully with fowl and eggs, raised on the spot, but also showed a profit of $238.72."[32] Although the NJH was located on Denver's outskirts, its grounds were limited to a growing number of modern treatment, administrative, and laboratory buildings, so the Schoenberg Farm was located some distance from the hospital. However, both the JCRS and Mount Sinai built chicken coops, a barn, and a dairy on their more spacious acreage. At NJH and the JCRS, for many years Jewish agriculturists supervised the farm. At Mount Sinai, however, after the first several years, management of the farm was turned over to local French-speaking gentile Québécois farmers. In 1920 a capable sanatorium orderly was persuaded to take over the job, with good success.[33]

A detailed description of the patients' routine at the NJH demonstrates how fresh air, diet, and enforced leisure informed treatment. "The patient passes the day as follows: He arises at 6 a.m. and after a shower bath, a walk and such light work as making up his bed, if he is able, he breakfasts at 7:30. From that moment until bedtime he must lead a life in the open. Lunch of milk, eggs or special diet when ordered is given at 9:30 a.m. ... Twelve o'clock is dinner hour; then an hour's rest. The patients then amuse themselves by playing games or walking about the grounds. Lunch is again furnished between 2 and 3 p.m.; supper at 5, and a glass of milk or eggs at 8; 9 o'clock is bed-time. Temperature is taken twice daily at 9 a.m. and 4 p.m."[34]

In addition to the accepted three-pronged approach to tuberculosis treatment that focused on diet, fresh air, and rest as the prescription for "chasing the cure," as the years passed, surgical intervention to treat TB patients was introduced, although it ultimately proved to be of uncertain value. The JCRS was a pioneer in this area. The goal of the operations was to "rest" the affected lung to allow it to recover. Artificial pneumothorax, for example, was a procedure that injected air into the cavity between the lungs and chest walls, collapsed the lung, and prevented patients from taking a full breath.[35] Once the procedure became more widely accepted in the 1920s, about one quarter of patients at TB sanatoriums were subjected to the "collapse" therapy. By 1920, Mount Sinai was reporting that in addition to the "usual regime of treatment," it had "resorted to more radical procedures such as artificial pneumothorax and thoracoplasty (a procedure in which several ribs were removed to limit lung mobility)."[36] The JCRS secured its own pneumothorax machine in 1911, soon after the device was perfected. From then until the late 1940s thousands of procedures were performed; 1,400 in 1948 alone.[37]

If the three institutions were remarkably similar in daily care, they differed radically in the "type" of patient they focused upon. In the early twentieth century, influenced by Progressive Era theories of efficiency, many sanatoriums admitted TB victims who only exhibited incipient or moderately advanced disease. It was commonly thought that attempting to treat advanced cases only wasted time and money that could be more profitably directed towards patients who had a good chance of recovery. At NJH, administrators decried the futility of devoting time, money, and energy to "hopeless" patients. As the First Annual Report declared, "our aim is to cure, not to provide a last home for incurables."[38]

Mount Sinai also initially focused on incipient cases, but because of the scarcity of TB beds and the urgent need to treat the increasing number of local Jewish victims of the disease, it was often called upon to admit more serious cases, and it adopted a more flexible approach than that at NJH. In an early annual report for 1914, the medical superintendent noted that the "sanatorium had been originally intended for the early cases only ... [but out of necessity] we have never refused entrance into our Sanatorium to patients in the most hopeless condition."[39] TB had clearly reached epidemic proportions in the Montreal Jewish community at the time, and these challenges persisted over the years. In 1920, it was reiterated that "originally this institution was designed for incipient cases of tuberculosis and those presenting a fair prospect for recovery ... but in the course of time, however, it was found expedient to exercise a certain amount of discretion."[40]

But by 1922, as revealed by the words of Mount Sinai president Salomon, the sanatorium administration did not consider it desirable to admit patients in all stages of the disease: "Seeing that our capacity is so limited, and the number of applicants for admission so large, we have tried to adhere to the policy of only admitting early cases and moderately advanced cases that we feel we can do something for."[41] Five years later, in 1927, he complained, "unavoidably, we have been accumulating year by year more and more incurable cases and this has hampered our work with the incipient cases for which our institution was originally founded." Salomon bemoaned the fact that since there was no other place for incurables nearby, the problem was becoming untenable, and he re-emphasized the need for larger, more spacious quarters that would at least allow patients at differing stages of illness to be isolated from one another.[42]

Even if the leaders at each of the three sanatoriums did not always agree on policy, they were certainly aware of the existence, expertise, and reputation of their counterparts across the border. It is interesting that in 1925, President Louis Salomon had once again emphasized the need for a new building to accommodate the growing patient population at Mount Sinai. He observed that good advice for suitable architectural pointers for such a building could be obtained from experts in Montreal or from leading US institutions like the "Trudeau Sanatorium at Saranac Lake, N.Y. or the Jewish Consumptives' Relief Society at Denver."[43] Mount Sinai's fundraising efforts eventually succeeded; the long awaited, beautiful new Art Deco facility, which opened in the fall of 1930, provided ninety-two beds, staff quarters, and the backdrop for more modernized treatment.

In sharp contrast to both NJH and Mount Sinai, as part of its underlying philosophy the JCRS purposefully and by choice admitted patients in all stages of the disease, including those who were in the last stages of life. Indeed, the JCRS motto, "He Who Saves One Life Saves the World," foreshadowed its commitment to caring for even terminal cases. The JCRS followed the national norm for TB treatment in many ways, but it also followed a unique path that could be directly traced to Spivak's influence. "He [Spivak] was a pioneer in a new and enlightened method of healing the sick and poor," one observer wrote.[44] In other words, Spivak channelled his early radical political convictions into more empathetic and humane treatment of patients in general and especially towards unconventional and path-breaking treatment for tuberculosis victims with severe cases of the disease, who generally had been marginalized by the medical mainstream.

It should also be noted that Mount Sinai treated a modest number of juvenile consumptives in addition to the adults who were its primary focus. In 1917, of the seventy-two patients discharged, eight were younger than fifteen. The percentage of young people was fairly stable, but in 1922, of the eighty-three patients discharged, twenty-nine were recorded as being in their first or second decade. Tuberculosis was no respecter of class, gender, or age, but as was the case throughout the United States and Canada at the time, it most often struck victims in their twenties and thirties, in the prime of life. This was reflected at Mount Sinai, NJH, and the JCRS as well.[45] The JCRS did not admit children, but in 1920, NJH established the Hofheimer Preventorium. It was designed to provide underprivileged children, who were thought to be most susceptible to tuberculosis, with a healthier environment. Like their older counterparts, the children received medical supervision, nutritious food, and exposure to sunlight and fresh air to build their resistance. A small group of children with TB of the bone and joints were also admitted as NJH patients and sometimes remained at the sanatorium for several years at a time.[46]

Let us now ask: How "Jewish" was the patient population and the environment at NJH, the JCRS, and Mount Sinai? All three institutions kept careful statistical records concerning the patients, and clearly the vast majority who were admitted at NJH, the JCRS, and Mount Sinai were Eastern European immigrants. Although both NJH and the JCRS were formally non-sectarian, in reality most patients were "Russian" Jews. Of the first 97 patients at the JCRS from 1904 to 1906, 73 or 75.3 percent came from Russia, and of 4,568 patients from 1904 to 1923, 3,153 or 69 percent were Russian-born.[47] At NJH, 82 or 55 percent of the hospital's first 149 patients for the year 1900 hailed from Russia. (Of course, many patients who were not born in Russia were also Jewish, making the percentage of Jewish patients at both sanatoriums even higher.)[48] A 1936 publication reported that of the 20,000 patients who had been admitted to NJH from 1900 to 1936, fully two thirds were Jewish.[49]

At Mount Sinai, of the 64 patients treated in 1914, 35 were from Russia and 15 from Romania. Nineteen housewives, 18 tailors, and 7 seamstresses led the list of occupations.[50] Similarly, in 1917, 43 of the mostly Jewish 72 patients discharged from Mount Sinai in that year hailed from Russia and 3 from Romania. Twenty-one of those patients were tailors by occupation, and there were 11 housewives.[51] This pattern persisted for a number of years. Tailors headed the list of occupations at NJH and the JCRS for many years as well, which fit the pattern for the era. As noted previously, in both the United States and Canada, many East European Jews worked in the burgeoning garment industry, and some sickened in the congested, unsanitary, poorly ventilated sweatshops. As time passed, Russian and other Eastern European Jewish immigrants continued to lead the patient lists, but tailors gradually gave way to other professions such as peddlers and clerks as the immigrants became more acculturated and moved up the economic and social ladder. The number of non-Jewish patients at Mount Sinai was reported only sporadically, but in 1920, for example, of the 47 patients treated, 5 were gentiles.[52]

Although the two Denver Jewish sanatoriums operated in a similar manner in day-to-day patient treatment, for many years NJH and the JCRS competed for funding locally and nationally and exhibited radically different philosophies. For example, NJH leader Rabbi Friedman criticized the JCRS policy of accepting patients at all stages of the disease: "The appeal of the JCRS extends an open invitation to the Jewish communities of the United States to send their penniless consumptives to Colorado ... The Society cannot possibly benefit the incurable consumptives and is a dangerous menace to Colorado."[53] A few years later an editorial in the JCRS publication *The Sanatorium* shot back a disdainful rejoinder. It criticized the increasingly popular Progressive Era scientific and sociological methods for dispensing aid incorporated at NJH. The editorial, probably written by Spivak or Hillkowitz, claimed that personal and human elements were entirely lacking in such an approach and urged instead that charity be "of the heart, and not the head," reflecting how philanthropy had been dispensed in Eastern Europe.[54]

Most patients at NJH and the JCRS were not Denver residents, but instead flocked to Denver from all parts of the United States. Fundraisers from both institutions, therefore, fanned out across America to raise money, and Ladies' Auxiliaries were established in almost every large and medium-sized city in the country to bolster support. NJH sought primarily wealthy contributors, while the JCRS, strongly influenced by Spivak's early socialist leanings, mostly solicited members of the working class. Early on he advised one of the JCRS travelling fundraisers that "if our Institution is to be a people's institution, it should be supported by the people only. Let us collect our moneys in dollars and quarters."[55] Although their donations were necessarily modest, they supported the institution en masse.

At first, income at Mount Sinai depended on a combination of donations, fundraising events, and yearly dues and subscriptions. Mount Sinai's supporters were generally affluent, but after 1915 the institution also received generous, long-sought-after funding from the Montreal municipal government, which lessened the burden on the Jewish community. In 1917, Mount Sinai also became a beneficiary of the new Jewish Federation of Montreal, which provided the sanatorium with a substantial yearly allocation and helped alleviate the need for multiple solicitations. Like their counterparts across North America, the established Jewish communities in Montreal and in Denver generally viewed the plight of their Eastern European counterparts with sympathy and a sense of obligation, but they also regarded these new immigrants, with their "Old World" religious traditions, cultural customs, Yiddish "jargon," and sometimes radical politics as a source of embarrassment and even as a threat to their own acceptance in American and Canadian society. They gave generously of their time and money to aid "Russian" Jews in need, but at the same time worked diligently to help them become acculturated as quickly as possible. As Abella put it with regard to the Canadian Jewish establishment, "up to the great migration at the end of the nineteenth century, the Jews of Ontario and Quebec were comfortable, well integrated and totally English Canadian in their culture, attitude, and language."[56]

The ambivalence of the elite German Jews towards the Russian Jews in Denver was reflected graphically at NJH. The sanatorium not only provided free, high-level care but also offered classes in English, civics, bookkeeping, and other vocational skills. As Seraphine Pisko, the executive secretary of NJH from 1911 to 1937, put it, "we taught Americanization before it became a national by-word."[57] Moreover, Yiddish, so dear to the heart of many Eastern European Jews, was often disparaged at NJH, as was traditional Jewish culture and religion. A 1905 NJH publicity pamphlet maintained that "we are making American citizens of the Russian men and women [patients] ... who came to us ignorant of all but the Yiddish language ... They learn quickly between the letters of the alphabet the true meaning of culture and freedom. The books they read at NJH help to disenthrall them from the narrowness of their Ghetto view of life."[58]

Although a Jewish chapel was built at NJH for religious worship in 1907 (and, in fact, the JCRS and Mount Sinai also featured beautifully constructed synagogues), and major Jewish holidays such as Rosh Hashanah, Yom Kippur, and Passover were celebrated, the first medical director at NJH maintained that following Jewish dietary laws at the hospital was "inadvisable for medical reasons," and insisted that milk, meat, and butter be served at all meals – a direct violation of Jewish dietary laws.[59] The director was a Jewish physician who was a member of the Reform Congregation Emanuel, and should have been aware of the potential backlash. Needless to say, this policy offended many Eastern European Jewish immigrant patients; even those who were not necessarily observant felt that such a move was mis-

Figure 8.4: Procession to celebrate a new Torah scroll at the Jewish Consumptives' Relief Society (JCRS) sanatorium, Denver, Colorado, 1930s. Courtesy Beck Archives, Special Collections, University Libraries, University of Denver.

guided at best as well as patently condescending. Even though Mrs. Pisko and other NJH administrators tried to please patients in 1921 by hiring a Jewish cook who could provide traditional Jewish dishes like chicken soup with noodles, a kosher kitchen was not established at NJH until 1923. When the kosher kitchen finally opened, it was lauded for promoting goodwill among the patients; but it was not viewed as a reflection of Jewish dietary imperatives.[60]

JCRS leaders Dr. Spivak and Dr. Hillkowitz, the son of Denver's senior Orthodox rabbi at the time, were themselves Eastern European immigrants and as such were exceptionally sensitive to the religious and cultural traditions of their brethren. Spivak had grown up in a traditional Jewish home but had been a radical revolutionary in his youth. He had fled Russia in 1882 at the age of twenty-one to avoid being arrested by the secret police, and ultimately received a degree in medicine from Jefferson Medical College in Philadelphia. He moved to Denver in 1896 due to his wife's ill health. The JCRS was founded in 1904 by a number of Eastern European immigrants who felt that NJH sometimes treated its largely destitute patients in a condescending manner and that it was often insensitive to the religious traditions of many Eastern European Jews. At the helm of the JCRS, Spivak was able to merge his fierce commitment to medicine and science with his complex socialist and Jewish roots.

The JCRS, founded and funded by Eastern European Jews, insisted that a Jewish environment was vital to the treatment of consumptive Russian Jews. As Dr. Spivak put it, "if he [the patient] feels at home in the place his recovery is hastened; otherwise it is retarded or prevented."[61] In May 1906, for example, Spivak approvingly recorded that "the [recent] Passover was celebrated this year with great éclat and enthusiasm ... The Seder was conducted in good old Orthodox fashion."[62] Moreover, from the beginning, Spivak maintained that the JCRS intended to "inaugurate a radical departure from similar organizations, by eliminating from the conduct and management of the Sanatorium, anything and everything that would tend to remind the inmates of the fact that they are 'public charges.'"[63]

Similarly, many annual reports for the Mount Sinai sanatorium refer to Jewish observances at the institution and note that the institution's leaders were very aware of the religious and cultural needs of their Jewish patients. This probably reflected the fact that Reform Judaism in Montreal at the time was a minority phenomenon and did not enjoy the same sort of prestige as it did in the United States during that era. As noted earlier, German-Jewish immigration to Canada in the nineteenth century was very modest compared to that to the United States, and the rise of Reform Judaism in America was closely tied to the development of the German-Jewish community. In addition, because of the strong English influence, "Canadian Jews tended to be more traditional in their religious practices than their American cousins."[64]

So it is very understandable that like the JCRS, Mount Sinai featured a strictly kosher kitchen from the beginning, with separate milk and meat dishes and food preparation areas. In 1914, it was noted that special festive meals were served for Jewish holidays, "the ceremonies observed in the strictest manner," and that "the services of a *schochet* [ritual slaughterer] at Ste. Agathe ensure fresh and kosher meat and the contentment that follows therefrom."[65] In the Montreal Jewish Federation's *First Annual Report* of 1917, it was recorded that "the usual services were conducted during the Holy Days and the Passover Festival was strictly observed," presumably with traditional Passover Seders and the elimination of leavened bread and other forbidden items from the menu.[66] In the 1919 *Third Annual Report*, reference was made to an expenditure of $30 for a cantor, who likely led synagogue services for the Jewish High Holidays of Rosh Hashanah and Yom Kippur.[67] Similarly, later in 1925, appreciation was extended to "those who rendered services and who helped make the Jewish religious holidays pleasant to the patients."[68]

Although Yiddish was discouraged at NJH, appreciation for the Yiddish language was certainly highly evident at the JCRS. Spivak played a central role in the Yiddish culture that permeated the JCRS, and he was perhaps best known internationally for the Yiddish dictionary he co-authored with Yehoash (Solomon Bloomgarden) in 1911. Yehoash was one of the most famous Yiddish writers living in America in the first decades of the twentieth century. A victim of TB, he arrived in Denver in 1899 to informally "chase the cure." Through his friendship with Spivak, Yehoash became active in the early JCRS, using his writing talents to help publicize the sanatorium's work. He also sometimes travelled to the East Coast to raise funds for the institution.[69] Also, the JCRS published sections of its annual reports in Yiddish and supported several patient publications that often featured Yiddish poems and stories.

As at the JCRS, there was a strong Yiddish culture at Mount Sinai, and indeed most of the Jewish patients for decades were Yiddish-speaking. In the early 1920s, the institution published a monthly bulletin called *The Tablets*, which featured articles in both Yiddish and English about tuberculosis treatment aimed at patients as well as the sanatorium's Jewish community supporters in Montreal. That articles were written in Yiddish confirm that the sanatorium leaders were well aware of the large population of Yiddish speakers in its midst.[70] One of its most famous was leading Yiddish writer Sholem Shtern, who emigrated from Poland to Montreal in 1927 at the age of twenty. Soon after, he contracted TB, and for several years was a patient at Mount Sinai, where he wrote poems that were printed in Jewish newspapers around the world. In the 1960s, he published a novel titled *The White House*, which was based on his earlier experiences at Mount Sinai.[71]

By the second decade of the twentieth century, the face of American and Canadian Jewry had been transformed and its leadership had begun to change hands from the earlier established Jewish community to the Eastern European immigrants and their children. As Abella observed of Canada, by 1914 it was no longer the "Anglicized, comfortable, integrated community" it had been thirty years before the arrival of "Yiddish-speaking, Orthodox, penurious immigrants."[72] Canadian historian Gerald Tulchinsky has noted that as early as 1900, Montreal's Jewish community exhibited "a more decidedly Jewish flavour" as a result of the newcomers.[73]

And by 1920 many of the Russian Jews in America, and in the following decades in Canada, had become successful and established in their own right. The Eastern European Jews not only influenced the development of NJH, the JCRS, and Mount Sinai, but the larger community as well. Although they had appreciated the generous efforts on their behalf by the Jewish establishment, they felt that the largesse was sometimes delivered with condescension, and they clearly longed to take the helm of their own self-help institutions. According to Spivak, writing in 1914, the success of the JCRS sanatorium demonstrated that "the first lesson [the JCRS] taught was that a national organization can be brought into the world without the midwifery of the rich and professional philanthropist ... It proved to the world that a national organization can be launched, built and maintained by small tradesmen and working-men, the so-called hoi-polloi."[74]

Patient treatment was remarkably similar across NJH, the JCRS, and Mount Sinai, but as we have seen, the three institutions differed in philosophy. Those differences, though, appear to have been largely rooted in class, ethnic structure, and background rather than in region. In both Denver and Montreal, the Jewish elite appears to have viewed the indigent incoming patients, who were predominantly traditional Yiddish-speaking Eastern European Jewish immigrants, in a similar manner and hoped to acculturate them as quickly as possible. They were certainly motivated in part by their concern that the newcomers not jeopardize the social status of the earlier acculturated Jews in the larger society. However, there were some significant nuances. The leaders at Mount Sinai Sanatorium appear to have been far more sensitive to the religious and cultural needs of their Eastern European patients than those at NJH.

This undoubtedly was a result of the fact that the early-established Montreal community was more diverse than that of the largely German-

Jewish early settlers in Denver. Early Canadian Jewry were mainly English, with some Sephardic, Prussian, and Polish members, along with a much more modest number of German Jews, who were more traditional in their religious observance. In Montreal by the 1850s, the Jewish community had already encountered Eastern European Jews and had begun to absorb groups of Polish immigrants, some of them impoverished. In addition, although Denver's first congregation was Reform, the first synagogues in Montreal were Orthodox. Montreal's Temple Emanu-El was not established until the early 1880s. Indeed, its founders were "a small minority upon whom the aims of American Reform Judaism had made an indelible impression," and who naturally "looked southward [to the United States] for leadership and assistance."[75] Reform Judaism, then, was largely an "import" from the United States; it arrived in Canada later in the community's development than it had in America, and it was weaker as well as slower to take hold. Thus, as early as the 1860s there were already various ethic, economic, and religious streams in the Montreal Jewish community.[76]

NJH certainly exhibited a different outlook than that of the leaders at the JCRS, who themselves were of the ranks of the Russian Jews; but in reality, through educational, vocational, and social programs, all three Jewish sanatoriums served as vehicles of acculturation for their patients, helping them to acquire better English skills and to accustom themselves to life in their new host country. For example, at the JCRS, despite the supportive Yiddish environment, American holidays like Thanksgiving and the Fourth of July were celebrated with great appreciation and enthusiasm, although the festivities included kosher refreshments and an emphasis on the compatibility between American and Jewish ideals. Patients were taught English, American customs, and practical skills, albeit in perhaps a more supportive environment. Jews had always exhibited a great respect for physicians, and the predominantly Eastern European patients at the JCRS held Spivak and Hillkowitz in high regard, for besides supplying high-quality medical care, they served as a "cultural brokers" who helped the patients navigate their acculturation to American life while respecting their religious and cultural origins. As time passed, NJH, the JCRS, and Mount Sinai all became self-contained quasi-towns, with their own patient wards and treatment rooms, kitchens, synagogues, libraries, farms, dairies, commissaries, laboratories, classrooms, and training centres.

As a leading medical and immigration scholar, Alan Kraut, has pointed out, health and disease played a major role in "international migration and cultural integration." This was a phenomenon clearly apparent at all three Jewish sanatoriums examined in this study. Moreover, Kraut noted that at the turn of the twentieth century, "the health care field [often] became a cultural battleground" between the established residents and the new, and sometimes "even among the newcomers themselves." Studying the development of the three early Jewish tuberculosis health care institutions in this chapter can teach us as much about issues of ethnic identity, social integration, and acculturation as medical issues.[77]

Through sanatorium treatment, public health measures, and education, and the discovery and use of such drugs as streptomycin (1944), para-aminosalicylic acid (1946), and Isoniazid (1953), the once dreaded disease of tuberculosis finally came under control in North America, although it has never been fully conquered. By the early 1950s, NJH, the JCRS, and Mount Sinai had all changed their focus from tuberculosis to other medical and health challenges. Today, although their names have changed, these three institutions continue to play an important role in maintaining the health and well being of the residents of Denver and Montreal. National Jewish Health, the successor to NJH, is a world leader in the treatment of respiratory and immune diseases; the JCRS has evolved into the respected AMC Cancer Research Center; and Mount Sinai Sanatorium has moved to Montreal, where it is known as Mount Sinai Hospital and currently special-

Figure 8.5: Bridge at Mount Sinai Sanatorium and entrance to the main building, Montreal, ca. 1930s. Courtesy Canadian Jewish Congress Charities Committee National Archives.

izes in respiratory diseases and high-level palliative and long-term care. All three reflect the transformation from the typical early-twentieth-century charitable and ethnic health care institution to the modern-day medical complex.

The connection between Jews, health, and medicine has a long history stretching back to Biblical times.[78] But as historian Jacob Jay Lindenthal put it in his seminal essay "Abi Gezunt: Health and the Eastern European Jewish Immigrant," in modern times tuberculosis was one of the diseases most feared by Jews, and "it was also the disease which most galvanized Jews into action resulting in endless fund drives and the establishment of a network of sanatoria."[79] NJH, the JCRS, and Mount Sinai were three of the best known and most effective of the North American Jewish sanatoriums that were built and maintained largely as the result of Jewish philanthropy. All three social welfare institutions ceased to function as tuberculosis sanatoriums over half a century ago, but inspired by age-old Jewish traditions of *tzedakah* and social responsibility, they have provided a legacy of healing and care that endures to this day.

Notes

1 Georgina Feldberg, *Disease and Class: Tuberculosis and the Shaping of Modern North American Society* (New Brunswick: Rutgers University Press, 1995), 40–46.

2 Unfortunately, Mount Sinai annual reports do not contain information about where its TB patients contracted the disease. At the JCRS and NJH, it was clear from documented statistics that almost all patients had migrated to Denver from cities across the United States, especially large urban centres like New York, Philadelphia, and Chicago, to specifically "chase the cure."

3 Health Committee of the City Club of Denver, *Tuberculosis in Denver*, 1925, 5; James Giese, "Tuberculosis and the Growth of Denver's Jewish Community: The Accommodation of an Immigrant Group to a Medium-Sized City, 1900-1920," Ph.D. diss., University of Colorado, 1979, 11.

4 For more on the Jewish Sheltering Home, see Jeanne Abrams, "For a Child's Sake: The Denver Sheltering Home for Jewish Children in the Progressive Era," *American Jewish History* 79 (Winter 1989–90): 181–202.

5 For a detailed study of early tuberculosis sanatoriums in Colorado, see Jeanne Abrams, *Blazing the Tuberculosis Trail* (Denver: Colorado Historical Society, 1990). Travelling to the American West to help cure pulmonary diseases, particularly tuberculosis, had become common by the early 1840s. See Abrams, "On the Road Again: Consumptives Traveling for Health in the American West, 1840-1925," *Great Plains Quarterly* 30 (Fall 2010): 271–85.

6 *NJH First Annual Report*, 63, National Jewish Hospital Collection, Beck Archives, Special Collections, University Libraries, University of Denver.

7 *JCRS First Annual Report*, 1905, 30–33, box 170, JCRS Collection, Beck Archives, Special Collections, University Libraries, University of Denver.

8 *100 Years: Mount Sinai Hospital Montreal 2008–2009 Annual Report*, 3.
9 *Third Annual Report of Mount Sinai Hospital*, 40–41, General Documentation Series ZC: Organization Files, file 12, Canadian Jewish Congress Charities Committee National Archives.
10 Cited in Annmarie Adams and Mary Anne Poutanen, "Architecture, Religion, and Tuberculosis in Sainte-Agathe-des-Monts, Quebec," *Scientia Canadensis* 32 (2009): 7.
11 See, for example, Abrams, *Blazing the Tuberculosis Trail*, 52, 65, 70.
12 Adams and Poutanen, "Architecture, Religion, and Tuberculosis," 7.
13 Irving Abella, *A Coat of Many Colours: Two Centuries of Jewish Life in Canada* (Toronto: Key Porter, 1990), 113.
14 Naomi Cohen, *Encounter with Emancipation* (Philadelphia: Jewish Publication Society, 1984), 114, 117.
15 Susan M. Chambre, "Parallel Power Structures, Invisible Careers, and the Changing Nature of American Jewish Women's Philanthropy," *Journal of Jewish Communal Service* 76 (Spring 2000): 206, 208.
16 Adams and Poutanen, "Architecture, Religion, and Tuberculosis," 2.
17 Abella, *A Coat of Many Colours*, 128.
18 See Ira Robinson, "'The Other Side of the Coin': The Anatomy of a Public Controversy in the Montreal Jewish Community, 1931," *Studies in Religion/Sciences*, 27 June 2011, http://sir.sagepub.com/content/early 2011/05/12/0008429811410816.
19 Gerald Tulchinsky, *Canada's Jews: A People's Journey* (Toronto: University of Toronto Press, 2008), 71.
20 For population statistics, see Ira Robinson, "Historical Introduction to the Jewish Community of Quebec," www.fedeartioncja.org/en/jewish-montreal/history; Allen DuPont Breck, *The Centennial History of the Jews of Colorado* (Denver: Hirschfeld Press, 1960), 321; and Tuchinsky, *Canada's Jews*, appendix.
21 *Dictionary of Canadian Biography Online*.
22 Gerald J.J. Tulchinsky, "'Justice and Only Justice Thou Shalt Pursue: Considerations on the Social Voice of Canada's Reform Rabbis," in *Religion and Public Life in Canada: Historical and Comparative Perspectives*, ed. Marguerie Van Die (Toronto: University of Toronto Press, 2001), 313–14.
23 Federation of Jewish Philanthropies, *First Annual Report of Federation of Jewish Philanthropies*, 1917, 15, Ctn. 025, Federation CJA Fonds 1001, Container 25, Jewish Public Library of Montreal.
24 For a more detailed description of the life of Frances Jacobs, see Jeanne Abrams, *Jewish Women Pioneering the Frontier Trail: A History in the American West* (New York: NYU Press, 2006).
25 Dr. Philip Hillkowitz, *JCRS First Annual Report*, 1905, box 170, JCRS Collection, Beck Archives.
26 Rabbi William Friedman, "Modern Methods of Fighting Tuberculosis: What the National Jewish Hospital for Consumptives Is Doing," address before the National Jewish Chautauqua Society, 1905, 8, 9, box 22, NJH Collection, Beck Archives.
27 Shana Korngold, *Zikhroynes* [Memories}," from an excerpt reprinted in *Rocky Mountain Jewish Historical Society Notes* 2 (March 1979): 3.
28 "Mount Sinai Sanatorium Report," in *Sixth Annual Report of the Federation of Jewish Philanthropies of Montreal*, 1922, 17, 19, Montreal Jewish Public Library.
29 Charles Spivak, *JCRS First Annual Report*, 1905, 60, JCRS Collection, Beck Archives. For an in-depth study of the life of Spivak, see Jeanne Abrams, *Dr. Charles David Spivak: A*

Jewish Immigrant and the American Tuberculosis Movement (Boulder: University Press of Colorado, 2009).

30 *NJH First Annual Report*, 1900, NJH Collection, Beck Archives.

31 "Mount Sinai Sanatorium Report," in *First Annual Report, Federation of Jewish Philanthropies of Montreal and Constituent Societies*, 1917, 70, Montreal Jewish Public Library.

32 "Mount Sinai Sanatorium Report of the President," in *Eleventh Annual Report of the Federation of Jewish Philanthropies of Montreal*, 1927, 42, 43, Montreal Jewish Public Library.

33 "Mount Sinai Sanatorium Report," in *Fourth Annual Report, Federation of the Jewish Philanthropies of Montreal*, 1920, 59, Montreal Jewish Public Library.

34 Friedman, "Modern Methods of Fighting Tuberculosis," 8, NJH Collection.

35 Frank Ryan, *The Forgotten Plague: How the Battle against Tuberculosis Was Won – and Lost* (Boston: Little, Brown, 1993), 28.

36 "Mount Sinai Report," in *Fourth Annual Report of Federation of Jewish Philanthropies of Montreal*, 1920, 64.

37 *45th Annual Medical Report of the JCRS*, 1948, 3, JCRS Collection, box 255, Beck Archives.

38 *NJH First Annual Report*, 1900, 17.

39 *Mount Sinai Sanatorium Third Annual Report for 1914*, 23, 27, CJCCC.

40 "Mount Sinai Sanatorium Report," in *Fourth Annual Reports of Federation of Jewish Philanthropies of Montreal*, 1920, 63.

41 "Mount Sinai Annual Report," in *Sixth Annual Report of the Federation of Jewish Philanthropies*, 1922, 15.

42 Mount Sinai Annual Report," in *Eleventh Annual Report of the Federation of Jewish Philanthropies in Montreal*, 41.

43 "President's Report," in *Ninth Annual Report of the Federation of Jewish Philanthropies of Montreal*, 1925, 43.

44 *Thirty Years of Saving Lives* (Denver: Jewish Consumptives' Relief Society, 1934), 29.

45 "Mount Sinai Annual Report," 1917, 65; "Mount Sinai Annual Report," 1922, 17; "Mount Sinai Annual Report," 1925, 44.

46 Mary Ann Fitzharris and Jeanne Abrams, *A Place to Heal: The History of National Jewish Medical and Research Center* (Boulder: Johnson Publishing, 1997), 27.

47 *JCRS Second Annual Report*, 1906, and *The Sanatorium* 18 (October–December 1924): 104–5, box 170, JCRS Collection, Beck Archives.

48 *NJH First Annual Report*, 1900, 63–65, NJH Collection, Beck Archives.

49 *News of the National* 4 (June 1936): 3, NJH Collection, Beck Archives, Box 10.

50 *Third Annual Report of Mount Sinai Sanatorium*, 26.

51 "Mount Sinai Sanatorium Report," in *First Annual Report of the Federation of Jewish Philanthropies of Montreal*, 72.

52 "Mount Sinai Sanatorium Report," in *Fourth Annual Report of the Federation of Jewish Philanthropies of Montreal*, 63.

53 *Jewish Outlook* (Denver), 15 April 1904, 7–8.

54 *The Sanatorium* 1 (March 1907): 41, JCRS Collection, box 170, Beck Archives.

55 Dr. Charles Spivak to Anna Hillkowitz, 14 May 1906, JCRS Collection, box 223, Beck Archives.

56 Abella, *A Coat of Many Colours*, 115.

57 Seraphine Pisko, undated NJH press release, ca. 1923, Pisko file, 1923–24, box 33, Pisko/Dauby/Grabfelder correspondence, NJH Collection.

58 "Throwing Out the Lifelines," October 1905, 10, NJH Collection, box 22.

59 *Jewish Outlook* (Denver), 7 October 1904.

60 Seraphine Pisko to Nathan Dauby, 14 June 1921, and unidentified clipping, "A Kosher Kitchen Is Installed at NJH," 7 April 1923, NJH Collection, box 33.

61 "Editorial," *The Sanatorium* 3 (September–October 1909): 253, JCRS Collection, box 170, Beck Archives.

62 "Seder Service," *The Sanatorium* 1 (May 1906): 55, JCRS Collection, box 170, Beck Archives.

63 *First Annual Report of the JCRS*, 60, JCRS Collection, box 170.

64 Ira Robinson and Mervn Butovsky, *Renewing Our Days: Montreal Jews in the Twentieth Century* (Montreal: Véhicule Press, 1995), 11–12.

65 *Third Annual Report for Mount Sinai Sanatorium for 1914*, 8, 9. CJCCC.

66 "Mount Sinai Sanatorium Report," in *First Annual Report of the Federation of Jewish Philanthropies of Montreal*, 63.

67 "Mount Sinai Sanatorium Report," in *Third Annual Report of the Federation of Jewish Philanthropies of Montreal*, 54.

68 "President's Report," in *Ninth Annual Report of the Federation of Jewish Philanthropies of Montreal*, 1925, 44.

69 "The Yehoash Receptions," *The Sanatorium* 2 (November 1908): 285, JCRS Collection, box 170, Beck Archives.

70 "Mount Sinai President's Report," in *Seventh Annual Report of the Jewish Philanthropies of Montreal*, 1923, 38.

71 Sholem Shtern, *The White House: A Novel in Verse*, trans. Max Rosefeld (Montreal and New York: Warbooke Publishers, 1974.) For more about consumptive Yiddish writers who were patients at the JCRS and Mount Sinai, see Ernest B. Gilman, *Yiddish Poetry and the Tuberculosis Sanatorium, 1900–1970* (Syracuse: Syracuse University Press, 2014).

72 Abella, *A Coat of Many Colours*, 103.

73 Tulchinsky, *Canada's Jews*, 109.

74 *The Sanatorium* 7 (September–December 1914): 95, JCRS Collection, box 170, Beck Archives.

75 Michael Brown, "The Beginnings of Reform Judaism in Canada," *Jewish Social Studies* 34 (October 1972): 324.

76 See Tuchinsky, *Canada's Jews*, 71–73; and Robinson and Butovsky, *Renewing Our Days*, 13–20.

77 Alan Kraut, "Foreign Bodies: The Perennial Negotiation over Health and Culture in a Nation of Immigrants," *Journal of American Ethnic History* 23 (Winter 2004): 17; and Kraut, *Silent Travelers: Germs, Genes, and the "Immigrant Menace"* (New York: Basic Books, 1994), 190.

78 See, for example, Mitchell B. Hart, *The Healthy Jew: The Symbiosis of Judaism and Modern Medicine* (New York: Cambridge University Press, 2007).

79 Jacob Jay Lindenthal, "*Abi Gezunt*: Health and the Eastern European Jewish Immigrant," *American Jewish History* 70 (June 1981): 434.

NINE

Performing Jewish?
Heinz Unger, Gustav Mahler, and the Musical Strains of German-Jewish Identity in Canada and the United States

Hernan Tesler-Mabé

"The hero ... suffers three blows of fate, of which the third fells him like a tree." This is how Alma Mahler – perhaps apocryphally – described the extra-musical significance of the three hammer blows in the finale to Gustav Mahler's Symphony No. 6 ("Tragic"). These words, meant as commentary on the tragedies the composer confronted, also describe those faced by one of his greatest devotees, the German-born Canadian conductor Heinz Unger. Unger, thrice the victim of fate, failed to complete his recording of Mahler's "Tragic Symphony" after suffering a fatal heart attack on 25 February 1965. This blow was but the second struck him; in 1933, the Jewish conductor was exiled from his native Germany after Hitler's rise to power. The third blow – his posthumous neglect by both the music community at large and the Jewish Canadian community to which he was tied by a faith to which he remained true throughout his life – resounds to this day.

Heinz Unger (1895–1965) was the product of a Central European milieu in which Jewish identity had evolved into a religious allegiance sub-

153

servient to the cause of the nation-state. Yet Unger's passion for Mahler's music was paradoxically also an expression of a cultural affinity predicated on the shared vernacular of an assimilated Jewish experience. Unger, although once described by American Reform rabbi Maxwell Dubin as "one of the few Jewish maestros who refused to compromise his faith," possessed an assimilated Jewish identity and artistic stance that failed to accord with prevailing Canadian Jewish modes of self-understanding. My hope is that this chapter will bring into relief the alternative sites of Jewish identity in Canada during the postwar period and in this way help us better comprehend Jewish identity in North America.

Because of the strength of the largely Eastern European Jewish community during much of the twentieth century, other narratives or expressions of Jewishness in Canada have long been subsumed. Rather than resist this orthodoxy, this chapter resituates the frame of reference, arguing that on account of the narrow bounds of Canadian Jewish identity and cultural expression from the late 1940s through to the mid-1960s, the admittedly smaller number of German Jews who settled in Canada remained tied to their fellow German Jews beyond national borders or in select geographical pockets rather than attempting to embed themselves in what was, for them, a foreign Jewish culture derived in large part from Eastern Europe. Indeed, the locus of German-Jewish identity did not lie within Canada but, reflecting instead the Diasporic experience, lay beyond it. This generated a loose network of German Jews who remained in regular contact through travel, correspondence, mutual advocacy, and – most important of all – a shared outlook or *Weltanschauung*. In sum, these German Jews maintained a community of their own long after they had been scattered around the world.

Given the breadth of this chapter's topic, I will be focusing on the life of the German-Jewish musician Heinz Unger as an example. The research will be structured as follows. First, I will provide a short sketch of Heinz Unger's life and accomplishments. Second, I will briefly discuss Jewish musicology, to demonstrate the distinct outlook of German Jews and how that outlook can in part be captured through an examination of Mahler's music. In doing so, I will also pay attention to how Jewish musicology developed in Canada and how – and why – that development was at odds with German Jewish artistic and cultural understandings. And third, I will address the matter of the links among German Jews and how they maintained networks spanning Canada, the United States, and even their home country of Germany that allowed them to remain connected despite living in locations often far removed from one another. I hope this chapter will help problematize the idea that identity is delimited by statehood, so as to recontour this idea in a way that allows us to better understand how the boundaries of identity do not necessarily accord with national borders and how a community's essence can be captured by examining the openness of networks rather than by focusing exclusively on geographic centres.

A Biography of Heinz Unger

Heinz Unger was born in Berlin in 1895. The son of a successful lawyer, he began by following in his father's footsteps. But he rejected this path after hearing Mahler's music for the first time in 1915. Inspired by the sonic landscape he had discovered, he decided to pursue a career in music instead, and made his professional debut with the Berlin Philharmonic in 1919, leading a performance of Mahler's First Symphony. By 1925 he had arranged his own annual concert series, and would lead the Berlin Philharmonic's *Gesellschaft der Musikfreunde* concerts for the better part of the next decade. During this period, Unger led significant performances, such as an early performance of Mahler's Eighth Symphony ("Symphony of a Thousand") in 1928, in which he directed the thousand massed musicians in a stirring rendition of this masterpiece. With the Nazis' rise to power in 1933, Unger like so many of his Jewish compatriots decided to leave Germany. After a brief and unhappy tenure as music director of the newly established Leningrad Radio Orchestra between 1934 and 1937, he moved to England with his wife and young daughter. During the war years, he remained in England, becoming music director of the Leeds-based Northern Philharmonic Orchestra, conducting the London Philharmonic Orchestra on a number of nationwide tours, and leading the British premiere of Mahler's Fifth Symphony in October 1945. Fearing a postwar Soviet domination of Europe, he decided that a new setting would be best for his family. So he resettled in Canada in 1947 after being advised by Leopold Stokowski that the "disturbed and crowded conditions" would prevent him from finding work in the United States.[1] Thereafter, he again slowly – and not altogether successfully – built up his career, creating the York Concert Society culled from the ranks of the Toronto Symphony Orchestra. He led these musicians in the Canadian premieres of Mahler's Second, Fifth, and Ninth symphonies, as well as the Canadian broadcast premiere of the Fourth symphony and the Toronto premiere of the Third. He also travelled extensively during his time resident in Canada, regularly appearing in Spain, throughout Latin America, and across Europe. In 1965, while preparing to premiere the Mahler Sixth, Unger suffered a heart attack that ended his life.[2]

Jewish Musicology and the Cultural Manifestations of a Jewish German Ethos

General Contours and the Modern Birth of the Idea of Jewish Music

While Jewish music undoubtedly existed before the modern period, the notion of a Jewish musicology only begins in the nineteenth century, at a time when the newly formed or defined nation-states of Europe were negotiating their existence. Indeed, it is interesting that the debate over Jewish music begins not with a discussion among Europe's Jews but with the German composer Richard Wagner's (1813–1883) anti-Semitic tract *Das Judentum in der Musik*.[3] Written under the pseudonym K. Freigedank ("Freethought"), Wagner's infamous essay began life as a contribution to the highly regarded and influential music journal *Neue Zeitschrift fur Musik* (Leipzig) in September 1850. On the surface, Wagner's article was a searing, vitriolic attack on two composers of Jewish descent, Felix Mendelssohn (1809–1847) and Giacomo Meyerbeer (1791–1864).[4] Wagner makes clear that the failings of these composers were not the result of deficiencies in their work but rather were a consequence of their Jewishness. Whether it be a result of – in the case of Mendelssohn – his "inability, while outside our footing, to have intercourse with us," or – in the case of Meyerbeer – his tendency to "dupe" and "profit from" German musical tastes, both these composers indicated to Wagner that the Jew was not a part of the *Volksgemeinschaft* or even a part of European culture but – in Wagner's odious phrase – an "unpleasant freak of Nature" standing outside its bounds.[5]

Jewish Musicology from Within: Eastern European Jewry Sets Its Musical Bounds

Seen through modern eyes, Wagner's mid-nineteenth-century article is a thoroughly reprehensible and tragic articulation of anti-Semitism. It is, however, also an attempt to delineate the bounds of German music, albeit by purging it of its "Jewish" elements. Interestingly, musicologist Klara Moricz has pointed out that the exclusionary rhetoric Wagner employed is reflected in many *Jewish* explorations of what constitutes Jewish music.[6] Although the racial element does not appear in the same manner, a similar exclusionary rhetoric is employed, in that certain composers are cast out not only for their failure to consciously synchronize their artistic efforts with what are deemed by some to be genuine expressions of Jewish feeling but sometimes also because the composer has arisen from a milieu deemed insufficiently "Jewish." As in Wagner's exclusionary formulation, these composers – and, by extension, musicians – of Jewish birth are treated by certain Jewish musicologists as "beyond the pale" – as bearing within them a set of qualities that are immutable and that will forever mark them as divorced from a Jewish milieu.

The studies of Jewish music bear a further similarity to Wagner's polemic: at their heart, they are attempts at self-definition by a cultural group in an era marked by strong currents of epistemological uncertainty. That is, they are attempts to work through issues of collective identity and to delimit a cultural group's sense of itself in times of historical crisis. Wagner's "Judaism in Music" was written in the wake of the revolutionary year 1848, a time during which German-speaking Central Europe was undergoing a series of upheavals that were to change Germans' self-perceptions as they navigated the stresses of a period that would culminate in the creation of Germany in 1871. In the case of Jewish musicology, meanwhile, the latter part of the nineteenth century and on to the middle of the twentieth was a period in Jewish history during which Jews were wracked by a series of upheavals (i.e., the rise of a modern anti-Semitism, pogroms, collective displacement, and the Holocaust), throughout which Jews were constantly reappraising their identity with respect to their neighbours, to say nothing of themselves and the bounds of their own communities. It comes as no surprise therefore that a great many studies of Jewish music undertaken by Jewish scholars reflected intentions and goals similar to those of their nineteenth-century German-speaking counterparts: to categorize music and conscript it as an ally in the quest for a sense of self that would serve as an element of identity-building.

Eastern European Jewish musicology takes as its point of departure the quest for self-definition that was a prerequisite for the creation of a Jewish nationalism. In the first decades of the twentieth century, Eastern European Jewish intellectuals – inspired by the nationalist projects undertaken by musicians and musicologists such as the Hungarian Béla Bartók – began to study and catalogue Jewish music. Between 1914 and 1932, Russian-born Abraham Idelsohn (1882–1938), widely considered the father of Jewish musicology, published his *Catalogue of Jewish Hebrew Oriental Melodies*, which served as a source of inspiration for many Jewish composers seeking to write explicitly Jewish music.[7] Thereafter, he would write the pioneering analysis of Jewish music, *Jewish Music: Its Historical Development*.[8] Idelsohn wrote *Jewish Music* near the end of a life devoted to the study of Jewish music, and it stands as a major accomplishment and a summation of his life's work. In this highly influential book and in his codification of Jewish melody, Idelsohn essentially created a canon of Jewish liturgical and folk music, surveying its development as a continuous sweep from the biblical period all the way through to the twentieth century.

In *Jewish Music*, Idelsohn's declared aim was to follow Jewish music's "history as a tonal expression of Judaism and of Jewish life."[9] In relying on his own understanding of "Jewish life," Idelsohn problematically created a schema wherein Eastern European Jewry was cast as "authentic" while Jews farther to the west had pursued a course that had allowed "foreign influences" to creep into their music and that ran counter to Jewish musical authenticity. As a result, Idelsohn tightly delineated Jewish music, casting aside not only those Jewish composers writing what he considered "non-Jewish" works (i.e., works clearly modelled on general sources) but even Jewish composers such as the Swiss-born American Ernest Bloch (b. Geneva, 1880–d. Portland, Oregon, 1959), who had succeeded in the realm of art music but whose compositions were often clearly informed and inspired by Jewish sources.[10] Given Bloch's self-identification as a Jew, as well as his use of Jewish material in many of his compositions, it is difficult to understand why Idelsohn rejected composers like him, whose only musical "fault" was to have arisen from the wrong (read "non–Eastern European") milieu.[11]

Idelsohn's work had a tremendous impact on Jewish musicology for decades to come. When Canadian Jewish musicology began to develop during the Second World War, the discipline was still very much grounded in the understandings and parameters established by Idelsohn half a world away. In 1940, the highly influential Jewish editor and writer Israel Rabinovitch (1894–1964), editor of Montreal's Yiddish-language daily *Der Keneder Adler* ("The Canadian Eagle"), produced his Yiddish-language text "Musik Bei Yidn."[12] In this work, Rabinovitch declared that only music that had been *consciously* crafted by Jews and that bore marks of biblical cantillation and other ancient Jewish musical modes could truly be classified as "Jewish" music. He put great stock in this connection between the ancient and the modern, arguing – like Idelsohn before him – that its Jewish cultural worth lay in its continuity from the ancient to the modern: "This, surely, is the power of these melodies, rooted in the Jewish soul, that with but a single touch upon the delicate string, they render the contemporary Jew at one with the generations of the past."[13]

Rabinovitch's text serves as a fascinating "time capsule" of Jewish musicological thought in a time and place once removed from its Eastern European Jewish roots that nevertheless espouses views entirely in keeping with utterances made as long before as half a century earlier halfway around the world. Rabinovitch's work was so suffused with the spirit of Old World musicological inquiry that he would go so far as to relight the embers of a decades-old feud, castigating the highly regarded Jewish musician and musicologist Lazare Saminsky (1882–1959) – who had become music director of Temple Emanu-El in New York in 1924 – as "anti-Yiddish" for suggesting that Jewish song and music were influenced by other sources and therefore not as "pure" as the Jewish musicologists that Rabinovitch so admired believed them to be.[14] In sum, while one can appreciate Rabinovitch for his enthusiasm for Jewish music, it is distressing to hear a leading member of Canada's Jewish community spouting inflammatory rhetoric that shamelessly alienated a great many Jewish musicians who did not fall within his tightly bounded definition of "genuine" Jewish music.

Jewish Music(s) Evolved: The Trouble with German-Jewish Music

Beginning with the Enlightenment, Central and Western European Jewry had been swept along by the same cultural changes taking place in general European society. During the *Haskalah* – the Jewish Enlightenment of the eighteenth century – Western and Central European Jews moved beyond the notion of remaining cloistered behind ghetto walls and embraced the idea of integrating with the emerging national communities of the nineteenth century. By the end of the nineteenth century, many European Jews considered themselves first and foremost not as Jews but as national citizens of the Mosaic faith.[15]

Swept along by the same wave of liberalism and national consciousness arising in the nineteenth century, European Jews outside the Russian Empire underwent the same educational and cultural processes as their countrymen. As a consequence, they became increasingly devoted to the same artistic pursuits as their non-Jewish countrymen. A corollary of the social development of Jews in Western and Central Europe was the fact that the art they created became ever more similar to what was being produced by others. In the case of music, we see more and more assimilated Jews composing and performing music virtually indistinguishable from what was being created by non-Jews. This music – commonly placed within the parameters of European art music and becoming a key element of the European art music canon – was therefore not the consequence of a conscious decision to move beyond the bounds of traditional Jewish culture but simply a result of the particular timing of Jewish emancipation across Europe.

But this did not mean that this music lay beyond the bounds of Jewish music, nor did it mean that certain Jewish contours could not be discerned – or, in the case of Wagner's attack, imagined into being. However odious Wagner's anti-Semitism might have been, he was correct in noting that some (but definitely not all) music composed by Jewish musicians did possess certain elements that (at times) stood out as incongruent with other works of the European art music canon.[16] Mahler's music, as well as his style of conducting, was just one such example of this ambivalence, lying as it did simultaneously within and beyond the European art music canon. Despite his success, Mahler was attacked violently by music critics, who associated his music with a Jewishness they found abhorrent. As music critic Rudolph Louis would state: "[Mahler's music] is repulsive to me because it *acts* Jewish. This is to say that it speaks musical German, but with an accent, with an inflection, and above all, with the gestures of an Eastern, all too Eastern Jew."[17]

However crude Louis's critique, verdicts concerning the Jewishness of Mahler and his music were seconded even by those more sympathetic to Mahler's cause. Even so sympathetic an observer as the German-speaking Czech Jewish author Max Brod (1884–1968) would, in attempting to make his case for Mahler's musical genius, note that the composer's music did not seem to speak in an organically German voice, pointing out that "it may be that Mahler's music, though apparently German, is instinctively recognized as non-German – which is indeed the case."[18] To all concerned, whether they favoured Mahler's art or disparaged it, the composer's music bore something that marked it as lying outside the German "norm."

Considering the rancour aroused by Mahler as both conductor and composer, it is not surprising that those who embraced his music – like Heinz Unger – were not outside this debate; indeed, they were key to its negotiation. In turn, Mahler's music was internalized not only as a key part of the German art music canon but also as central to a German-Jewish musical canon very different from what was being forged to the east. In sum, devotion to Mahler's music in the first half of the twentieth century became part of a sort of quasi-religious Jewish expression – culturally, socially, and spiritually – for many Central European Jews who had lost something of themselves in the transition to general society and who had not yet found a way to replace that something. To steal a phrase from the German-speaking Czech and Jewish writer Franz Kafka, "[most Jews] who began to write German wanted to leave Judaism ... but with their little hind legs they were still glued to the Jewishness of their fathers and with their little front legs they found no new ground."[19]

Here, then, lies the explanation for the gap between Heinz Unger and the Jewish community of Canada. Neither Idelsohn nor Rabinovitch possessed the historical experience to accept or assimilate a music that had, to their ears, far transcended the bounds of Jewish music and, by extension, Jewish culture. For whatever the religious belief shared by Russian and German Jews, the cultural expression of their faith and identity sounded very different on account of their very different historical experiences. While much of the Canadian Jewish community – informed by the musicological and cultural utterances of leading cultural figures such as Israel Rabinovitch – positioned themselves culturally behind defences that clearly delineated who had access to the Jewish Canadian world, those who had experienced a very different trajectory to Jewish modernity bore within themselves a set of values far removed from those of their Canadian co-religionists. In essence, their cultural productions and preferences became their difference. And the demographic contours of Canadian Jewry – with German Jews representing but a small percentage of an overall Canadian Jewish population that was largely Eastern European and had been so since at least the early years of the twentieth century – meant that this difference became the source of German-Jewish exclusion from the main currents of Jewish life in Canada.[20]

This situation was, however, far removed from that experienced by German Jews who settled in the United States. During the middle decades of the nineteenth century (approximately 1840 to 1880), the United States had seen a significant wave of German-speaking immigrants, who included a large number of Jews. And while the latter part of the nineteenth century and the beginning of the twentieth had seen the arrival in the United States of large numbers of Russian and Eastern European Jews fleeing from anti-Semitism, those arrivals did not entirely overwhelm the previously established contours of the American Jewish community and its life, as had happened in Canada. German Jews, despite now representing a minority vis-à-vis Eastern European Jewish immigrants, continued to represent a vibrant part of American Jewish culture.[21]

These circumstances had further cultural implications leading into the twentieth century. In the 1930s, a large community of German-Jewish émi-grés formed in the Los Angeles area, where a great many of German-speaking Europe's leading musical and artistic talents – including musicians like the avant-garde composer Arnold Schoenberg (b. Vienna, 1874 – d. Los Angeles, 1951), Max Steiner (b. Vienna, 1888 – d. 1971, Los Angeles), and Erich Korngold (b. Brno, 1897 – d. 1957, Los Angeles) – had moved to escape Nazi persecution.[22] Thus, while German Jews who settled in the United States (or even paradoxically in Israel)[23] were able to re-form their community bonds after the Second World War and play out their lives with the European art music canon as a sonic and cultural backdrop that represented not just their displacement from Europe but also their German-Jewish identity, Heinz Unger and the few other German Jews who settled in Canada – save those who were more religiously inclined – were unable to engage with the Jewish community more generally because their own soundtrack was an entirely different one from the prevailing norm. In sum, the synchronicity between culture and community was not in evidence as in the aforementioned contexts, and Unger and his fellow German Jews had to actively seek one another out, and not just within the bounds of Canada; they also often had to search beyond Canada to restore the integrity of their cultural identity.

The Community Atomized, or the Creation of Hybrid Identities

A large part of Heinz Unger's difficulty in embedding himself in the Canadian Jewish community arose from the fact that his German-Jewish identity – and the manner in which he expressed it culturally – presented a challenge to Canadian Jewry and its self-understanding. Remember that Unger came from a Central European milieu in which the contours of identity and the integrationist impulses that had taken hold among German Jewry over the course of the nineteenth century were at odds with those familiar to the vast majority of Canadian Jews, who had arrived from an Eastern Europe where understandings of Jewishness were very different and (at least initially) treated with far more suspicion.[24] And while postwar Canadian Jewry underwent a process whereby members of the Canadian Jewish community, in the words of Franklin Bialystock, "were bent on advancing from the fringes of the Canadian mosaic into the mainstream of Canadian society," the contours of the community would have still been informed by its antecedents.[25] In other words, the preconditions for what Canadian historian Harold Troper has called the "whitening of Euro-ethnics" could not have entirely eradicated the self-understandings accrued over the course of centuries in the Old Country as well as in the first fifty years of life in their adopted new Canadian homeland.[26] Canada, which welcomed far fewer German Jews in the postwar period than its neighbour to the south, remained a space where the views of a (once) Eastern European Jewry dominated the national Jewish ethos, which was still negotiating its own space in the evolving Canadian mosaic. In this context, the German-Jewish immigrants of the immediate postwar period were as islands in a stream, having come from a different milieu than the majority of Canada's Jews, who, while undergoing a process of liberalization in the postwar period and breaking many of the contours of a formerly parochial community, continued to view themselves – and just as importantly, continued to be viewed by other Canadians – as part of a distinct community within Canada, however much they may have "gained the acceptance of most Canadians."[27]

Moreover, we cannot discount the rather obvious fact that German Jews bore distinctly German features. German Jews remained Jews, but the ways in which they expressed themselves often contained elements – everything from their more formal mode of dress to their preferences in music, literature, and the arts, and their decidedly German-inflected speech – that would have served as painful reminders for Canadian Jews who had very recently seen with their own eyes the vile manifestation of the very culture that German Jews carried within them.[28] In short, how could Canadian Jews stomach the cultural expressions of German Jews, who seemed to them eerily similar to those Germans who had slaughtered millions of Europe's Jews?

Such crude formulations aside, Heinz Unger was not ostracized by all parts of the Canadian Jewish community. While his difficulties in embedding himself on account of his interwoven German-Jewish identity may have contributed to his frustration in his first years in Canada, he still managed to begin a dialogue with the more reform-minded segments of Toronto's Jewish community. Although he managed but one appearance with a professional ensemble in his first years in Canada – a Proms concert with the Toronto Philharmonic in 1948 – he did in fact manage to make a series of new acquaintances who would propel his Canadian career in the years to come. The main thrust of his career in these years lay with the Forest Hill Village Community Orchestra, a mixed amateur and professional ensemble that he led in a series of concerts in the early 1950s. His professional advancement in Canada, however slow it may have been, depended on his social success in the neighbourhood of Forest Hill, which was, in the words of Gerald Tulchinsky, a key site for a number of upwardly mobile Canadian Jews: "Some more affluent Toronto Jews moved away from the areas of first and second settlement up to swanky Forest Hill … Many of the new arrivals shed their 'old-fashioned' ways – abandoning Orthodox religious observances, for example – and adopted upper-class norms."[29]

Heinz Unger, once a regular conductor with the Berlin Philharmonic, was now the leader and artistic director of what some perhaps viewed as a lowly community orchestra in Toronto. But his move also marked the beginning of a relationship – albeit a tenuous and selective one – with more liberal segments of Canada's Jewish community, who had succeeded – like their predecessors in Europe – in elucidating, encapsulating, and living a Jewish life beyond the exclusive bounds of the Jewish community.

The more liberal-minded Jews of the area, moreover, did not reject art music as had Rabinovitch and his Eastern European models. Instead, they acknowledged and took pride in the Jewish composers who had succeeded in interweaving their Jewish and other identities into an inseparable new understanding. In 1953, therefore, members of this community would provide Unger with sufficient support to establish the York Concert Society, an organization comprising musicians of the Toronto Symphony Orchestra. From 1953 until Unger's death in 1965, he would lead these musicians in brief concert series (usually four or five springtime concerts held at the Eaton Auditorium or – when required by the concert program – at Massey Hall), performing key works of the musical canon. It should be noted, furthermore, that the York Concert Society became the orchestra with which Unger would lead the Canadian premieres of many of Mahler's symphonies.

In Forest Hill, too, Unger would find not only supporters but also his closest friends. Among its upwardly mobile residents, Unger would become closest to Mark Levy and his wife, who would advocate for him on many occasions. In 1958, the Levys would even attempt to help him achieve his long-held dream of conducting the Israel Philharmonic Orchestra. It is telling that Unger's main goal in this regard was to conduct Mahler's work with the IPO, preferably in time for the Mahler centenary of 1960. Unger's desire to conduct this composer's work in Israel was not a coincidence; it was, rather, a sign of his belief that Mahler and his music represented a vital aspect of Jewish identity, an identity he valued so highly that he considered it libellous to suggest otherwise.[30]

Lamentably, and despite the personal involvement of Mark Levy on a 1958 trip to Israel, during which he met with a board member of the Israel Philharmonic, Unger's dream of conducting the orchestra would never come to fruition, nor would his desire to lead, in Israel, a performance of Mahler – the composer who represented Unger's most vital connection to his Jewishness. Even so, during the 1950s and into the 1960s, the support of the Levys, as well as friendship with Holy Blossom's Rabbi Gunther Plaut, the soon-to-be music director of the National Archives Helmut Kallmann – himself a German Jew who had immigrated to Canada – and with grocery store magnate Leon Weinstein, speak to Unger's ability to embed himself in a Canadian Jewish context, albeit one that did not include many of Canada's more orthodox Jews, who could not understand how a man who spoke with so heavy a German accent could also be a good Jew.[31]

But Unger's network far transcended Toronto or even Canada. He had become convinced of Mahler's musical worth on a brisk November night in Munich in 1915 when he first heard Mahler's *Das Lied von der Erde*, conducted by Bruno Walter (1876–1962). Walter, a German Jew who as a young musician had served as Mahler's assistant and had become one of Mahler's greatest exponents as well as one of his closest friends, had departed Central Europe like Unger at the time of the Nazis' rise to power. He did not settle in Canada, like Unger; instead, fortuitously and more wisely, he chose to settle in the United States. Safely ensconced in Los Angeles's German émigré community, which consisted largely of German-Jewish artists fleeing Nazi persecution, Walter would live out the balance of his life in happy circumstances, surrounded by people he had known since his youth and with whom he shared a common outlook if not religion (Walter had renounced his Jewish faith at the end of the nineteenth century, embracing Catholicism just as Mahler had done). Illustrating the anti-parochial stance of German Jewry, Walter's conversion did not signal the demise of the friendship between Unger and Walter; they remained close friends until Walter's passing, corresponding frequently and visiting each other whenever possible. That said, it is ironic that Walter remained close to German-Jewish artistic luminaries like Max Steiner and Erich Korngold – both of whom wrote film scores for some of the most famous films of Hollywood's golden era, and achieved great artistic success in doing so – while Unger struggled to find those who could understand his artistic–cultural aspirations.

Bruno Walter was not Unger's only friend in the Los Angeles area. Unger could also count among his intimates Hugo Strelitzer (1896–1981), a friend since their youth in Germany. Strelitzer, a German Jew who had been able to escape Germany after the eminent conductor Wilhelm Furtwängler interceded on his behalf, and who would serve as choir master for the premiere of the jointly composed oratorio *Genesis Suite*, would resettle – like many of Unger's friends and acquaintances – in Los Angeles, and maintain contact with Unger until the latter's passing.[32]

But Unger's most intriguing friendship in the Los Angeles area by far was with Maxwell Dubin, the long-serving assistant rabbi at Temple Emanu-El on Wilshire Boulevard.[33] It is not known how the two men first met, and not much is remembered of Dubin. However, their correspondence clearly illustrates the affection each held for the other. In 1959, Dubin did all he could to bring Unger to Los Angeles to fill the position of conductor of the Los Angeles Philharmonic, speaking to members of the Philharmonic board such as Dorothy Chandler to see what might be done.[34] In the end, Dubin's advocacy on Unger's behalf came to nothing, and he was never formally considered for the post. Nor did Dubin's attempt to have concert impresario Sol Hurok (1888–1974) – agent to some of the greatest musical talents of the time, including Marian Anderson, Vladimir Ashkenazy, Van Cliburn, Emil Gilels, David Oistrakh, Jan Peerce, Mstislav Rostropovich, Arthur Rubinstein, and Isaac Stern – represent Unger succeed, partly on account of Unger's 1949 support for German conductor Wilhelm Furtwängler (1886–1954) in his quest to secure an appointment with the Chicago Symphony Orchestra. The American Jewish community – backed by many leading artists – succeeded in preventing Furtwängler from assuming a post he had been offered by the Chicago Symphony board, amid rumours concerning his wartime support of the Nazi regime.[35] Only a few outspoken individuals – including Unger and Yehudi Menuhin – came to Furtwängler's defence, highlighting the German conductor's moral correctness if not his decision to remain in Germany during the Second World War. While Dubin's repeated support for Unger proved unsuccessful, his actions speak of a faithful friendship and an affection on both the personal and professional planes. Just as importantly, they illustrate the importance borne by their shared Jewish convictions, as reflected clearly in this personal appeal the rabbi made to Hurok: "Not only is Dr. Unger a distinguished conductor; he is, in addition, one of the few Jewish maestros who refused to compromise with his faith and accept baptism in order to further his career. As a rabbi, this has made him doubly close to me."[36]

Unger was also invested in German-Jewish culture in the United States through his relationship with Mahler's widow, Alma Mahler-Werfel. Given his total devotion to Mahler, Unger had maintained close ties with Mahler's widow, and this had borne fruit when she asked him to join the board of directors of the newly created Gustav Mahler Society of America in June 1958.[37] In the wake of this honour and after a life spent toiling on behalf of Mahler's music, Unger was honoured with the Bruckner Society of America's Mahler Medal in 1959, an award bestowed upon a select few individuals, institutions, and orchestras that had done vital work disseminating Mahler's music and creed. Heinz Unger was the first Canadian to receive this award, and his being honoured in this way (alongside other recipients such as Bruno Walter, Eugene Ormandy, Dmitri Mitropolous, Otto Klemperer, William Steinberg, and Leonard Bernstein) is further indication of how close he had remained to the pulse of German Jewry by way of a devotion to Mahler that was perhaps best appreciated beyond Canadian borders.

It should also be noted that despite the actions of the Nazi regime and the trauma that its actions caused him, Unger did not break ties with his native Germany, nor to its Jewish community. In 1956, he returned to Germany for the first time since his 1933 escape, to conduct a series of concerts in his native Berlin. There, he reconnected with his German-Jewish identity, an element that had played but a peripheral role in his life for a number of years, all at once. His German-Jewish rebirth was heightened by the rapidly approaching 1960 centenary of Gustav Mahler's birth. Mahler, as we have seen, represented a nexus of German-Jewish identity for Unger; the conductor viewed him as a kindred emotional spirit, his music serving as his own personal gospel. Reflecting on the Mahler centenary, Unger – perhaps for the first time in his life – now understood that Mahler and his music represented for him a universe of German *and* Jewish meaning; as he noted at the time, "the year 1960 will bring the 100th birthday of Gustav Mahler, one of the most important composers of Jewish origin, to whose music I as you know have devoted my whole life."[38] Heinz Unger, after years of wandering, had, by way of Mahler's music, reconnected with his roots, with his youth, and with the world he thought he had lost when the Nazis rose to power. So it was no coincidence that in that very year, Unger donated to the *Zentralrat der Juden in Deutschland* an honorarium he had received from the *Westdeutschen Rundfunks* in Köln (Cologne) for a concert conducted the previous year.[39]

But to mention only Unger's Jewish networks of affiliation would be to seriously distort his life and self-understanding. For as a German Jew living in the Double Diaspora imposed by the process of emancipation and the turbulent events of the twentieth century, Unger had moved beyond an exclusively Jewish self-understanding and was bound up in a modernity wherein Germanness and Jewishness coexisted and could not be divorced from each other.[40] Thus, we would be failing to accurately convey the nature of Unger's networks if we were to overlook the fact that, alongside his Jewish networks of affiliation within and beyond Canada's borders, Unger maintained networks of affiliation that transcended the Jewish sphere. Indeed, some of Unger's closest friends in Canada – like the managing director of Volkswagen Canada, Karl Barths – were themselves part of a German Canadian community that had been ostracized in postwar Canada, where there was a common misunderstanding that all Germans were Nazis.[41] And with the balm of time, Heinz Unger also moved closer to the Germany he had abandoned as a consequence of Nazi persecution. On 24 February 1960 – during Mahler's centenary year – he conducted the Toronto Symphony Orchestra in a performance of Mahler's *Das Lied von der Erde* at Massey Hall. That concert was followed by a reception hosted by the Consul of the Federal Republic of Germany, Gottfried von Waldheim. And just two weeks before his passing, Unger was honoured with the West German award of the *Verdienstkreuz*, a tremendous professional honour for him and one that served a curative purpose on a more personal level, granted as it was, in Unger's words, "in an effort to mend what the years of darkness [the Nazi period] have done to me and so many others."[42] Moreover, that one of the most recent mentions of Heinz Unger can be encountered in Gerhard Bassler's 1991 survey of German Canadians is surely evidence of the impact that the German-Jewish conductor had on the German Canadian community before his death.[43]

Conclusion

In this chapter we have used one individual's social and cultural contexts to show that Canadian Jewish culture has borne within it a multitude of voices that have not often been recognized or heard until recently. To accomplish this, we have built an argument that explores how intellectual, cultural, and social trends in Europe beginning in the nineteenth century created a situation where the majority sentiment of Canadian Jewry failed to allow for a minority of Canada's Jews to immerse themselves completely in the Canadian Jewish milieu. Given these circumstances, Heinz Unger – as our representative of a minority voice within Canadian Jewry – established networks of affiliation that transcended the borders of Canada and placed him in a network of commonality with Jews beyond Canada, whether in the United States or his native Germany. While Unger was able to find a community in the greater Toronto area that understood his German-Jewish cultural and artistic outlook, a greater number of his friends and people with a similar disposition and outlook were in the United States. This in turn resulted in Unger maintaining close ties to the German-Jewish émigré community in the United States – and particularly in the greater Los Angeles area – despite the great geographical distance between them and his limited opportunities to interact with them directly. Much of this was a result of a common understanding of the German-Jewish identity that he shared with German Jews around the world and forces us to reconsider the national boundedness of Jewish communities, whether in Canada, the United States, or beyond.

I end this chapter by returning to the issue of cultural production and identity, for this lies at the heart of our discussion. However important Unger's embeddedness or isolation in a social milieu, to only discuss networks and connections would be to discount a major reason for the gulf between parts of the Jewish community in Canada – music and culture. In brief, musical creations, like other artistic constructions, are cultural products that embody deep personal meanings. Canada's Central European Jews continued to express – as they had in Europe – their Jewish identity by way of an allegiance to cultural expressions consistent with their emancipatory experience that brought them closer to German Jews beyond Canada's borders than to their co-religionists within the nation's borders. This meant that their lives would – at least culturally – be vastly different from those lived by their majority Eastern European Canadian co-religionists, drawing them closer to their German-Jewish brethren to the south.

Unger's devotion to Mahler was not simply aesthetic. It also built upon cultural values that he – like other Central European Jews – had internalized as essential to his Jewish identity and, just as critically, as a type of ritualized observance that allowed him to connect to his German-Jewish identity. Interestingly, this same set of values carried over into the German art music canon, creating a paradoxical situation in which even non-Jewish compositions (i.e., those created by Mozart and perversely even Richard Wagner) would be transformed into what musicologist Philip Bohlman has called a German-Jewish "ethnic music."[44] And while this may seem a problematic construction, it is by no means an untrue one. So just as paradoxically, German Jews – resident both in Canada and beyond – saw the music that had been denied a Jewish meaning by East European or Canadian musicologists as the very expression of their own Jewishness, and this only widened the gap and increased the cultural misunderstandings not only between parts of the Jewish Canadian community but also within the Jewish community across the Diaspora. Culture, therefore, lay at the heart of the gap in the Canadian Jewish community. We hope that this chapter, which traverses Europe and the Americas across three centuries, has helped remind us of the importance of art as an extension of the self and how artistic expressions not only align with issues of identity abstractly but also can help us better understood how communities understand themselves, wherever they may be found.

Notes

1   Letter from Leopold Stokowski to Heinz Unger, 20 December 1947. Library and Archives Canada (LAC), MUS 56, box 1, file 10.

2   Heinz Unger Fonds, LAC, MUS 56.

3   The title of the piece, "Das Judentum in der Musik," is most accurately translated as "Jewishness in Music" but is more commonly translated as "Judaism in Music," an alteration that lessens the visceral nature of Wagner's anti-Semitism and paints the diatribe as less of a blatantly anti-Semitic attack (which it most certainly is) and renders it a seeming critique of the formal aspects of Jewish religiosity in music.

4   Felix Mendelssohn was a renowned German composer of the Romantic period. The grandson of the renowned Jewish philosopher and father of the Jewish Enlightenment (*Haskalah*) Moses Mendelssohn, Mendelssohn was baptized in 1816 along with his entire family. As a composer, his fame spread across Europe, especially in England, where he made numerous appearances and where his music has always retained its popularity. Giacomo Meyerbeer was a Jewish-born German composer best known for his operatic compositions. Meyerbeer was a highly popular and successful composer, though his fame faded somewhat after his death.

5   Richard Wagner, *Judaism in Music*, trans. William Ashton Ellis (London: London Wagner Society, 1894).

6   Moricz has noted that "the invocation of Wagner did not serve as a shibboleth, for opinions about his ideas hardly differentiated anti-Semites and the proponents of Jewish music … Authors of all stripes have readily endorsed his essentialist views of Jewish composers." Klara Moricz, *Jewish Identities: Nationalism, Racism, and Utopianism in Twentieth-Century Music* (Berkeley: University of California Press, 2008), 4–5.

7   Idelsohn's *Catalogue of Jewish Hebrew Oriental Melodies* (also known as the *Thesaurus of Hebrew-Oriental Melodies*) was published in ten volumes and first appeared in print between 1914 and 1932. Originally published by Breitkopf and Haertel (Leipzig) and reprinted by Ktav Publishing House (New York) in 1973.

8   Abraham Idelsohn, *Jewish Music: Its Historical Development* (New York: Dover Publications, [1938]1992).

9 Ibid., xix.

10 Violinist Zina Schiff argues that Bloch's 1938 Violin Concerto, for instance, bears numerous Jewish hallmarks, including "the same interval (fifth) as in the beginning of both the *Vidui* [Contrition] and *Simchat Torah* [Rejoicing] in *Baal Shem* [which] is also a traditional interval for blowing the shofar, the ram's horn, on the High Holy Days of Rosh Hashanah and Yom Kippur." Zina Schiff, liner notes to Ernest Bloch (Violin Concerto; Baal Shem; Suite Hebraique) (Naxos 8.557757) 2000, 2.

11 In a 1906 letter to his friend and collaborator Edmond Fleg, Bloch noted: "I have read the Bible – I have read fragments about Moses. And an immense sense of pride has been surging within me! My entire being reverberated. It is a revelation. I shall find myself again in this – I could not continue reading, for I was afraid. Yes, Fleg, I was afraid of discovering too much of myself, of feeling everything which had gradually accumulated, glued to me, fall away in one sudden blow; of finding myself naked again, naked within this entire past which lives inside me, of standing erect as a Jew proudly Jewish … and of no longer being able to stand the conditions in which I live." David Z. Kushner, "Religious Ambiguity in the Life and Works of Ernest Bloch," http://www.biu.ac.il/hu/mu/min-ad04/BLOCH-1.pdf.

12 The work would be expanded and translated – with the help of Canadian Jewish poet A.M. Klein in 1952 – retitled *Of Jewish Music, Ancient and Modern*.

13 Israel Rabinovitch, *Of Jewish Music, Ancient and Modern*, trans. A.M. Klein (Montreal: Book Center, 1952), 137.

14 Prior to his arrival in the United States in 1920, Lazare Saminsky had been one of the first members of the Society for Jewish Folk Music. Saminsky's views on the inauthenticity of folk sources are discussed in Neil Levin's authoritative notes to the Milken Archive CD "Jewish Music of the Dance." Neil W. Levin, "Jewish Music of the Dance" (Naxos, 8.559439).

15 The historian Jacob Katz neatly encapsulates the change in Jewish identity during this period: "In the first period [the decade 1760–70] a Jew might have been designated as English, French, or German depending on his land of residence. At that time, however, this was only a geographical description and gave, perhaps, a hint of some collective characteristics that the members of each respective community may have manifested. A hundred years later, if a person was called a French, English or German Jew, he was taken to belong in some way to both the social units implied in the compound expression: he belonged to one of these nations and was, in addition, a Jew." Jacob Katz, *Out of the Ghetto: The Social Background of Jewish Emancipation, 1770–1870* (Cambridge, MA: Harvard University Press, 1973), 1.

16 That said, we should not discount the importance of musical reception. For example, Felix Mendelssohn's music, though possessing little Jewish material save perhaps a tendency toward the use of Old Testament texts in some of his oratorios, was forbidden during the Nazi period on account of its alleged ability to pollute the German nation, being cast as Degenerate music (*Entartete Musik*) on account of the composer's race. This – and of course Wagner's attack, published admittedly but three years after Mendelssohn's death – has left us with the perception that Mendelssohn wrote "Jewish" music. The point is not in this case, however, whether he did or did not, but rather, that his music has become a part of the Jewish musical canon by way of accrued historical understandings. In January 2009, for instance, to help celebrate the bicentennial of Mendelssohn's birth, a series of heretofore unknown compositions by the composer were presented at New York's Museum of Jewish Heritage under the working title "Mendelssohn: Lost Treasures

and the Wagner Suppression." See Leslie Kandell, "Bicentennial Celebration," in *American Record Guide*, May–June 2009, 17–18.

17 Rudolph Louis, *Die deutsche Musik der Gegenwart* (Munich: G. Mueller, 1912). As quoted and cited in Francesca Draughon and Raymond Knapp, "Gustav Mahler and the Crisis of Jewish Identity," in *ECHO: A Music-Centred Journal* 3, no. 2 (Fall 2001).

18 Max Brod, *Israel's Music* (Tel Aviv: Sefer Press, 1951), 31.

19 Arnold J. Band, "Kafka: The Margins of Assimilation," in *Modern Judaism* 8, no. 2 (May 1988), 139–55. The quotation from Kafka appears on page 144.

20 For a general history of the Canadian Jewish Community – one that includes ample evidence of the demographic and cultural predominance of Eastern European Ashkenazim since the early decades of the twentieth century – see Gerald Tulchinsky, *Canada's Jews: A People's Journey* (Toronto: University of Toronto Press, 2008). See also Louis Rosenberg, *Canada's Jews: A Social and Economic Study of Jews in Canada in the 1930s* (Montreal and Kingston: McGill–Queen's University Press, 1993).

21 See Hasia R. Diner, *A Time for Gathering: The Second Migration, 1820–1880* (Baltimore: Johns Hopkins University Press, 1992), 231–35.

22 For a fuller discussion of this community, see Dorothy Lamb Crawford, *A Windfall of Musicians: Hitler's Emigres and Exiles in Southern California* (New Haven: Yale University Press, 2009).

23 Even in Israel, German-speaking Jews – called *Yekkes* – re-formed the contours of their community, creating cultural institutions and meeting regularly at concerts where the key works of the Central European art music canon (including – illicitly – the music of Richard Wagner) were performed. See Philip Bohlman, *The Land Where Two Streams Flow: Music and the German-Jewish Community of Israel* (Champaign: University of Illinois Press, 1989).

24 For a discussion of the absent dialogue between Eastern European Jewish immigrants to Canada and the citizens of the country to which they had moved around the turn of the twentieth century, see Gerald Tulchinsky, *Taking Root: The Origins of the Canadian Jewish Community* (Toronto: Lester Publishing, 1992).

25 Franklin Bialystock, *Delayed Impact: The Holocaust and the Canadian Jewish Community* (Montreal and Kingston: McGill–Queen's University Press, 2000), 69.

26 In his magisterial account of Jewish life in the Americas, Irving Howe makes this precise point with a beautiful nuance that bears repeating: "Cultures are slow to die; when they do, they bequeath large deposits of custom and value to their successors; and sometimes they survive long after their more self-conscious members suppose them to have vanished. A great many suburban Jews no longer spoke Yiddish, a growing number did not understand it, some failed to appreciate the magnitude of their loss; but their deepest inclinations of conduct, bias, manner, style, intonation, all bore heavy signs of immigrant shaping. What Jewish suburbanites took to be 'a good life,' the kinds of vocations to which they hoped to lead their children, their sense of appropriate conduct within a family, the ideas capable of winning their respect, the moral appeals to which they remained open, their modes of argument, their fondness for pacific conduct, their views of respectability and delinquency – all showed the strains of immigrant Yiddish culture, usually blurred, sometimes buried, but still at work." Irving Howe, *World of Our Fathers* (New York: Simon and Schuster), 618.

27 Bialystock, *Delayed Impact*, 69.

28 Philip Bohlman points out that the German Jews who settled in Israel exhibited social characteristics that set them apart from the other segments of Jewish society. Presumably,

the same tendencies would have been in evidence in Canada as well as in other contexts. See Bohlman, *The Land Where Two Streams Flow.*

29 Tulchinsky, *Canada's Jews,* 417.

30 "On one occasion a New York management told me that the administration of the [Israel Philharmonic] orchestra believes me to be baptised, a libellous error, which I have rectified straight-away." Letter from Heinz Unger to Mrs. Levy, 5 June 1958. LAC, MUS 56, box 1, file 11.

31 Rabbi Gunther Plaut (1912-2012) was born in Munster, Germany, fled from Nazi Germany in 1935, and immigrated to the United States. After serving in the Second World War as a chaplain, he assumed religious directorship of the Mount Zion Temple in St. Paul, Minnesota (1948–1961); thereafter he moved to Toronto and became the rabbi at Holy Blossom between 1961 and 1977 as well as serving as president of the Canadian Jewish Congress. According to Sharon Drache, his non-traditional religious views placed him "firmly within the secular Jewish camp." Sharon *Drache, "Gunther W. Plaut,"* in *The Canadian Encyclopedia* (Toronto: Hurtig Publishers, 1988).

Helmut Kallmann (1922–2012) was born in Berlin and, like Unger, escaped Nazi Germany in 1939. After a brief time in England, where he was interned as a German citizen, Kallmann moved to Canada, where he was again interned between 1940 and 1943. Thereafter, he studied music in Toronto and eventually moved on to work in the CBC music library between the years 1950 and 1970. In 1970, he was appointed director of the newly created Music Division at the National Library of Canada, working in that capacity until his retirement in 1987. See "Helmut Kallman" in *The Encyclopedia of Music in Canada.*

32 Hugo Strelitzer arrived in Los Angeles in 1936 and had the honour of serving as chorus master at the 18 November 1945 Los Angeles premiere of the *Genesis Suite,* a collaboratively composed work that musically depicted the major events of the Biblical book of Genesis. The composers who came together to each compose one portion of the seven-part work were the Austrian Arnold Schoenberg (1874–1951), New York–born Nathaniel Shilkret (1889–1982), the Polish-born Alexandre Tansman (1897–1986), Frenchman Darius Milhaud (1892–1974), Italian Mario Castelnuovo-Tedesco (1895–1968), Vienna-born Ernst Toch (1887–1964), and the Russian Igor Stravinsky (1882–1971). The project was the brainchild of Nathaniel Shilkret. All but Stravinsky were Jewish, and all were resident in the greater Los Angeles area at the time. See James Westby's informative notes to the Milken Archive's recording of the *Genesis Suite.* Naxos 8.559442 (2004).

33 Little information is to be found relating to Rabbi Maxwell Dubin. In their survey of American synagogues, Kerry Olitzky and Marc Lee Raphael note that "in 1926, Maxwell Dubin was appointed to the position of Director of Religious Education and Social Activities" at the Wilshire Boulevard Temple. According to Olitzky and Raphael's account, Dubin never rose to the position of Senior Rabbi of the Wilshire Boulevard Temple. Kerry Olitzky and Marc Lee Raphael, *The American Synagogue: A Historical Dictionary and Sourcebook* (Westport: Greenwood Press, 1996), 51.

34 The post had just recently become vacant after its director, the Dutch conductor Eduard van Beinum (1900–59), had suddenly died of a heart attack the previous month. Acting on the conductor's inquiries, Rabbi Dubin informed Unger that he had "taken the liberty of sending your clippings to Mrs. Norman Chandler," whom the rabbi charmingly described as being "very active in the Los Angeles Philharmonic Society." Letter from Rabbi Dubin to Heinz Unger, dated 12 May 1959. LAC, MUS 56, box 1, file 12. In his letter to Mrs. Chandler, Dubin made clear his admiration for Dr. Unger, calling him a "conductor of outstanding ability [that] would bring to our Orchestra the stature and

leadership it requires." Letter from Rabbi Dubin to Mrs. Chandler, dated 12 May 1959. LAC, MUS 56, box 1, file 12. Mrs. Norman Chandler is in fact Dorothy Buffum Chandler (1901–97), the wife of the publisher of the *Los Angeles Times* from 1945 to 1960. Dorothy Chandler spent a large part of her life revitalizing the Los Angeles Arts scene. In honour of her tireless work in its creation, the Los Angeles Music Center's main orchestral hall (completed 1967) was named the Dorothy Chandler Pavilion. It served as the home of the Los Angeles Philharmonic between 1964 and 2003, when it was replaced by the newly built Walt Disney Concert Hall.

35 There is a vast literature on Wilhelm Furtwängler, and even today there is a heated debate on whether partaking in an "internal migration" to set oneself apart from the regime under which one lives and works is a morally acceptable course of action. For a fuller account of Furtwängler's activities and positions during the Nazi era, see Michael H. Kater, *The Twisted Muse: Musicians and Their Music in the Third Reich* (Oxford: Oxford University Press, 1997). Also interesting and particularly relevant to the matter of Furtwängler's de-Nazification is David Monod's *Settling Scores: German Music, Denazification, and the Americans, 1945–1953* (Chapel Hill: University of North Carolina Press, 2005). See especially Chapter 4, "Learning to Keep Quiet: Wilhelm Furtwängler and the End of Denazification."

36 Letter from Maxwell Dubin to Sol Hurok, dated 9 September 1959. LAC, MUS 56, box 1, file 12.

37 The official letter of invitation from Alma Mahler-Werfel, signed in her odd, large script, lies in LAC, MUS 56, box 1, file 4. The official letter is accompanied by a personal note to Heinz Unger as well as by a letter to his wife, indicating that all three knew one another and shared a cordial friendship.

38 Letter from Heinz Unger to Mrs. Mark Levy, dated 5 June 1958. LAC, MUS 56, box 1, file 11.

39 In a letter thanking him for the donation, the *Zentralrat der Juden in Deutschland* Secretary Dr. van Dam explicitly mentions that the money will be used for the training and education of a Jewish teacher ("fur die Ausbildung eines judischen Lehrers verwandt"). Letter from the *Zentralrat der Juden in Deutschland* to Heinz Unger, dated 15 December 1960. LAC, MUS 56, box 1, file 13. The total amount of the honorarium was DM720.

40 For a fuller elaboration of this idea, see Todd Samuel Presner, *Mobile Modernity: Germans, Jews, Trains* (New York: Columbia University Press, 2007).

41 Numerous examples could be drawn to support the fact that Unger frequently fraternized and was close friends with non-Jewish Germans. Shortly after receiving the *Grosskreuz des Verdienstordens der Bundesrepublik Deutschland*, the managing director of Volkswagen Canada, Karl Barths, sent Unger a warm letter congratulating him on his honour. See letter from Karl Barths to Heinz Unger, dated 2 February 1965. LAC, MUS 56, box 1, file 16. For perceptions of Germans in Canada in the postwar period, see Alexander Freund, "Troubling Memories in Nation-Building: World War II Memories and Germans' Interethnic Encounters in Canada after 1945," *Histoire Sociale/Social History* 39, no. 77 (2006): 129–56.

42 Letter from Heinz Unger to Peter Johnston (First Secretary to the Canadian High Commissioner in London), dated 9 December 1964. LAC, MUS 56, box 1, file 16.

43 Gerhard P. Bassler, *The German Canadian Mosaic Today and Yesterday: Identities, Roots, and Heritage* (Ottawa: German-Canadian Congress, 1991), 2.

44 Bohlman, *The Land Where Two Streams Flow.*

TEN

East Meets West
Sephardic and Mizrahi Jews in Canada and the United States

Kelly Amanda Train

When the Eastern Sephardim (Jews from Arab lands) first arrived in the United States and Canada they were greeted in the same way by the established Jewish communities of both countries. In both places, their Ashkenazi brethren did not understand how they could "truly" be Jewish since they did not speak Yiddish and exhibited a great many other cultural differences. Although it was understood by Ashkenazic Jews that the Eastern Sephardim were Jews, their identities were unfamiliar, and therefore "not Jewish," to the Ashkenazi majority. In the case of Mizrahi Jews from India, Canadian and American Ashkenazi community leaders and members were shocked to discover that there were Indian Jews and questioned how it was possible to be both Jewish and Indian. Hence, Indian Jews had to constantly "prove" to Ashkenazi Jews that they were in fact "real" Jews and not Hindu or Muslim Indians who had converted.[1]

This chapter explores Sephardic and Mizrahi Jewish immigration and settlement in Canada and the United States as a basis for discussing Western and Eastern Sephardim and Sephardi–Ashkenazi relations in both countries. It emphasizes the distinct Canadian and American immigration policies and nation-building strategies, as well as global social, economic, and political forces that profoundly shaped the construction of Jewish communities in North America. I argue that the construction of an *authentic* Jewish identity has masked diverse Jewish experiences and ways of being Jewish, while simultaneously marginalizing non-Ashkenazic Jewish identities, particularly those of Eastern Sephardic and Mizrahi Jews.

The historical framework of immigration provides a basis for examining the relationship between Sephardim and Ashkenazim in both countries. Specifically, Eastern Sephardic and Mizrahi Jews were marginalized and excluded from the construction of an *authentic* Jewish identity. The identity that did evolve unified the broader American and Canadian Jewish community identities and essentialized these as synonymous with an Eastern European Ashkenazi identity. Ironically, early hegemonic Jewish community identities in both Canada and the United States had been dominated by "Western Sephardic" identities. But as the Jewish population in both countries became increasingly dominated by Ashkenazi, and as community institutions became increasingly led by Ashkenazi, an essentialist Jewish identity that reflected an Eastern European Ashkenazi identity emerged.

This chapter's research was based on eighteen interviews with North African Jews in Canada, including five community leaders, as well as sixteen interviews with Indian Jews in Canada, including seven community leaders. Community archival materials were also used. The Canadian research is part of an ongoing research project; the American materials rely largely on secondary sources. This chapter begins by defining the distinct historical and cultural contexts in which the groupings of Ashkenazi Jews, Western and Eastern Sephardic Jews, and Mizrahi Jews emerged. I also examine the immigration policies of Canada and the United States and how they had shaped Jewish communities in each country.

Who Are the Ashkenazi Jews? Who Are the Eastern and Western Sephardic Jews? Who Are the Mizrahi Jews?

The Jewish world is, broadly speaking, divided into two large and diverse groups: the Ashkenazim and the Sephardim. In the late tenth and early eleventh centuries, Ashkenazim and Sephardim emerged as the two main groups of Jews around the world.[2] Ashkenazi Jews are understood within the global Jewish community as the Jews who settled in northern France and western Germany during the Middle Ages. As a result of persecution and expulsion, Ashkenazi Jews migrated east, settling in various parts of Central and Eastern Europe. In the seventeenth and eighteenth centuries, some Ashkenazi Jews returned to Western Europe to escape the anti-Semitic *pogroms* that had broken out in Eastern Europe as well as the poverty that faced them there.[3] Generally speaking, Ashkenazi Jews lived under Christian rule in Europe. The histories, cultures, and identities of Western and Eastern Ashkenazi Jews reflect their experiences in different parts of Christian Europe.

In North America between the 1880s and 1950, Western Ashkenazim descended from German, British, French, and Central European Jews differentiated themselves from their Eastern Ashkenazi counterparts, referring to the latter as "uncivilized."[4] By the 1920s, however, it was Eastern Ashkenazim who dominated the Jewish community's leadership and membership throughout Canada and the United States. Moreover, by the mid-1920s, when Jewish immigration to Canada and the United States almost ground to a halt, the descendants of Western and Eastern Ashkenazi Jewish immigrants had become highly Canadianized or Americanized, and their identities were largely commingled by 1950.[5]

Sephardim are defined as the descendants of Jews who settled on the Iberian Peninsula in the Middle Ages. After 1391, much of Iberian Jewry was forcibly converted to Christianity. Many of these converts, known as New Christians or *Conversos*, continued to secretly practise Judaism or quietly identify as Jews. As a result of the continued secret practice of Judaism, the Inquisition was established in Spain in 1478. Concerned that unconverted Jews and those who secretly practised Judaism were encouraging New Christians to stray from their new faith, the Catholic monarchs of Spain expelled the Jews from their realms in 1492. It is estimated that at least half of these Spanish Jewish exiles resettled in Portugal.[6] In 1497, however, the Portuguese rulers forced Jews to convert to Catholicism; this was followed by an Inquisition established in 1536 to enforce Church dogma.[7]

When the Sephardic Jews were exiled from Iberia in the late fifteenth century, some of these crypto-Jews and their descendants migrated to Western and Northwestern Europe (including the Netherlands, the Bordeaux region of France, and England) as well as to the New World colonies. These Sephardic Jews became known as the Western Sephardim. Significant numbers of Sephardic Jews fleeing the Iberian Inquisitions also settled in various lands under Islamic rule, especially the Ottoman Empire and Moroccan Sultanate. On their arrival these crypto-Jews found long-established Jewish communities. Throughout the sixteenth and seventeenth centuries, the Jews of the Ottoman Empire constituted the largest Jewish community in the world. Although they were a diverse group with different linguistic, cultural, and historical backgrounds, these Jews became known collectively as the Eastern Sephardim.[8]

Some scholars and Sephardic community members have argued that all Eastern Sephardic and Mizrahi Jews should be referred to as "Sephardim"; other scholars and community members have argued that such a broad term ignores the diverse backgrounds, cultures, and histories of the different Sephardic and Mizrahi groups. For example, Daniel Elazar and Joseph Papo contend that a narrow definition of Sephardim as the descendants of the Jews of Iberia only is historically and culturally inadequate.[9] Instead, they claim that because of the influence and transmission of Sephardic culture and practices throughout the Middle East, North Africa, and India, the term "Sephardic" is an appropriate categorization for Jews who lived in all of those regions. Elazar and Papo also maintain that the Jews who lived throughout the Middle East, North Africa, and India should be considered Sephardim since Jews whose religious rituals and traditions are not Ashkenazi consider themselves to be part of the Sephardic world. Since the early 1990s, various scholars – including Ella Shohat, Yehuda Shenhav, Rebecca Torstrick, Zion Zohar, and Aziza Khazzoom – have noted that the word "Mizrahi" has replaced the derogatory term *bnei edot hamizrah* ("descendants of the Oriental ethnicities"), especially since Eastern Sephardic Jews are no longer being referred to as "Sephardic" because they are entirely associated with Arab and Levantine origins, without any historical connection to Iberia. "Mizrahi" came to be used in the Israeli context as a term of political resistance that challenged and rejected depictions of Arab Jews, Indian Jews, and Ethiopian Jews as "inferior," "backward," and "uncivilized."

Shohat and Shenhav use the term "Arab Jew" in the same way that "Mizrahi" has come to be used in the Israeli context: as a political term of resistance meant to disrupt the essentialist and binary categories of "Arab" and "Jew" and to reject and challenge the ways in which non-Ashkenazi Jewish identities have been denoted as inferior to the "real" Ashkenazi Jewish identity. The term "Arab Jew" problematizes how "Jew" has become synonymous with white Ashkenazi Jewish identity and how "Arab" has become synonymous with Muslim identity. Shohat and Shenhav use "Arab Jew" as a term of defiance and empowerment to highlight the distinct histories and the complex, diverse, and nuanced identities of the Jews from Arab lands in a manner that is "strategically essentialist."[10] In the Canadian and American contexts, diverse Eastern Sephardic groups refer to themselves as "Sephardic," as well as by the country from which they or their ancestors came (e.g., "Turkish Jews," "Greek Jews," "Moroccan Jews," "Iraqi Jews," "Persian Jews"). I use the term Eastern Sephardim to include the Jews who settled in the Eastern Hemisphere after their expulsion from Iberia, as well as the Jews from Arab lands, since my own findings illustrate that all identify as Sephardim.[11]

The Bene Israel and the Cochin Jews of India do not consider them-selves "Sephardic," although they share Sephardic liturgy and religious cus-toms. Rather, they classify themselves by their specific cultural, regional, and linguistic identities as "Bene Israel" or "Cochin Jews," or as descen-dants of the "Jews of India." Only the "Baghdadi Jews" of India who are the descendants of Iraqi Jews who settled in India under the British conquest refer to themselves as "Sephardic." Baghdadi Jews also point to their specific linguistic, cultural, and historical identity apart from Iraqi Jews, the Bene Israel, and the Cochin Jews.[12] It is appropriate to use the term "Mizrahim" as a broad term to refer to the diverse Indian Jewish communities, as well as to other non-Ashkenazi Jews who settled in North America who do not identify as Sephardim.

Ben-Ur argues that what is most important to recognize is how non-Ashkenazi Jews who arrived in the United States saw themselves as distinct social groups from one another in terms of language, region, culture, and identity, and organized their communities in the United States accord-ingly.[13] In Canada, Sephardic and Mizrahi Jews organized some of their institutions around their own linguistic, regional, and cultural identities; for example, North African Jewish synagogues were based in French or Spanish, as well as the city or region from which families descended. The Indian Jewish congregation was organized by members of the Bene Israel community residing in the Greater Toronto Area and therefore is based largely on Bene Israel and Cochin traditions, since Cochin Jewish religious leaders and rites historically shaped Bene Israel religious practices. The Indian Jewish congregation welcomes the Baghdadi Jews and incorporates their traditions and prayers, as well as the religious customs of Ashkenazim, Sephardim, and other Mizrahi groups. Other institutions, such as the Sep-hardic Jewish day school, were collectively organized as broadly Sephardic and incorporate the histories, cultures, and customs of all Eastern and Western Sephardic groups, while also acknowledging those of Ashkenazim and Mizrahim. The relatively small size of the Sephardic community in Toronto means that that school relies on the Sephardic community, but also on Mizrahi and Ashkenazi Jews, for students and financial support.[14]

For the purposes of this chapter, however, it is important to distinguish between Western and Eastern Sephardim as well as Mizrahim in order to document the different historical times and contexts in which immigration and settlement of diverse Jewish groups occurred in North America. More-over, it is important to understand that the terms "Sephardic" and "Mizrahi" refer to a highly diverse and broad group of non-Ashkenazi Jews. In reality, Sephardic and Mizrahi Jews constitute multiple and diverse groups of Jews who have very different linguistic, cultural, regional, and historical legacies.

The terms "Eastern Sephardim," "Western Sephardim," and "Mizrahim" are used in this chapter to distinguish between the different historical, cultural, ethnic, class, and immigration experiences of these various Jewish groups – experiences that in turn shaped their relations with Ashkenazi Jews and other Sephardic and Mizrahi Jews as well as with the larger American and Canadian societies. I use the terms "Eastern Sephardim," "Western Sephardim," and "Mizrahim" throughout this chapter as broad terms in ways that are "strategically essentialist." It is necessary to recognize how the various Sephardim and Mizrahim regarded themselves as distinct and different from one another, and to acknowledge the complex, diverse, and nuanced identities among Sephardim and Mizrahim.

Immigration of Western and Eastern Sephardic and Mizrahi Jews to North America

Prior to 1750, Western Sephardic colonists dominated Jewish settlement in North America. By the mid-eighteenth century the number of Ashkenazi Jews immigrating to the British North American colonies had begun to surpass the existing Sephardic Jewish population. They came originally from Great Britain (until 1776), then from Central Europe (1785–1880) and finally from Eastern Europe (1881–1924).[15] In Canada, the early Sephardim came either from the United States or directly from Britain. Some of these early Jewish settlers were Western Sephardim and had names that suggested Iberian roots.[16] However, except perhaps for a few, the Sephardim had disappeared from the Canadian Jewish population by 1768, relocating to other colonies or the United States, or assimilating with non-Jews.[17]

Few Sephardim resided in Canada until the second half of the twentieth century. The first wave of Sephardic settlers had disappeared by 1768; also, immigration restrictions that focused on building Canada as a white settler nation excluded all Sephardic and Mizrahi immigration until after the mid-1950s. White, European Jews faced almost no immigration restrictions from the 1890s until the outbreak of the First World War in 1914; immigrants from across Asia (from Turkey to the Far East) were considered "undesirable" and faced numerous immigration restrictions.[18] Immigration officials were given discretion to reject any potential immigrant deemed "unsuitable," and bigotry often played a significant role.[19]

Canada's exclusion of Sephardim and Mizrahim, and of other non-European immigrants, was solidified by an Order in Council issued in 1923 that excluded "any immigrant of any Asiatic race." The terms "Asia" and "Asiatics" applied to the entire region of the Eastern Hemisphere that was not considered part of Europe.[20] Asia referred to the region along the southern border of Russia and the Black Sea and included the eastern and southern coasts of the Mediterranean. Hence, all of Turkey, North Africa, and the Middle East was considered part of Asia. At the same time, severe restrictions on Jewish immigration from non-preferred countries, especially Eastern Europe, were implemented from 1919 to 1923 on the basis that Jews were "unable to assimilate" to Canadian cultural norms, and thus were a threat to society because of their activism in communist and anarchist movements.[21]

As a result, any potential Eastern Sephardic immigration in the first half of the twentieth century was impossible. Sephardic and Mizrahi immigration to Canada did not begin until the 1950s, when Canadian immigration policy changed to allow non-European immigration to Canada, but only from the Middle East. Visible minority immigrants, such as those from India, Asia, and Africa, were not allowed into Canada until 1962, when the Non-Discriminatory Immigration Regulations were enacted, including a points system. This change allowed Jews from North Africa and the Middle East, especially Morocco, to enter and settle in Canada after 1956, and the Jews of India after 1962.

American immigration policy, in contrast, allowed for the immigration of Eastern Sephardic Jews from the various Arab nations throughout the Ottoman Empire, including Turkey, the Balkans, and Greece after 1896, when the Ottoman Empire lifted its restrictions on emigration. An estimated 3,413 Eastern Sephardic immigrants arrived in the United States from all parts of the Ottoman Empire between 1899 and 1908.[22] Drawn by economic opportunity and repelled by military conscription, significant numbers of Eastern Sephardim arrived in the United States between 1908 and 1924, in the wake of political upheavals and rising nationalism throughout the Ottoman Empire.[23] Hebrew Immigrant Aid Services (HIAS), the Jewish agency assisting Jewish immigration and settlement in the United States, recorded that 2,865 Eastern Sephardic Jews arrived between 1909 and 1912.[24] By 1926, the number of Sephardic immigrants in the United States had risen to about 23,763.[25] Papo argues that this latter number is low, since it does not account for Eastern Sephardim who failed to tell American immigration officials that they were "Hebrews" and were therefore recorded as "Turks," "Greeks," "Serbs," "Syrians," and so on. Factoring this in, Marc Angel and Hasia Diner estimated that around 30,000 Jews from Arab lands, especially the Balkans, Turkey, and Greece, arrived between 1890 and 1924.[26] Most of these Eastern Sephardic immigrants came from the Ottoman Empire and spoke Ladino (Judeo-Spanish). Some of them were Greek-speaking Jews from Greece or Arabic-speaking Jews from Arab lands, especially Syria.[27]

Between 1880 and 1920 the vast majority of immigrants arriving and settling in the United States were from Eastern and Southern Europe, including Jews, Poles, Russians, Hungarians, Italians, Greeks, and Ukrainians. As the numbers of Eastern and Southern European immigrants increased, so did nativist attitudes and xenophobia.[28] In response to heightened anti-immigrant sentiments, American policy-makers began to institute immigration restrictions between the 1880s and the 1920s that reflected their desire to maintain a white, Anglo-Saxon, Protestant nation (these efforts included the Chinese Exclusion Act in 1882 and the Gentlemen's Agreement in 1908 to end Japanese immigration). The Quota Laws of 1921 and 1924 were established to severely reduce all non-Northern and non–Western European immigration. The 1921 Quota Law limited the number of immigrants from any one country to no more than 3 percent of the foreign-born persons from that country who were living in the United States in 1910; thus, the annual total number of immigrants from outside of Northern and Western Europe could not surpass 357,800.[29] The 1924 Quota Law reduced Southern and Eastern European immigration further by limiting the number of immigrants from any one country to a maximum of 2 percent of the number of foreign-born persons from that country living in the United States in 1890. By shifting immigration quotas to reflect the 1890 rather than 1910 census, immigration policy overwhelmingly favoured Northern and Northwestern European immigration. In the case of non-Ashkenazi Jewish immigrants, the 1924 Quota Law was especially restrictive of Eastern Sephardic and Mizrahi immigration since, based on the 1890 census, their numbers were limited to between one hundred and three hundred per country annually.[30] Eastern Sephardic and Mizrahi immigration to the United States would not resume until the 1950s.

In the post–Second World War era, Canada and the United States began to change their immigration policies. In 1947 the Canadian government defined "Asia" as all countries outside of Europe situated in the Eastern Hemisphere, including the Middle East, Turkey, Egypt, and Morocco. Thus, all immigration from the Middle East was prohibited under Canadian immigration regulations that excluded all *Asian* immigration. However, the selection criteria were liberalized after 1956 so as to allow a large number of applicants from the Middle East to be admitted to Canada. By the mid-1950s, the Middle East, including North Africa, was no longer considered part of "Asia," and immigration from the Middle East was actually encouraged.[31] This opened the way for Sephardic immigration to Canada from the Middle East.

In 1957 the US Congress passed the Refugee-Escapee Act, which broadened the definition of refugee to include a person from any country in the Middle East (from Libya to Pakistan, and from Turkey to Ethiopia and Saudi Arabia) who could not return to his or her country of origin for fear of being persecuted for reasons of race, religion, or political opinion.[32] Some of these Sephardic refugees were Holocaust survivors from the Balkan states. Jews from Arab lands began to seek emigration in light of the rise of anti-Semitism as Middle Eastern countries gained independence from their colonial rulers, and especially in the aftermath of the Six-Day War in 1967. While many of these emigrants fled to Israel or France, significant numbers came to North America.[33] Nonetheless, although the quota system had been liberalized to allow for immigration from the Middle East and for greater numbers of refugees and escapees, especially from communist-dominated and communist-occupied countries, numerical restrictions on non-European immigrants had not been removed altogether.[34]

In the 1960s, both Canada and the United States stopped emphasizing race, ethnicity, and nationality in their immigration criteria to focus instead on work skills. In 1962, new Canadian immigration regulations were implemented to address what the government considered to be the "poor quality of sponsored workers" and Canada's increasing need for skilled labour. This entailed creating a new priority system for selecting immigrants to ensure that well-qualified workers with the skills necessary for Canadian labour market needs would be granted admission, and that others would be kept out.[35] By 1967, these new selection criteria were being referred to as the points system, which was intended to serve as a fair and objective tool for assessing all immigration applicants, regardless of country of origin. It had nine criteria, which included education and training, work experience, employment opportunities and location in Canada, and knowledge of French or English, as well as personal suitability and relatives in Canada. To be considered as immigrants, applicants had to score at least 50 out of a possible 100 points.[36] Although the points system seemed to have eliminated racial discrimination, many scholars have argued that racism continued to permeate the process. For example, the Canadian government spent most of its immigration recruitment budget in Western countries, and Canadian immigration officials were granted substantial discretionary power in that they were allotted control over 15 points of the 100 points to determine an applicant's "personal suitability."[37] Even so, the new regulations allowed people of colour to immigrate to Canada for the first time. This facilitated the arrival of Mizrahi Jews from India.

In the United States, the 1965 Immigration Act eliminated the quota system that restricted non-European immigration and replaced it with a preference system. The act gave priority to professional and skilled workers, especially in occupations where there were labour shortages, as well as to refugees from communist countries and the Middle East and to members of extended families.[38] The act reinforced the 1957 provision that allowed for the immigration of Eastern Sephardim escaping the upheaval of decolonization in the Middle East. By 1965, most Western European countries were economically prosperous. As a result, few Western Europeans were interested in immigrating. Those who *were* interested were unable to pass the mandatory health requirements, known as the "LPC [likely to become a public charge] clause." By 1965, Eastern Europeans were not free to emigrate from the Communist Bloc. The elimination of restrictions based on race and ethnicity, combined with the emphasis on professional and skilled workers, allowed for significant numbers of immigrants from Asia, including Mizrahim and Eastern Sephardim, as well as Indian and Persian Jews seeking emigration, especially after Iran's Islamic Revolution of 1979.[39]

The 1957 provision and the 1965 act allowed for the immigration of Eastern Sephardic Jews from Iraq, Egypt, Morocco, Lebanon, Syria, and Iran throughout the 1950s and 1960s. Since 1973, Sephardic and Mizrahi immigration to the United States has been comprised of Eastern Sephardic as well as Mizrahi Jews, such as the Jews of India, coming from Israel. While most Eastern Sephardic and Mizrahi Jews settled in New York City, other communities were established in Atlantic City, Rochester, Syracuse, New Rochelle–Scarsdale, Washington, D.C., Hartford, Indianapolis, Detroit, Cincinnati, Chicago, Atlanta, Miami, Seattle, Portland, Los Angeles, and San Francisco.[40]

In the late 1970s, Jews were slightly less than 3 percent of the total US population, and around 3 percent of American Jews (180,000) were Sephardic (including Western and Eastern Sephardim and Mizrahim).[41] By the mid-2000s, out of about six million Jews in the United States, around 250,000 were non-Ashkenazi; they included 75,000 Eastern Sephardim of Ladino-speaking origins, 50,000 Syrian Jews, 40,000 Bukharian Jews, 30,000 to 40,000 Iranian Jews, 30,000 Yemeni Jews, 15,000 Iraqi Jews, and fewer than 1,000 Indian Jews.[42] It is likely that these demographic figures currently remain the same; the *American Jewish Year Book 2012* reported that the total Jewish population in the United States was between 6 and 6.4 million.[43]

In Canada, Sephardic and Mizrahi immigration from the Middle East and India occurred between 1957 and 1980. Since 1980, non-Ashkenazi immigration to Canada has been comprised of Eastern Sephardic and Mizrahi Jews from Israel.[44] North African Jews, especially from Morocco, represent the largest group of Sephardic Jews in Canada – at least one-third of the non-Ashkenazic population in Canada, and probably more if we include Israelis of North African origin in these numbers. Besides North African

Jews, the Sephardic and Mizrahi Jewish population in Canada includes very small numbers of Sephardic and Mizrahi Jews from Tunisia, Algeria, Iraq, Egypt, Iran, Lebanon, and Syria, including an Indian Jewish population of two to three hundred.[45]

Many of the Sephardim from French-speaking Middle Eastern countries, especially French-speaking North Africa, settled in Montreal.[46] Between 75 and 80 percent of all Sephardic and Mizrahi Jews in Canada live in or near Montreal.[47] Smaller numbers of French-speaking Sephardic Jews, and most Spanish-speaking Sephardic Jews from Morocco, have settled in Toronto.[48] English-speaking Sephardic and Mizrahi Jews (such as Iraqi and Indian Jews) have settled mainly in Toronto, with small numbers establishing themselves in Montreal, Vancouver, and Ottawa.[49] It is estimated that 15 to 20 percent of all Sephardic and Mizrahi Jews settled in Toronto, with smaller numbers in Vancouver and Ottawa and handfuls in other Canadian cities such as Winnipeg, Calgary, Edmonton, Kingston, and Hamilton.

It has become commonplace for Ashkenazim in Canada to view all Sephardim as North African Jews, and more specifically as "Moroccan Jews." Between 1957 and 1980, 17,000 to 18,000 Sephardim from North Africa immigrated to Canada.[50] According to Haim Hazan, by 1987 there were around 25,000 Sephardim in Montreal.[51] In 2001, the Canadian Jewish Appeal (CJA) Federation of Montreal stated that there were close to 21,215 Sephardic Jews residing in Montreal.[52] As of 1991, more than 8,000 Sephardic Jews were living in Toronto whose families had immigrated to Canada directly from North Africa.[53] Hazan stipulated that this figure did not include Sephardic Jews who arrived from Israel, of whom there were between 5,000 and 25,000. The 1991 Canadian Census revealed that, based on the combined categories of "Jewish as ethnicity," "Jewish as religion," place of birth, and mother tongue, there were between 18,870 and 25,805 Sephardic and Mizrahi Jews in Canada.[54] The Sephardic and Mizrahi population in Canada is estimated at between 26,000 and 46,000, out of a total of 370,505 Jews as recorded by the 2001 Canadian Census, with the vast majority residing in Toronto and Montreal.[55] In 2011 the Canadian Jewish population was recorded as 385,000.[56] It is estimated that the Canadian Sephardic and Mizrahi Jewish population, as of 2011, is between 27,000 and 48,000.

Western and Eastern Sephardic Jewish Relations in the United States

When Eastern Sephardim and Mizrahim immigrated to the United States in the early 1900s, they encountered two different Jewish communities: Western Sephardim and Ashkenazim. This experience was specifically American since there was no Canadian equivalent. The Canadian Jewish community was entirely Ashkenazi in the early 1900s, and Canadian immigration policy did not allow Eastern Sephardim or Mizrahim to immigrate. The Spanish and Portuguese Synagogue (also called Shearith Israel) in Montreal created by the early Western Sephardic and Ashkenazi settlers flourished as the oldest synagogue in Canada; it continued to follow Western Sephardic rites, customs, and traditions for prayer services, with English as the language of instruction.[57]

For the Eastern European Ashkenazi Jews who began arriving in Canada in large numbers after the 1880s, Western Sephardic practices were foreign and associated with the snobbishness of the upper-middle-class British Jews. As Eastern European Jews began to dominate the Canadian Jewish community through their sheer numbers, so did their customs and identities. Eastern European Jews established their own synagogues and religious schools, as well as political and social organizations comprised of brethren from their own country or town of origin. These organizations were rooted in Ashkenazi customs, melodies, and rites, with Yiddish as the language of instruction.[58] By the 1920s, Eastern European Ashkenazi Jews numerically dominated the Canadian Jewish community; they had also monopolized the leadership positions in all political and social Canadian Jewish community organizations, such as the Canadian Jewish Congress.

In the United States, Eastern Sephardim faced disdain from their Western Sephardic counterparts, as well as the refusal by Ashkenazi Jews to recognize their Jewish identities. Western Sephardic Jews identified with the upper class and emphasized their royal ancestral roots, whether real or imagined. They used these claims of noble blood, their high social status, and accounts of Western Sephardic contributions to science and literature during the Golden Age of Spain to shield their families from anti-Semitism, which from the late 1800s until the postwar era was generally experienced by the new Ashkenazi Jewish immigrants from Eastern Europe. By the early 1900s, Western Sephardim had become highly acculturated and Americanized into white Christian society, often boasting about their role in the American colonies and the American Revolution.[59] Many Western Sephardim had married upper-middle-class non-Jews, or Ashkenazim who had made their way into gentile, white Anglo-Saxon American society.

The more recently arrived Eastern Sephardim were also "Sephardic," but their religious customs and culture were distinctly "Arabic," not Western. Eastern Sephardim did not have any connections to a crypto-Jewish ancestral past since they had generally lived under Muslim rule in the Ottoman

Empire. The ancestors of Eastern Sephardim had chosen expulsion over conversion. Unlike Western Sephardic American Jews, the new Sephardic immigrants were largely poor and working class. Nonetheless, many Western and Eastern Sephardim shared an identity based on their common history with the Spanish and Portuguese Inquisitions and a similar Sephardic liturgy; they also spoke similar languages (Ladino and modern Spanish). All of these things served as a basis of their Jewish identity.[60] Other Eastern Sephardim did not share a history of the Inquisitions since their origins, identities, and traditions were rooted in Arabic cultures, within which they spoke Judeo-Arabic.

Western Sephardim saw that the newcomers could help rebuild the Sephardic community. Intermarriage among Western Sephardim, Ashkenazim, and non-Jews had resulted in diminishing numbers of Sephardim. In theory, Western Sephardim were glad to receive the new Eastern Sephardic immigrants, whom they saw as revitalizing the Sephardic community. The newcomers needed the financial help, charity, and guidance of the established Sephardic community to integrate into American society. The newcomers were pleased to have the assistance of the Western Sephardic community. Nonetheless, issues arose. The Sisterhood activists of the Spanish and Portuguese Synagogue in New York City (sharing the same name, Shearith Israel) were especially keen on helping the newcomers. The Spanish and Portuguese Synagogue was the centre of the Western Sephardic community in North America and served as the community's leadership. Since it is the oldest Jewish congregation in the United States, it was associated with the elite status of its seventeenth-century founders. The Sisterhood members sympathized with the plight of the new immigrants and wanted to provide whatever services they needed. But they also imposed their elitist ideas about acculturation on the newcomers in paternalistic and demeaning ways. Instead of recognizing the immediate daily needs of newcomers, they emphasized that settlement and acculturation meant adopting the traits and pastimes of the upper class. One Sisterhood activist stated that she would take on the responsibility of making sure that Sephardic girls learned to play the piano and speak modern Spanish to replace Ladino.[61] Eastern Sephardic immigrants were offended and felt misunderstood.

In 1913, the spiritual leader of the Spanish and Portuguese Synagogue acknowledged that Eastern Sephardim preferred to pray according to their own rituals and should be supported in doing so. Therefore, the congregation's leaders established parallel religious services for the Eastern Sephardim so that they could preserve their distinctive traditions. But although these services were organized specifically for Eastern Sephardim, they were conducted according to Western Sephardic liturgy and rituals, and they did not include the Ladino or Judeo-Arabic prayers that were part of Eastern Sephardic religious rites and traditions. By 1913, these separate services and places of worship had all been consolidated into Berith Shalom. A religious school was also established. The Western Sephardic Sisterhood paid the rent for the synagogue and the religious school, in addition to teacher salaries. Since the Spanish and Portuguese Synagogue administered the Eastern Sephardic school and synagogue, it was heavily influenced by Western Sephardic traditions and customs.

Eastern Sephardim liked the idea that their own religious institutions would be closely affiliated with those of the Western Sephardic community, for this would bring them status and respect for their own community in the eyes of the larger, Ashkenazi-dominated Jewish community. In 1914, Eastern Sephardim who worshipped at Berith Shalom were allowed to become associate members of the Spanish and Portuguese Synagogue through the payment of monthly dues. Many Eastern Sephardim embraced associate membership. However, in 1925 the Eastern Sephardic members broke away from the Spanish and Portuguese Synagogue affiliation, citing "irreconcilable differences," largely on the basis of class disparities and the elitist attitude of the Western Sephardic community. For example, as late as 1933, the spiritual leader of the Spanish and Portuguese Synagogue recommended that Eastern Sephardim be offered "gradual associate membership" conditionally based on upward mobility.[62]

Class was not the only basis on which the Eastern Sephardim felt demeaned by the Western Sephardic community. In 1911, the Hebrew Immigrant Aid Society (HIAS) established a charitable office specifically to aid Sephardic immigrants. In 1912, the office became officially known as the "Bureau for Sephardic Immigrants." However, Western Sephardic community leaders pressured the HIAS to change the name to "Oriental Bureau." At the same time, a group of Eastern Sephardim formed their own charitable organization, which they named the "Federation of Sephardic Societies," and asked the Spanish and Portuguese Synagogue for assistance in meeting the most urgent needs of the new immigrants. The congregation was willing to provide support, but only if the organization changed its name from "Sephardic" to "Oriental."[63] The leader of the Western Sephardic community, David de Sola Pool, claimed that "Oriental" was more fitting for the organization than "Sephardic" since its users were primarily from Turkey, Syria, Morocco, and other Middle Eastern countries. Hence, the organization became the "Federation of Oriental Jews."

The Western Sephardic community continued to fight for hegemony over the term "Sephardic" when, in 1914, the HIAS announced that it was establishing a "Committee on Sephardic Jewish Immigrants." Pool pressured the HIAS leadership to change the name to "Committee on Oriental Jewish Immigrants," and he won, even though the HIAS considered the term inappropriate. One HIAS official argued that the American public would misconstrue "Oriental and Eastern" as meaning "Chinese" or "Japanese." "Levantine" was probably a more appropriate term, except that at the time, it was American slang for "cheats" and "swindlers." He further argued that the term "Sephardic" was the closest term to refer to the group of people it sought to aid. Note that all of the organizations that later superseded the Federation of Oriental Jews expunged the term "Oriental" and replaced it with "Sephardic," including the Sephardic Community of New York (1920–22), the Sephardic Jewish Community of New York (1922–32), and the Central Sephardic Jewish Community of America (1941).[64] In 1972, all of these Sephardic community organizations were subsumed under the newly created American Sephardi Federation. In 1978, the term "Sephardic" was officially adopted to refer to all non-Ashkenazi Jews. Western Sephardic community leaders sought to preserve their elite heritage by distancing themselves from Eastern Sephardim, largely through terminology.[65] The Western Sephardim provided Eastern Sephardic newcomers with assistance. But at the same time, Western Sephardic community leaders were desperate to preserve their elevated social status by distancing themselves from their poor, working-class, "foreign" Eastern counterparts.

Pool tried to preserve the elite status of the Western Sephardic community, but he also recognized the importance of Eastern Sephardic rites, rituals, and customs. In 1936, he published a new Sephardic prayer book, which was adopted by many congregations across the United States and around the world, including South America and the Caribbean. In his prayer book, Pool tried to merge Western and Eastern Sephardic traditions, customs, and practices. In the second edition, published in 1941, he acknowledged textual additions that were specifically from the rituals and customs of Eastern Sephardim. Pool's prayer book, *The Book of Prayers*, now in its twelfth edition, published by the Union of Sephardic Congregations (1997), amounted to a significant deviation from the way that Western Sephardic community leaders sought to impose Western Sephardic rites, traditions, and customs on the Eastern Sephardic newcomers in the early days of immigration. At that time, the establishment viewed Western Sephardic rites as "authentic" and treated Eastern Sephardic traditions as superficial additions.[66] Pool's prayer book helped bring the Sephardic communities together at a time when Western Sephardic communities were on the verge of extinction as a result of acculturation into white Christian American society, the "Ashkenazification" of Western Sephardim through intermarriage and absorption, and the death of large numbers of Western Sephardim in the Holocaust.[67] The immigration of thousands of Sephardi and Mizrahi Jews from the Middle East and Asia helped revitalize Western and Eastern Sephardic congregations; however, most established their own congregations with their own distinctive customs and traditions. Pool's prayer book helped bring together Western and Eastern Sephardim rituals, along with those of Mizrahim, so that Sephardic communities could view themselves as united by the group identity "Sephardic."[68] Pool's prayer book is still being used by non-Ashkenazi congregations, including Western and Eastern Sephardic and Mizrahi congregations, such as Congregation Bene Israel of North America (BINA), a congregation of Indian Jews. The prayer book is acknowledged as a means to unify non-Ashkenazi Jewish communities through a broad Sephardic and Mizrahi group identity, although each community uses its own melodies, customs, and traditions.

Sephardi–Ashkenazi Jewish Relations in Canada and the United States

When Eastern Sephardim arrived in the United States in the early 1900s, their Ashkenazi brethren did not recognize them as Jews. The Ashkenazi Jews they encountered were largely Eastern European immigrants or the second American generation of these immigrants, who primarily spoke Yiddish and generally defined Jewishness according to German and Eastern European Ashkenazi culture, both secular and religious (*Yiddishkeit*; Jewish culture). Ashkenazi Jews could not believe that these "Turks," "Greeks," or "Arabs" were actually Jews, and assumed they were gentiles.[69] Ashkenazi Jews assumed that the only true markers of Jewish identity were cultural: kosher versions of German and Eastern European foods, various dialects of Yiddish (Judeo-German), the customs and traditions associated with the Ashkenazi form of Judaism, the Ashkenazi pronunciation of Hebrew, Eastern European and German names, and Eastern and Western European dress.[70] In other words, German and Eastern European Ashkenazi identity was the "standard" by which Jewish identity was determined. At the same time, Eastern Sephardic and Mizrahi Jews felt uncomfortable in Ashkenazi institutions since they spoke Ladino, Arabic, or Greek rather than Yiddish and were unfamiliar with the Ashkenazi pronunciation of Hebrew prayers, which made it impossible for them to participate in religious worship in Ashkenazi synagogues.

Eastern Sephardim regarded Ashkenazi Jewish identity and culture as unfamiliar, but they did not doubt the "Jewishness" of Ashkenazim. Eastern Sephardic and Mizrahi Jews had been aware of the existence of Ashkenazi

Jews globally prior to immigrating to the United States. In contrast, Eastern Sephardic and Mizrahi Jews encountered outright rejection as Jews by Ashkenazim, except for the odd rabbinical leader who took on the responsibility of educating his congregants about the "authenticity" of Eastern Sephardic and Mizrahi Jewishness. It was not unusual for Ashkenazi Jews to question Eastern Sephardic Jews about their names and their inability to speak or understand Yiddish and on that basis refuse to acknowledge their "Jewishness."[71] Similarly, Ashkenazi Jews saw Eastern Sephardic foods, traditional dress, and leisure pursuits (such as drinking Turkish coffee and smoking waterpipes, or hookah) as "Turkish" or "Arabic" and therefore as not Jewish. Moise Gadol, the founder of the Sephardic newspaper *La America*, wrote in 1910 that before his newspaper existed, Ashkenazim refused to believe that Eastern Sephardim were Jews, even when they showed the Ashkenazim their prayer shawls. According to Gadol, it was only when Ashkenazi Jews saw that the Ladino newspapers used Hebrew letters that they began to understand that the Eastern Sephardim were in fact Jews and that their language – Judeo-Spanish – was a dialect of Spanish that reflected their Jewish identity. In sum, it was Ashkenazi Jews in the United States who were unaware of the existence of Sephardic Jews around the world, not the other way around.[72]

Since Ashkenazi HIAS officials did not recognize Eastern Sephardic or Mizrahi Jews as Jews, it was not unusual for the newcomers to arrive unnoticed and miss out on the assistance for which they were eligible. An early Sephardic activist in the United States, Gadol became the voice of the immigrant Sephardic community by establishing the *La America* (published weekly in Ladino) to provide essential information to immigrant Eastern Sephardim on how to find employment, the kinds of services and opportunities available to them, and generally how to integrate into American society. Gadol persuaded HIAS leaders to establish a special agency that would serve the specific needs of the Sephardic newcomers. In 1911, the "Oriental Bureau" was created, with Gadol as the first secretary. It provided assistance to Sephardic immigrants as they arrived at Ellis Island in New York. It also helped newcomers deal with other issues as they settled in New York City, for example, by helping them fill out citizenship papers and providing employment advice.

The predominance of Yiddish as a marker of Jewish identity was not the only factor that prevented Eastern Sephardim from being recognized as Jews. Sephardic activists found it almost impossible to participate in Jewish community organizations, since the meetings were entirely in Yiddish. US government publications that focused on guiding the integration of new immigrants were published in a variety of European languages, English as well as Yiddish, but not in Ladino or Arabic; thus, Eastern Sephardim had no access to such information.[73] This indicates that among the American public, German and Eastern European Ashkenazi Jewish identity was the *only* Jewish identity.

Eastern Sephardic community activists like Gadol were certain that once Eastern Sephardic Jewish communal organizations, such as the HIAS's "Oriental Bureau" and *La America*, were established to address the needs and concerns of the newcomers, Eastern Sephardic and Mizrahi Jews would be recognized as "authentic" Jews by their Ashkenazi brethren. Indeed, these organizations did help the Ashkenazi-dominated American Jewish community recognize Eastern Sephardim as Jews, but this did not mean that Sephardim were given equal treatment. In particular, the dominance of Yiddish in Jewish organizations, including social service organizations, prevented Eastern Sephardic and Mizrahi Jews from using these services to escape poverty, gain social mobility, and integrate into the American Jewish community and society in general.[74]

Eastern Sephardim and Mizrahim internalized the "Otherness" imposed on them by the Ashkenazi establishment. According to Joseph Sutton, Syrian Jewish immigrants referred to themselves as "Syrians" while referring to Ashkenazim as "Jews" because "Jews" and Jewish culture in the American context referred specifically to Ashkenazi Jews both within the American Jewish community and in American society at large.[75] By the 1950s, Ashkenazi American Jews had largely become "white," and were rising into the middle and upper classes – a movement that was largely denied to most people of colour.[76] After the 1950s, Hollywood portrayed Ashkenazi Jews as no different from other white Americans. Eastern Sephardic and Mizrahi culture threatened the whiteness of American Ashkenazi Jewry. Although Eastern Sephardim sought recognition and inclusion within the established American Jewish community, they also affiliated themselves with Arab culture, which was not specifically Jewish, in order to retain their distinct Arab-Jewish identity.[77]

Eastern Sephardic Jews who came to Canada entered a Jewish community that was almost completely Ashkenazic. Canadian Jewry was by no means monolithic; Ashkenazi differed from one another on the basis of political affiliation, class, and length of time in Canada. That said, by the 1950s the Canadian Jewish community was dominated by English-speaking, Canadian-born Jews of Eastern European descent who had risen to the middle and upper classes and were highly "Canadianized."[78] As a result, the term "Sephardic" in the Canadian context referred specifically to Eastern Sephardic Jews, especially Moroccans, who represented the majority of Sephardim settling in Canada after 1956.[79]

Eastern Sephardic Jews from North Africa were the first non-Ashkenazi Jews to settle in Canada since the earliest days of British Quebec. These Sephardic Jews were the first non-European Jewish newcomers to the Canadian Jewish community. In the 1960s and 1970s, most Jewish immigrants to Canada were coming from North Africa. Significant numbers of these Sephardic immigrants were French-speaking and settled in Montreal and Toronto. The number of North African Jews who arrived in Canada during this period was so significant that Jewish Immigrant Aid Services (JIAS, the Canadian version of HIAS) organized an integration program, the Moroccan Integration Program, specifically aimed at addressing their particular needs.[80] Canadian Jews became aware that noticeable numbers of North African Jews were settling in Canada. These Jews did not face questions about their Jewishness from Canadian Jews, however. Instead, they were marginalized as non-European.

Even so, the Canadian Jewish infrastructure made a tremendous effort to help North African Jews immigrate and integrate. The JIAS played a crucial role in getting their immigration applications processed. Once these Jews arrived in Canada, the JIAS provided them with full access to all the services and resources the organization was able to offer. The JIAS met the newcomers at their point of arrival, arranged housing, and provided clothing, basic household items, furniture, rent, and a living allowance until the head of the household secured employment, which was usually with the assistance of Jewish Vocational Services, the Jewish community's employment agency.[81]

Shortly after immigrating to Canada in 1957, as one of the first Eastern Sephardim to arrive in Toronto, Maurice Benzacar convinced the JIAS that Eastern Sephardic newcomers would integrate more easily if they were met on arrival in Canada by an Eastern Sephardic JIAS official (i.e., rather than an Ashkenazi) who could speak with them in French and Spanish and was familiar with Eastern Sephardic cultural identities. Benzacar was soon hired to act in this capacity.[82]

Eastern Sephardi and Mizrahi Jews were welcome to participate in Ashkenazi organizations, such as synagogues and Jewish parochial schools, but they, like their American counterparts, felt uncomfortable when doing so. Ashkenazi Jews were aware that Eastern Sephardim were Jews, but they regarded their Jewishness as "inauthentic" and "wrong" since they did not meet the norms associated with Ashkenazi Jewish identity with regard to language, food, rituals, and other cultural traits.[83] Thus, while already by the 1950s English had replaced Yiddish as the "mother tongue" of the community, Yiddish continued to be a cultural marker of Jewish identity in Canada.[84] Influenced by the cultural importance of Yiddish, many Canadian

Jews wondered how Sephardim could be Jewish when they did not speak Yiddish.[85]

Eastern Sephardim received formal assistance from the JIAS and other Jewish community organizations, but they also encountered demeaning condescension from Ashkenazi Jews. In particular, Ashkenazi Jews assumed that Eastern Sephardim were unfamiliar with Western cultural norms and that they were "backward" and "unenlightened" in their secular and religious practices, values, and beliefs. In an official JIAS document produced in 1972, a top executive complained that the children of Eastern Sephardic Jewish families had significant high school dropout rates, as well as high rates of unemployment, criminal behaviour, and drug abuse; he blamed all of this on Eastern Sephardic family values. The same official claimed that these values were the reason why Sephardim were failing to adapt to Jewish life in Canada and to Canadian society as a whole.[86] Statements like these reinforced the marginalization of Eastern Sephardim within the established Jewish community and their distrust of Ashkenazi Jews generally.

Eastern Sephardic schoolchildren and their families were treated as "inferior" Jews by the religious Ashkenazi Jewish day school establishment.[87] Eastern Sephardic community leaders sought acceptance for themselves within the Orthodox Jewish community by encouraging Eastern Sephardic families to send their children to strictly religious Jewish day schools. Eastern Sephardic schoolchildren started attending Orthodox Ashkenazi Jewish day schools in the fall of 1967. Many of them, as the children of low-income new immigrants, were subsidized by the schools (which received funding from the Jewish Federation of the United Jewish Appeal, via the Board of Jewish Education), as well as by private sources. This process was expedited between 1968 and 1974 by a decline in the number of Ashkenazi students at Orthodox Ashkenazi day schools, as the level of religiosity of Canadian Jews began to wane.

But Eastern Sephardic schoolchildren found themselves demeaned and demoralized: they were forced into separate classes from Ashkenazi students, viewed as less intelligent and culturally inferior, and treated as if their Jewish identity, customs, practices, and traditions were simply "wrong." As well, their Eastern Sephardic histories, rites, prayers, melodies, and traditions were entirely absent from the curriculum. As one former (and now adult) Eastern Sephardic schoolgirl, Alegria Levy Benhaim (alias) explained, the only correct Jewish practices, customs, and histories were those of Ashkenazi Jews. Anything else was considered non-Jewish and "unkosher." Discussions of modern Jewish history revolved entirely around the persecution that Ashkenazi Jews had endured in the Holocaust. The persecution of Spanish and Portuguese Jews during the Inquisitions was never mentioned. Nor were the experiences of Jews in Arab lands, including the hostility they endured after Israel's independence in 1948.

Eastern Sephardic Jews were (and continue to be) depicted as "Arabs" within the Canadian Jewish community.[88] As a result, Eastern Sephardim in Canada, like their American counterparts, were constantly reminded of their "Otherness" and "foreignness" within the established Ashkenazi-dominated community. Much like their American counterparts, Eastern Sephardic Jews in Canada – especially the children of the newcomers – internalized the "Otherness" imposed on them by the Canadian Jewish community. They were subjected to "Ashkenazification," that is, the process by which Sephardic Jews adopt elements of Eastern European Jewish culture, which are not necessarily connected to religious practices, and abandon their distinct Sephardic cultural identity in order to be recognized within religious and secular Ashkenazi-dominated Jewish communities, in both Canada and the United States.[89]

The Eastern Sephardic children of immigrants and the Eastern Sephardic religious leaders sought to escape being regarded as "inferior" by Ashkenazi Jews and the Ashkenazi establishment by abandoning their Sephardic identities and adopting Ashkenazi traditions, Eastern European Jewish foods, the Ashkenazi pronunciation of Hebrew, and Ashkenazi prayer tunes, and by using Yiddish phrases. Maklouf Elcabas (alias) explained that as a minority within a minority, you end up giving up your distinct Sephardic Jewish identity and adopting Ashkenazi practices and culture in order to be recognized as a Jew by both the Jewish community and broader gentile society. Abraham Elfassy (alias) explained that the Sephardic rabbis tried to gain acceptance from the established religious community by wearing traditional Eastern European Ashkenazi male dress – a black hat, a long beard, and sidelocks (payot) – and by adopting Ashkenazi prayer melodies and Hebrew pronunciation, and even by using Yiddish terms. The French-speaking Sephardic Jews in Quebec responded to the marginalization and disparaging remarks they experienced from the Ashkenazi community by identifying politically and socially with French-speaking non-Jews. Even today, tensions exist between the French-speaking Sephardim and the English-speaking Ashkenazi community in Montreal.[90]

Mizrahi–Ashkenazi Jewish Relations in Canada and the United States

For Indian Jews who arrived in Canada between 1964 and 1980 and in the United States between the 1950s and the early 1970s, the Ashkenazi-dominated Jewish community had (and continues to have) difficulty understanding how they could be Jewish since their skin colour was not even remotely "white," according to Ashkenazi standards of Jewish identity.[91] In contrast, while the skin colour of Eastern Sephardim was "tanned," it was still "light." Therefore, Ashkenazi Jews viewed these newcomers as Indians, not as Jews, falsely assuming they were Hindus or Muslims who possibly had converted to Judaism.[92]

Indian Jewish immigrants to North America during the mid- and late twentieth century were educated professionals and highly skilled workers who spoke English, unlike the Eastern Sephardim. When Indian Jews began immigrating to Canada in the mid-1960s, the JIAS encouraged large numbers of Jewish newcomers to settle in Toronto and Winnipeg. It provided immigration and settlement assistance to Indian Jews; however, virtually all Indian Jews who immigrated between 1964 and 1980 were able to find employment on their own and support themselves within the first few months of arriving in Canada.[93]

One Indian Jewish leader, Sarah Reuben (alias), who settled in Toronto in 1966, reported that although a JIAS worker at the airport met her and her husband, the social worker had not arranged for them to be placed in a Jewish neighbourhood, nor had he asked whether they needed accommodation for kosher meals or to be within walking distance of a synagogue. Instead, she stated, he looked through a newspaper, called a non-Jewish boarding house ad, and dropped them off at the boarding house, leaving them to fend for themselves and pay for their own accommodations.[94] Reuben discovered years later that the JIAS was supposed to provide immigration services that included arranging for an apartment for new immigrants (not boarding house accommodation), paying their rent for a number of months, providing them with basic personal and household items (such as furniture, kitchenware, and clothing suitable for the Canadian climate), helping new immigrants find jobs, and connecting them with a Canadian Jewish family to mentor them and serve as a support network. Reuben stated that even after asking various JIAS workers for help on a number of occasions during the first few weeks after her arrival, she received none of these services. At this point, she gave up on the JIAS and through family connections in India contacted an Indian Jewish family acquaintance who had immigrated to Toronto earlier. Instead of the JIAS, she relied on this family acquaintance for advice and mentoring in the first years of settlement in Toronto. Reuben attributed her experiences to how she was not recognized as "Jewish" by Canadian Jewish community workers, even though she was eligible for Jewish immigrant aid and other services on the basis of being Jewish.

Indian Jews were formally welcome to participate in Ashkenazi institutions such as synagogues and Jewish parochial schools, but they felt uncomfortable, even demoralized, in these places, especially since they were repeatedly questioned about their "Jewishness." Joan Roland writes that few Indian Jews in the United States tried to integrate into Ashkenazi congregations, although some older Bene Israel attended Sephardic synagogues. She asserts that Indian Jews found the Ashkenazi pronunciation of Hebrew and liturgical melodies so different that they were unable to participate, despite being well versed in the prayer services.[95]

At the same time, they were uncomfortable dealing with questions from their Ashkenazi counterparts surrounding their "Jewishness."[96] In Canada, Indian Jews were regularly questioned by Ashkenazi Jews about how they could be Jewish on the basis that they did not "look" Jewish according to the Ashkenazi Jewish standard (i.e., "white"). Lily Jacob (alias) describes how she was forced to "prove" that she was a "real" Jew because of her skin colour. Ruby Benjamin noted that when she worked at the Canadian Jewish Congress shortly after arriving in Canada, her employer told her she could not come to work because, dressed in a sari, she looked "Indian" rather than "Jewish."

The only way that Ashkenazi Jews could make sense of Indian Jewishness was through the concept of conversion. Thus, Indian Jews found themselves regularly having to explain their "legitimacy" and "authenticity" as "real" Jews by tracing their Jewish lineage and by informally educating Ashkenazi Jews about the history of the Jews in India in social conversations. Sally Joseph (alias) stated that Canadian Jews would assume either she or one or both of her parents had converted to Judaism, and that she was constantly having to explain the history of the Jews of India and how they arrived in India 2,500 years ago after the destruction of the Second Temple in CE 70. Sarah Reuben recalled an Indian Jewish friend's encounter with a well-known Ashkenazi rabbi (a community leader from the 1950s to the 1980s) who, to her face, rejected the notion that Indian Jews could exist except through conversion.

Ashkenazi Jews rejected the "Jewishness" of Indian Jews primarily on the basis of skin colour and culture. For Ashkenazi Jews, "real" Jewishness was associated with whiteness and "Europeanness." Hence, Indian Jewish traditional dress, languages such as Judeo-Marathi, and foods that were viewed by Ashkenazi Jews as symbols of "Indianness" all contradicted the "true" and "authentic" Jewish identity, which was a white European identity. Like their Eastern Sephardi counterparts, Indian Jews were questioned by Ashkenazi Jews about how they could be Jewish if they were unfamiliar with Yiddish, which was viewed by Ashkenazi Jews as the "authentic" language of Jewish identity and culture, especially before 1980. Similarly, Ashkenazi Jews could not understand the "Jewishness" of Indian Jews since they were unfamiliar with Eastern European Jewish foods and culture, which Ashkenazi Jews viewed as symbols of "true" or "authentic" Jewish identity. David Musleah, a Baghdadi Jewish respondent, stated that when he went to the homes of Canadian Jews, he was often questioned about how he could be Jewish since he was unfamiliar with *gefilte fish*, as well as other Eastern European Jewish foods.

Indian Jews found it demoralizing and demeaning not to be recognized as "real" Jews by their Ashkenazi counterparts. Furthermore, this meant that they found themselves symbolically and materially denied membership and access to Jewish community resources. In the early 1970s, the young son of a religious Indian Jewish family in Toronto died suddenly. The family did not belong to any synagogue, organization, or association that had burial plots reserved for its members, since these organizations were almost entirely Eastern European Ashkenazi. At the time, there was no Jewish cemetery for the unaffiliated. Because of their Indian identity, the family had a very difficult time finding a synagogue or society that would bury their son. They were constantly asked to "prove" their Jewish identity in order to obtain a burial plot for their son. The family found themselves humiliated by the Ashkenazi-dominated establishment, which questioned their Jewish identity even while they were mourning their son.

Like their Eastern Sephardic Jewish counterparts, Indian Jewish schoolchildren found their Indian Jewish identities, histories, practices, traditions, and cultures entirely absent from Jewish parochial school curriculums. Many were told by their teachers that their Jewish cultural practices and traditions were "wrong." Joanna Saul noted that when she and her sister attended an Orthodox Jewish day school they only learned Eastern European Jewish history, such as how Ashkenazi Jews were persecuted in the Holocaust. Instruction also stated that Ashkenazi tunes, customs, traditions, and pronunciation of Hebrew were the only "right" way to practise Judaism. She and her sister would adamantly insist to their parents that what they learned in school was "right" and reject any and all Indian Jewish melodies, customs, and traditions. Hence, like their Eastern Sephardic Jewish counterparts, Indian Jewish children sought to escape their "Otherness" by abandoning Indian Jewish identities and adopting Ashkenazi traditions and dress.[97] Yet many Indian Jews found that they still remained outcasts within the broader Jewish community on the basis of their skin colour.

The Creation of Sephardic and Mizrahi Jewish Institutions

In response to Eastern Sephardic and Mizrahi Jewish experiences of marginalization in both the United States and Canada, the members of these communities sought to establish their own Jewish institutions separate from the Ashkenazi-dominated and Western Sephardic communal institutions. The ones they founded provided different and complementary services to the established Jewish communal services that already existed, catering to the specific needs of their own communities while also cultivating Eastern Sephardic and Mizrahi Jewish identity. Most importantly, these institutions, which were sometimes established with the assistance of Ashkenazi benefactors, celebrated non-Ashkenazi Jewish identities, educated the greater Ashkenazi-dominated community about non-Ashkenazi Jewish identities and cultures, enabled Eastern Sephardic and Mizrahi Jews to practise their own Jewish traditions and customs in their own communal spaces, and fostered pride among Eastern Sephardic and Mizrahi Jews, especially their North American–born children, about their specific Jewish identities.

In both the United States and Canada, Eastern Sephardic and Mizrahi Jews established synagogues, Jewish parochial schools, community centres, homes for the elderly, veterans' groups, and clubs that were specific to their practices, traditions, and customs. In the United States, Eastern Sephardic and Mizrahi Jews also established an independent press to provide their communities with a social and political voice within the established Ashkenazi-dominated Jewish community structures.[98]

Eastern Sephardic and Mizrahi communities founded institutions to support the needs of their communities that were being ignored by Ashkenazi community structures.[99] These institutions and organizations supported Sephardic and Mizrahi culture and identity. They provided the Eastern Sephardic community with its own social and political voice so that its members could meet the material needs of their own community and celebrate and continue Eastern Sephardic and Mizrahi Jewish traditions. This included raising awareness among North American Ashkenazim of their distinctive heritage through educational forums and the media. The effectiveness of these institutions and organizations is best measured by each Sephardic and Mizrahi group's refusal to be silenced and marginalized. By instilling pride and respect for the distinctive heritage of Sephardic and Mizrahi Jews, they are ensuring the survival of these exceptional cultural identities for future generations.

Conclusion

American and Canadian Eastern Sephardic and Mizrahi Jews faced many hardships integrating with the Jewish communities of both countries. They had been permitted to immigrate to the United States early in the twentieth century since American immigration policy allowed for some immigration from the Middle East prior to the 1921 and 1924 Quota Laws. On arrival, Sephardic and Mizrahi Jews encountered an established Ashkenazi-dominated community that regarded the newcomers as "inauthentically" Jewish. Although established charities provided assistance to the immigrants, American Jews did not know what to make of the newcomers since their non-European, Middle Eastern backgrounds were alien to them.

In Canada, Eastern Sephardic and Mizrahi Jews did not arrive until the 1950s, since Canadian immigration policy did not allow non-Europeans to enter Canada before then. When the newcomers arrived, they encountered a Jewish community that was almost entirely Eastern European Ashkenazi. Although Canadian Jews were aware that Eastern Sephardic Jews were "Jewish," they regarded the new immigrants as having a "wrong" or "inauthentic" Jewish identity since they used Ashkenazic *Yiddishkeit* as the rubric for measuring Jewishness. Indian Jews were constantly having to "prove" their Jewishness to Canadian Jews and explain how they were not Hindu or Muslim Indians who had converted to Judaism.

The concept of an "authentic" Jewish identity is highly problematic, as demonstrated in this chapter. Eastern Sephardic and Mizrahi Jews brought to light how in both Canada and the United States an "authentic" Jewish identity can mask the diversity of Jewish cultures by marginalizing non-Ashkenazi Jewish identities, particularly those of Eastern Sephardic and Mizrahi Jews. The concept of an "authentic" Jewish identity has had tangible consequences in the lives of those who are marginalized as a result of this construction. While Eastern Sephardic and Mizrahi Jews were able to receive communal assistance for immigration and settlement, they were also demeaned and demoralized by not being recognized as legitimate Jews.

The Eastern Sephardic and Mizrahi Jewish communities resisted marginalization by establishing their own institutions and organizations. In creating these, however, they did not intend to separate themselves from the established Jewish community. Rather, these institutions were intended to seek wider community acknowledgment so that their diverse identities and needs would be included within a larger political and social agenda in meaningful and practical ways. Eastern Sephardic and Mizrahi institutions such as religious, educational, and political organizations, community centres, retirement and assisted living homes, and social clubs have been designed to meet the specific needs of Eastern Sephardic and Mizrahi people, as well as bring about an awareness of Jewish multiculturality within the Jewish communities of Canada and the United States in order to better address the needs of all members.

Notes

1 Sheldon Kirschner, "Minority within a Minority: India's Jews Face Racial Prejudice," *Canadian Jewish News*, 21 April 1978, 15; Prithi Yelaja, "Their Tiny Slice of India Is Jewish," *Toronto Star*, 13 September 2007, http://www.thestar.com; Joan Roland, "Transforming Identities: Bene Israel Immigrants in Israel and the United States," in *Transnational Traditions: New Perspectives on American Jewish History*, ed. Ava F. Kahn and Adam D. Mendelsohn (Detroit: Wayne State University Press, 2014), 244.

2 Daniel Elazar, *The Other Jews: The Sephardim Today* (New York: Basic Books, 1989), 14–17.

3 Esther Benbassa and Jean-Christophe Attias, *The Jew and the Other* (Ithaca: Cornell University Press, 2002), 98–109; Elazar, *The Other Jews*, 14–17; Steven Lowenstein, *The Jewish Cultural Tapestry: International Jewish Folk Traditions* (New York: Oxford University Press, 2000), 19–48; and Zion Zohar, "A Global Perspective on Sephardic and Mizrahi Jewry: An Introductory Essay," in *Sephardic and Mizrahi Jewry: From the Golden Age of Spain to Modern Times*, ed. Zion Zohar (New York: NYU Press, 2005), 4–19.

4 Aviva Ben-Ur, *Sephardic Jews in America: A Diasporic History* (New York: NYU Press, 2009), 13–16; Sander L. Gilman, *Jewish Self-Hatred: Anti-Semitism and the Hidden Language of the Jews* (Baltimore: Johns Hopkins University Press, 1986), 299–302; Aviva Khazzoom, *Shifting Ethnic Boundaries and Inequality in Israel, Or, How the Polish Peddler Became a German Intellectual* (Stanford: Stanford University Press, 2008), 104–26.

5 Aviva Ben-Ur, "Diasporic Reunions: Sephardi/Ashkenazi Tensions in Historical Perspective," *Conversations: Journal of the Institute for Jewish Ideas and Ideals* 13 (2012): 1–15; Franklyn Bialystok, *Delayed Impact: The Holocaust and the Canadian Jewish Community* (Montreal and Kingston: McGill–Queen's University Press, 2000), 69–70; Karen Brodkin, *How Jews Became White Folks and What That Says about Race in America* (New Brunswick: Rutgers University Press, 1998), 138–74; Daniel Elazar and Harold M. Waller, *Maintaining Consensus: The Canadian Jewish Polity in the Postwar World* (Lanham: Jerusalem Center for Public Affairs, University Press of America, 1990), 3–36.

6 Lowenstein, *The Jewish Cultural Tapestry*, 36.

7 Elazar, *The Other Jews*, 21; Chaim Raphael, *The Sephardi Story: A Celebration of Jewish History* (London: Vallentine Mitchell, 1991–93), 132–36.

8 Ben-Ur, *Sephardic Jews in America*, 13–15; Benbassa and Attias, *The Jew and the Other*, 99-100; Lowenstein, *The Jewish Cultural Tapestry*, 36; Joseph M. Papo, *Sephardim in Twentieth Century America: In Search of Unity* (San Jose: Pele Yoetz Books; and Berkeley: Judah L. Magnes Museum, 1987), 52; Zohar, "A Global Perspective," 6.

9 Elazar, *The Other Jews*, 23–25; Papo, *Sephardim in Twentieth Century America*, 7.

10 Yehouda Shenhav, *The Arab Jews: A Postcolonial Reading of Nationalism, Religion, and Ethnicity* (Stanford: Stanford University Press, 2006), 1–17; Ella Shohat, "The Invention of the Mizrahim," *Journal of Palestine Studies* 29, no. 1 (1999): 5–20; Shohat, "Rupture and Return: Zionist Discourse and the Study of Arab Jews," *Social Text*, 21, no. 2 (2003): 49–74; Shohat, *Taboo Memories, Diasporic Voices* (Durham: Duke University Press,

2006), 330–58; Shohat, "Dislocated Identities: Reflections of an Arab Jew," in *An Introduction to Women's Studies: Gender in a Transnational World*, ed. Inderpal Grewal and Caren Kaplan (New York: McGraw-Hill, 2006), 440–42; Rebecca Torstrick, "'Educating for Democracy' in Israel: Combating or Perpetuating Racism?," *Identities: Global Studies in Culture and Power* 1, no. 4 (1995): 367–90; Zohar, "A Global Perspective on Sephardic and Mizrahi Jewry," 3–19; Aviva Khazzoom, *Shifting Ethnic Boundaries and Inequality in Israel, Or, How the Polish Peddler Became a German Intellectual* (Stanford: Stanford University Press, 2008), 104–26.

11 Kelly Train, "Authenticity, Identity and the Politics of Belonging: Sephardic Jews from North Africa and India within the Toronto Jewish Community," Ph.D. diss., York University, 2008, 481; Train, "Am I *That* Jew? North African Jewish Experiences in the Toronto Jewish Day School System and the Establishment of Or Haemet Sephardic School," *Diaspora, Indigenous, and Minority Education: Studies of Migration, Integration, Equity, and Cultural Survival* 7, no. 1 (2013): 6–20.

12 Joan G. Roland, *The Jewish Communities of India: Identity in a Colonial Era* (New Brunswick: Transaction Publishers, 1998), 1–7; Train, "Authenticity, Identity, and the Politics of Belonging," 481.

13 Ben-Ur, *Sephardic Jews in America*, 23–50; see also Marc D. Angel, "Sephardic Culture in America," in *A Coat of Many Colours: Jewish Subcommunities in the United States*, ed. Abraham D. Lavendar (Westport: Greenwood Press, 1977), 277–80; Angel, *La America: The Sephardic Experience in the United States* (Philadelphia: Jewish Publication Society of America, 1982), 3–105; Elazar, *The Other Jews*, 162–83; Jack Glazier, "Stigma, Identity, and Sephardic–Ashkenazic Relations in Indiana," in *Persistence and Flexibility: Anthropological Perspectives on the American Jewish Experience*, ed. Walter P. Zenner (Albany: SUNY Press, 1988), 43–60; Abraham D. Lavendar, "The Sephardic Revival in the United States: A Case of Ethnic Revival in a Minority-within-a-Minority," in *A Coat of Many Colours*, 305–14; Papo, *Sephardim in Twentieth Century America*, 43–66; and Joseph A.D. Sutton, *Magic Carpet: Aleppo-in-Flatbush* (New York: Thayer-Jacoby, 1986), 3–33.

14 Train, "Authenticity, Identity," 277–79, 326–97; Train, "Am I *That* Jew?," 6–20; see also Jean-Claude Lasry, "A Francophone Diaspora in Quebec," in *The Canadian Jewish Mosaic*, ed. Morton Weinfeld, William Shaffir, and Irwin Cotler (Toronto: John Wiley and Sons, 1981), 221–40; Lasry, "Sephardim and Ashkenazim in Montreal," in *The Jews in Canada*, ed. Robert J. Brym, William Shaffir, and Morton Weinfeld (Toronto: Oxford University Press, 1993), 395–401; Sarah Taieb-Carlen, "Assessment of a Small Group Ethnic Identity: The Jews in North Africa and the North African Jews in Toronto," Ph.D. diss., York University, 1989, 209–95; Taieb-Carlen, "Monocultural Education in a Pluralist Environment: Ashkenazi Curricula in Toronto Jewish Educational Institutions," *Canadian Ethnic Studies* 24, no. 3 (1992): 75–86; and Taieb-Carlen, "The North African Jews in Toronto Today: Assimilation or Survival," in *From Iberia to Diaspora: Studies in Sephardic History and Culture*, ed. Yedida K. Stillman and Norman A. Stillman (Boston: Brill, 1999), 151–67.

15 Jacob Rader Marcus, "The American Colonial Jews: A Study in Acculturation," 6–19; Marcus, *United States Jewry 1776–1985*, vol. 1, 19–45; Marcus, *United States Jewry 1776–1985*, vol. 2 (Detroit: Wayne State University Press, 1989), 11–21; Marcus, *United States Jewry, 1776–1985*, vol. 4 (Detroit: Wayne State University Press, 1989), 9–175.

16 B.G. Sack, *History of the Jews in Canada* (Montreal: Harvest House, 1964), 35–56; Gerald Tulchinsky, *Taking Root: The Origins of the Canadian Jewish Community* (Toronto: Stoddart Publishing, 1992/1997), 8–21; Tulchinsky, *Canada's Jews: A People's Journey* (Toronto: University of Toronto Press, 2008), 13–36.

17 Irving Abella, *A Coat of Many Colours: Two Centuries of Jewish Life in Canada* (Toronto: Key Porter, 1990/1999), 1–22; Elazar, *The Other Jews*, 162–83; Louis Rosenberg, *Canada's Jews: A Social and Economic Study of the Jews in Canada in the 1930s* (1939; repr. with introduction by Morton Weinfeld, Montreal and Kingston: McGill–Queen's University Press, 1993), 9–11; Sack, *History of the Jews in Canada*, 35–46; Taieb-Carlen, "Assessment of a Small Group Ethnic Identity," 197–204; Harold Troper and Morton Weinfeld, "Canadian Jews and Canadian Multiculturalism," in *Multiculturalism, Jews, and Identities in Canada*, ed. Howard Adelman and John H. Simpsom (Jerusalem: Magnes Press, 1996), 11–36; Tulchinsky, *Taking Root*, 8–21; Tulchinsky, *Canada's Jews*, 13–36; Morton Weinfeld, *Like Everyone Else … But Different: The Paradoxical Success of Canadian Jews* (Toronto: McClelland and Stewart, 2001), 58–59.

18 Abella, *A Coat of Many Colours*, 103–46; Lisa Jakubowski, *Immigration and the Legalization of Racism* (Halifax: Fernwood, 1997), 10–22; Harold Troper, "New Horizons in a New Land: Jewish Immigration to Canada," in *From Immigration to Integration: The Canadian Jewish Experience*, ed. Ruth Klein and Frank Dimant (Toronto: Institute for International Affairs, B'nai Brith Canada, Malcolm Lester, 2001), 3–18; and Tulchinsky, *Taking Root*, 231–54.

19 Jakubowski, *Immigration and the Legalization of Racism*, 10–22.

20 Freda Hawkins, *Critical Years in Immigration: Canada and Australia Compared* (Montreal and Kingston: McGill–Queen's University Press, 1991), 20–21.

21 Abella, *A Coat of Many Colours*, 147–78; Troper, "New Horizons in a New Land," 3–18; Gerald Tulchinsky, *Branching Out: The Transformation of the Canadian Jewish Community* (Toronto: Stoddart, 1998), 32–62; Bernard Vigod, *The Jews in Canada* (Ottawa: Canadian Historical Association, 1984), 11–15.

22 Papo, *Sephardim in Twentieth Century America*, 21.

23 Angel, *La America*, 11–13; Elazar, *The Other Jews*, 162–83; Glazier, "Stigma, Identity," 43–62; Papo, *Sephardim in Twentieth Century America*, 21–22; Victor D. Sanua, "Contemporary Studies of Sephardi Jews in the United States," in *A Coat of Many Colours: Jewish Subcommunities in the United States*, ed. Abraham D. Lavendar (Westport: Greenwood Press, 1977), 281–88; Sutton, *Magic Carpet*, 6–8.

24 Ben-Ur, *Sephardic Jews in America*, 33.

25 Papo, *Sephardim in Twentieth Century America*, 22.

26 Angel, *La America*, 6; Diner, *The Jews of the United States*, 81.

27 Elazar, *The Other Jews*, 162–83; Glazier, "Stigma, Identity," 43–62; Lavendar, "The Sephardic Revival," 305–14; Sutton, *Magic Carpet*, 6–8; Walter P. Zenner, "Streams of Immigration: Sephardic Immigration to Britain and the United States," in *From Iberia to Diaspora: Studies in Sephardic History and Culture*, ed. Yedida K. Stillman and Norman A. Stillman (Boston: Brill, 1999), 139–50.

28 John Higham, *Strangers in the Land: Patterns of American Nativism, 1860–1925* (New Brunswick: Rutgers University Press, 2011), 87–105.

29 Ben-Ur, *Sephardic Jews in America*, 25–26; Roger Daniels, *Guarding the Golden Door: American Immigration Policy and Immigrants since 1882* (New York: Hill and Wang, 2004), 45–55; Arthur Hertzberg, *The Jews in America* (New York: Columbia University Press, 1997), 230–33; Michael C. LeMay, *From Open Door to Dutch Door: An Analysis of US Immigration Policy Since 1820* (Westport: Praeger), 73–86; Michael C. LeMay, "Enacting Racism into Law: Restrictionism and the Asian Exclusion Immigration Laws," in *Transforming America: Perspectives on US Immigration*, vol. II: *The Transformation of a Nation of Nations: 1865 to 1945*, ed. Michael C. LeMay (Santa Barbara: Praeger, 2013), 175–96.

30 Papo, *Sephardim in Twentieth Century America*, 21.

31 Freda Hawkins, *Canada and Immigration: Public Policy and Public Concern* (Montreal and Kingston: McGill–Queen's University Press, 1988), 94–95, 123, 284–85.

32 Daniels, *Guarding the Golden Door*, 126-128; Papo, *Sephardim in Twentieth Century America*, 29.

33 Elazar, *The Other Jews*, 162–83; and John J. Schulter, "Washington's Moroccan Jews: A Community of Artisans," in *A Coat of Many Colours: Jewish Subcommunities in the United States*, ed. Abraham D. Lavendar (Westport: Greenwood Press, 1977), 289–95.

34 Daniels, *Guarding the Golden Door*, 126–28.

35 Hawkins, *Canada and Immigration*, 124; Jakubowski, *Immigration and the Legalization of Racism*, 10–22.

36 Hawkins, *Canada and Immigration*, 162; Jakubowski, *Immigration and the Legalization of Racism*, 10–22; and Troper, "New Horizons in a New Land," 17.

37 Jakubowski, *Immigration and the Legalization of Racism*, 10–22.

38 Daniels, *Guarding the Golden Door*, 136–37; Michael C. LeMay, "An Overview of Immigration to the United States, 1945–2010," in *Transforming America: Perspectives on U.S. Immigration*, vol. 3, ed. Michael C. LeMay (Santa Barbara: Praeger, 2013), 1–18; Aristide R. Zolberg, *A Nation by Design: Immigration Policy in the Fashioning of America* (Cambridge, MA: Harvard University Press, 2006), 333.

39 Daniels, *Guarding the Golden Door*, 136–37; LeMay, *From Open Door to Dutch Door*, 109–14; LeMay, "An Overview of Immigration to the United States, 1945–2010," 1–18; Zolberg, *A Nation by Design*, 338.

40 Elazar, *The Other Jews*, 167–80; Glazier, "Stigma, Identity," 48; Papo, *Sephardim in Twentieth Century America*, 43; Roland, "Transforming Identities," 237; Sanua, "Contemporary Studies," 282–85; Schulter, "Washington's Moroccan Jews," 289; Saba Soomekh, *From the Shahs to Los Angeles: Three Generations of Iranian Jewish Women between Religion and Culture* (Albany: SUNY Press, 2012), 2; Sutton, *Magic Carpet*, 3–9.

41 Lavendar, "The Sephardic Revival," 305.

42 Ben-Ur, *Sephardic Jews in America*, 196, 219–20n80, Sookmekh, *From the Shahs to Los Angeles*, 2; Roland, "Transforming Identities," 237.

43 Ira M. Sheskin and Arnold Dashefsky, "Jewish Populations in the United States, 2012," in *American Jewish Year Book 2012*, ed. Arnold Dashefsky and Ira M. Sheskin (Dordrecht: Springer, 2013), 152.

44 Elazar, *The Other Jews*, 181–83; Taieb-Carlen, "Assessment of a Small Group Ethnic Identity," 197–248; Taieb-Carlen, "The North African Jews in Toronto Today," 162–64; Train, "Authenticity, Identity," 264–65, 315–16.

45 Elazar, *The Other Jews*, 182–83; Train, "Authenticity, Identity," 318.

46 JIAS Information Bulletin, no. 355, 15 March 1974, Ontario Jewish Archives; JIAS Information Bulletin, no. 382, 30 June 1975, Ontario Jewish Archives; Joseph Kage, "Able and Willing to Work: Jewish Immigration and Occupational Patterns in Canada," in *The Canadian Jewish Mosaic*, ed. Morton Weinfeld, William Shaffir, and Irwin Cotler (Toronto: John Wiley and Sons, 1981), 27–48; Lasry, "A Francophone Diaspora in Quebec," 221–40; Taieb-Carlen, "Assessment of a Small Group Ethnic Identity," 197–204; Morton Weinfeld, Randal F. Schnoor, and David S. Koffman, "Overview of Canadian Jewry," in *American Jewish Year Book 2012*, ed. Arnold Dashefsky and Ira M. Sheskin (Dordrecht: Springer, 2013), 63.

47 James Torczyner, "A Community Snapshot: The Socio-Economic Dimensions," in *From Immigration to Integration: The Canadian Jewish Experience: A Millennium Edition*, ed.

Ruth Klein and Frank Dimant (Toronto: Institute for International Affairs, B'nai Brith Canada, Malcolm Lester, 2001), 246–48.

48 Elazar, *The Other Jews*, 181–83; Taieb-Carlen, "Assessment of a Small Group Ethnic Identity," 197–248; Taieb-Carlen, "The North African Jews in Toronto Today," 154; Torczyner, "A Community Snapshot," 246–48; Train, "Authenticity, Identity," 263.

49 Saul Joel, "Bene Israel Immigration and Its Social-Cultural Background," MSW research report, McGill University, 1967, 159; Train, "Authenticity, Identity," 317.

50 Lasry, "A Francophone Diaspora in Quebec," 221–40; Taieb-Carlen, "Assessment of a Small Group Ethnic Identity," 197–204.

51 As cited in Tulchinsky, *Canada's Jews*, 452.

52 Federation CJA: The Central Address for Jewish Philanthropy and Community Services, "Demographics of the Montreal Jewish Community," http://www.federationcja.org/jewish_montreal/demographics/#sthash.R5eJsFNv.dpbs.

53 Taieb-Carlen, "The North African Jews in Toronto Today," 151.

54 Torczyner, "A Community Snapshot," 246–48.

55 Canadian Jewish Congress Charities Committee National Archives, "Population and Statistics: Canadian Population Census Figures, 2001," Canadian Jewish Congress Charities Committee National Archives, http://www.cjccc.ca/en/community-faq/jewish-life-in-canada/population-and-statistics.

56 Weinfeld, Schnoor and Koffman, "Overview of Canadian Jewry," 60.

57 Tulchinsky, *Taking Root*, 10; Tulchinsky, *Canada's Jews*, 19–20.

58 Stephen A. Speisman, *The Jews of Toronto: A History to 1937* (Toronto: McClelland and Stewart, 1979), 117–27.

59 Ben-Ur, *Sephardic Jews in America*, 81–107; Stephen Birmingham, *The Grandees: America's Sephardic Elite* (Syracuse: Syracuse University Press, 1997), 23–48.

60 Angel, "Sephardic Culture in America," 277–80; Ben-Ur, *Sephardic Jews in America*, 81–107.

61 Angel, *La America*, 88–105; Ben-Ur, *Sephardic Jews in America*, 81–107; Papo, *Sephardim in Twentieth Century America*, 51–65.

62 Ben-Ur, *Sephardic Jews in America*, 81–107; Papo, *Sephardim in Twentieth Century America*, 54.

63 Angel, *La America*, 88–105; Ben-Ur, *Sephardic Jews in America*, 81–107; Papo, *Sephardim in Twentieth Century America*, 51–58.

64 Ben-Ur, *Sephardic Jews in America*, 81–107; Papo, *Sephardim in Twentieth Century America*, 51–65.

65 Angel, *La America*, 88–105; Ben-Ur, *Sephardic Jews in America*, 81–107; Papo, *Sephardim in Twentieth Century America*, 51–58.

66 Ben-Ur, *Sephardic Jews in America*, 102–3.

67 Angel, *La America*, 39–60; Ben-Ur, *Sephardic Jews in America*, 102–4; see also Kelly Amanda Train, "Carving Out a Space of One's Own: The Sephardic Kehila Centre and the Toronto Jewish Community," in *Claiming Space: Racialization in Canadian Cities*, ed. Cheryl Teelucksingh (Waterloo: Wilfrid Laurier University Press, 2006), 41; Train, "Authenticity, Identity," 66–69; Train, "Am I *That* Jew?," 4–5; for an explanation of "Ashkenazification" in the Canadian context.

68 Ben-Ur, *Sephardic Jews in America*, 102–7.

69 Angel, *La America*, 39–60; Ben-Ur, *Sephardic Jews in America*, 108–49; Ben-Ur, "Diasporic Reunions," 1–15; Glazier, "Stigma, Identity," 50–54; Papo, *Sephardim in Twentieth Century America*, 43–44; Sutton, *Magic Carpet*, 22.

70 Ben-Ur, *Sephardic Jews in America*, 108–49; Ben-Ur, "Diasporic Reunions," 1–15; Glazier, "Stigma, Identity, and Sephardic–Ashkenazic Relations in Indiana," 50–54; Papo, *Sephardim in Twentieth Century America*, 43–44; and Train, "Authenticity, Identity and the Politics of Belonging," 269–70.

71 Angel, *La America*, 39–60; Ben-Ur, *Sephardic Jews in America*, 108–49; Ben-Ur, "Diasporic Reunions," 1–15; Papo, *Sephardim in Twentieth Century America*, 43–44.

72 Angel, *La America*, 14, 39–60; Ben-Ur, *Sephardic Jews in America*, 26–27, 114–17; Ben-Ur, "Diasporic Reunions," 1–15.

73 Angel, *La America*, 42; Ben-Ur, *Sephardic Jews in America*, 120–23; Ben-Ur, "Diasporic Reunions," 1–15.

74 Angel, *La America*, 56–60; Ben-Ur, *Sephardic Jews in America*, 122–26.

75 Sutton, *Magic Carpet*, 20–22; see also Ben-Ur, *Sephardic Jews in America*, 127; Ben-Ur, "Diasporic Reunions," 1–15.

76 Brodkin, *How Jews Became White Folks*, 138–74; and Eric L. Goldstein, *The Price of Whiteness: Jews, Race, and American Identity* (Princeton: Princeton University Press, 2006), 212.

77 Ben-Ur, *Sephardic Jews in America*, 182–83.

78 Bialystok, *Delayed Impact*, 57–58; Troper, "New Horizons in a New Land," 17; Harold Troper, *The Defining Decade: Identity, Politics, and the Canadian Jewish Community in the 1960s* (Toronto: University of Toronto Press, 2010), 85–86; Weinfeld, *Like Everyone Else …*, 99.

79 Elazar, *The Other Jews*, 181–83; Lasry, "A Francophone Diaspora in Quebec," 221–40; Lasry, "Sephardim and Ashkenazim in Montreal," 395–401; Taieb-Carlen, "Assessment of a Small Group Ethnic Identity," 197–204; Taieb-Carlen, "Monocultural Education in a Pluralist Environment," 75–86; Taieb-Carlen, "The North African Jews in Toronto Today," 151; Train, "Authenticity, Identity," 261–62; Train, "Am I *That* Jew?," 6–20; Troper, *The Defining Decade*, 44–46; Tulchinsky, *Canada's Jews*, 449–45; Weinfeld, *Like Everyone Else …*, 76–78.

80 Proposal-Integration-North African Jewish Community in Metro Toronto, September 1972, Ontario Jewish Archives.

81 Lasry, "A Francophone Diaspora in Quebec," 221–40.

82 Anna Morgan, "Maurice Benzacar to be Honoured for His Devotion to Community," *Canadian Jewish News*, 25 January 2001, 14; Sheri Shefa, "Moroccan Community Marks 50 Years in Toronto," *Canadian Jewish News*, 2 January 2008, http://www.cjnews.com.

83 Elazar, *The Other Jews*, 162–81; Lasry, "A Francophone Diaspora in Quebec," 221–40; Taieb-Carlen, "Assessment of a Small Group Ethnic Identity," 197–248; Taieb-Carlen, "Monocultural Education," 75–86; Taieb-Carlen, "The North African Jews in Toronto Today," 53; Train, "Carving Out a Space of One's Own," 41–64; Train, "Authenticity, Identity," 269–70; Train, "Am I *That* Jew?," 6–20; and Morton Weinfeld, "The Jews of Quebec: An Overview," in *The Jews in Canada*, ed. Robert J. Brym, William Shaffir, and Morton Weinfeld (Toronto: Oxford University Press, 1993), 171–92.

84 Weinfeld, "The Jews of Quebec," 171–92; Weinfeld, *Like Everyone Else …*, 99.

85 Taieb-Carlen, "Assessment of a Small Group Ethnic Identity," 197–248; Taieb-Carlen, "The North African Jews in Toronto Today," 51–53.

86 Proposal-Integration-North African Jewish Community in Metro Toronto, September 1972.

87 See my previous publications – Train, "Authenticity, Identity," 343–83; and "Am I *That* Jew?," 6–20 – where I did the original research on this topic.

88 Lasry, "A Francophone Diaspora in Quebec," 221–40.

89 Elazar, *The Other Jews*, 185–89; Norman A. Stillman, *Sephardi Religious Responses to Modernity* (Luxembourg: Harwood Academic, 1995), 76–86.

90 Tulchinsky, *Canada's Jews*, 450.

91 Roland, "Transforming Identities," 244; Train, "Authenticity, Identity," 343–83, 418–28; see also Train, "Am I *That* Jew?," 6–20.

92 Sheldon Kirschner, "Minority within a Minority: India's Jews Face Racial Prejudice," *Canadian Jewish News*, 21 April 1978, 15; Yelaja, "Their Tiny Slice," 13 September 2007, http://www.thestar.com.

93 Joel, "Bene Israel Immigration," 157; Train, "Authenticity, Identity," 317–18.

94 Again, this is from my fieldwork for "Authenticity, Identity," 320–455; and "Am I *That* Jew?," 6–20.

95 Roland, "Transforming Identities," 237–38.

96 Ibid.

97 Train, "Authenticity, Identity," 422–37.

98 Angel, *La America*, 19–38; Papo, *Sephardim in Twentieth Century America*, 129–78; Ira Robinson, "Historical Introduction to the Jewish Community of Quebec," Jewish Montreal Federation CJA: The Central Address for Jewish Philanthropy and Community Services, http://www.federationcja.org/en/jewish_montreal/history/#sthash.sPbyb8Dc .dpbs; Roland, "Transforming Identities," 238–39; Sephardic Kehila Centre Grand Opening Celebration, 2 September 1997; Train, "Authenticity, Identity," 384–97, 440–55. Examples include, in the American context, *La America* (1910–1925), the Federation of Oriental Jews (1912–17), the Sephardic Community of New York (1920–22), the Sephardic Jewish Community of New York (1922–32), the Central Sephardic Jewish Community of America (1941–72), and the American Sephardi Federation (1972–present), and for Indian Jews, Congregation BINA (Bene Israel of North America) (New York City) (1981), and, in the Canadian context, the North African Jewish Association (1959), the Francophone Sephardic Association (1966), L'École Maimonide Primary (1969) and Secondary (1975) Schools, Or Haemet Sephardic School (1975), the Communauté Sepharde du Québec (1978), the Ontario Sephardic Association (1980), and the Sephardi-Ashkenazi Relations Committee, a joint project of the Association of Jewish Communal Services, Canadian Jewish Congress, and the Communauté Sepharde du Québec (1985), the Sephardic Kehila Centre (1997), and for Indian Jews, Congregation BINA (Bene Israel of North America) (Toronto) (1979).

99 Lasry, "A Francophone Diaspora in Quebec," 221–40; Taieb-Carlen, "Assessment of a Small Group Ethnic Identity," 197–248; Taieb-Carlen, "Monocultural Education," 75–86; Taieb-Carlen, "The North African Jews in Toronto Today," 151–54; Train, "Authenticity, Identity," 384–97, 440–55; Train, "Am I *That* Jew?," 6–20.

About the Contributors

Jeanne Abrams received her Ph.D. in American History from the University of Colorado at Boulder. She is a professor at the Center for Judaic Studies and the University Libraries at the University of Denver, as well as a lecturer in America History at the University of Colorado at Denver. Her latest books include *Dr. Charles David Spivak: A Jewish Immigrant and the American Tuberculosis Movement* (2009) and *Revolutionary Medicine: The Founding Fathers and Mother in Sickness and in Health* (2013). She is also the author of numerous articles and essays in many academic journals and popular magazines.

Zev Eleff is Chief Academic Officer of Hebrew Theological College in Skokie, Ilinois. He is the author of several books and more than thirty scholarly articles in the field of American Jewish history. His most recent books are *Who Rules the Synagogue: Religious Authority and the Formation of American Judaism* (2016) and *Modern Orthodox Judaism: A Documentary History* (2016).

Howard Gontovnick, Ph.D., is an Adjunct Professor at SUNY Plattsburgh, New York, in the Department of Interdisciplinary Studies. He has authored numerous articles in psychology and religion, with a specialization in the history of Jewish farming colonies in Canada. His latest publication is a chapter on East European Jewish migration and its impact on farming colonies in Canada (in Ira Robinson, ed., *Canada's Jews: In Time, Space and Spirit*, 2013). He is also a publisher of the latest works of Alvin R. Mahrer,

Ph.D., Professor Emeritus University of Ottawa and a psychotherapist with a private practice.

Susan Landau-Chark, Ph.D., is Associate Director of the Zelikovitz Centre for Jewish Studies, Carleton University, Ottawa. Her most recent publication is the chapter "Canada," written for *The Jewish Emigrant from Britain 1700–2000: Essays in Memory of Lloyd P. Gartner* (2013). The chapter focuses on the early British Jewish settlers and explores the ease with which British Jews were able to emigrate and integrate into Canadian society. Her present project explores Canadian Jewry's response to Confederation.

Lillooet Nördlinger McDonnell, Ph.D., is a scholar of modern Jewish history. Originally from British Columbia, she is a Research Associate with Carleton University's Zelikovitz Centre for Jewish Studies. She lives in Brooklyn, New York.

Ira Robinson is Professor of Judaic Studies and Director of the Institute for Quebec and Canadian Jewish Studies at Concordia University, where he has taught since 1979. Dr. Robinson has published extensively on Canadian Jewish Studies and has received several distinguished awards for this scholarship and service. A recent book of his is *Canada's Jews: In Time, Space and Spirit* (2013).

Jonathan Sarna is University Professor and Joseph H. & Belle R. Braun Professor of American Jewish History and Chair of the Hornstein Jewish Professional Leadership Program at Brandeis University, as well as Chief Historian of the National Museum of American Jewish History in Philadelphia.

Barry L. Stiefel received his Ph.D. in Historic Preservation from Tulane University. He is an Associate Professor in the Historic Preservation and Community Planning program at the College of Charleston in South Carolina, as well as a Research Associate at the Max and Tessie Zelikovitz Centre for Jewish Studies at Carleton University in Ottawa. His research focuses on the preservation of Jewish heritage, from which he has published (or co-published) several scholarly articles and books. He also serves as President of the Association of Canadian Jewish Studies.

Hernan Tesler-Mabé obtained his Ph.D. in History at the University of Ottawa. He is a regular part-time Professor in the Department of History at the University of Ottawa and serves also as a Research Associate at the Max and Tessie Zelikovitz Centre for Jewish Studies, Carleton University,

Ottawa. His dissertation, *A Jewish Conductor, A Devoted Mahlerite, and a Delicate String: The Musical Life of Heinz Unger, 1895–1965*, explored the manner in which the strands of German-Jewish identity converged and were negotiated by a musician who lived a sizable portion of his life in a double diaspora (in the Jewish diaspora as well as exiled from his European home). Alongside his ongoing interest in Jewish history, Dr. Tesler-Mabé's areas of specialization include modern Europe, European integration, and cultural history. He is a board member of the Association for Canadian Jewish Studies.

Kelly Amanda Train holds a Ph.D. in sociology from York University in Toronto. She has published several articles and book chapters on race, ethnicity, Canadian immigration policy, and Jewish identity and is currently writing a book on North African and Indian Jews within the Toronto Jewish community. She teaches in the Department of Sociology at Ryerson University in Toronto.

Index